WHAT FUTURISTS BELIEVE

A WORLD FUTURE SOCIETY BOOK

WHAT

FUTURISTS

BELIEVE

Joseph F. Coates
Jennifer Jarratt
J. F. Coates, Inc.

Published by
LOMOND
1989

Library of Congress Catalog Number: 88-82961

ISBN: 0-912338-66-0 (Clothbound)
ISBN: 0-912338-67-9 (Microfiche)

A World Future Society Book

Published by:
Lomond Publications, Inc.
P.O. Box 88
Mt. Airy, Maryland 21771

and

The World Future Society
4916 St. Elmo Avenue
Bethesda, Maryland 20814

TABLE OF CONTENTS

FOREWORD

by Edward Cornish
President, World Future Society
Editor, *The Futurist*

The term "futurist," in its current meaning, did not become part of our language until the 1960s, when it began appearing in U.S. magazines as a handy way to describe people who are seriously interested in what may happen in the years ahead. Until then, it seems, such people were sufficiently rare that the absence of a word for them was not a serious problem, though one *Fortune* magazine writer in the pre-futurist days was driven to invent the phrase "wild bird" as a name for the visionary thinkers who were moving into corporations.

During the sixties, futurists multiplied in the excitement over space exploration and the abundance of scientific and technological breakthroughs, and *Time* magazine devoted a major essay in 1965 to describing these "futurists." This usage of the term in its new sense—it had previously been used to describe an early-twentieth-century art movement—seems to have been the impetus that made the term what it is today. The World Future Society named its initial newsletter (later a magazine) *The Futurist*, and today "futurist" is widely used as a catch-all term for people interested in long-term issues. It received a kind of official status in 1985 when the President of the United States invited a group of people described as "futurists" to have lunch with him at the White House.

Many people now described as futurists might prefer to call themselves something else—long-range planner, forecaster, social theorist, trend analyst, etc.—but the public cannot get very excited over niceties of word and meaning; the term "futurist" is easily understood, and being called one is no longer the worst of fates. Society has come to accept futurists as people worth listening to, not because they have the right answers, but because they do have the right questions—those that concern the serious long-term issues that our society faces.

Since the sixties, futurists have acquired steadily increasing respect in government, business, education, and other areas. The U.S. Congress now has its own futurist "club:" the Congressional Clearinghouse on the Future, to which several-score senators and representatives belong. Top business leaders participate in futurist activities and hire futurists to advise their companies. And futurists at universities have established numerous courses dealing with the future.

The growing respect accorded futurists does not mean that there is agreement on just what a futurist really is—or should be. Some futurists want the term to apply only to people professionally engaged in studying or planning for the future; they want futurists to be a professional group, with the usual accouterments of such—academic degrees, peer review, etc. Other futurists insist on a more democratic approach, arguing that the future belongs to everyone and should not be made a private preserve for specialists. This conflict has resulted in a World Future Society policy: People of all kinds are admitted to membership, but there is also a professional section with its own journal and members-only meetings.

Though anyone interested in the long-term future may be called a futurist, the term strongly implies an interest in a broad range of issues, not just those in a particular specialty. The interconnections among the many different aspects of our society become abundantly clear to anyone who tries seriously to explore the future: new technology will influence education, which will mold the work force of the future, and the new work force will have values that may encourage an entirely new direction for technology. Nothing in our society exists all by itself; each element is connected to every other element by subtle and intricate chains of cause and effect. Thus, good futurist thinking is holistic.

Futurists insist on a rational or even scientific basis for their speculations about the future. They have little patience with mystical predictions (palmistry, astrology, etc.), but are generally ready to listen to a very wide range of opinions based on scientific or historical evidence. As a group, they are pragmatic rather than ideological: They want to know what will "work;" that is, what will really be effective in improving the human condition over the long term. Though they distrust ideologies, they are very hospitable to social experiments and innovations.

The reality of human choices in shaping the future is one of the basic tenets of today's futurists. They do not see the future as predetermined by fate or divine providence, but as constantly being shaped and reshaped by human actions based on human choices. We humans determine the future, so we think about the future not to predict what will happen, but to create a better future than we will otherwise have. Each of us is an active participant in the historic process of determining mankind's future.

Futurists thus share a basic orientation toward the world that provides the framework for fruitful dialogue. Because they are broad-gauge in their thinking habits and generally open to new ideas and experience, they have considerable flexibility in their thinking and are more willing than most people to change their minds and adopt new positions.

The broad, long-term perspective of futurists means that they have a lively appreciation of the complexity of society and the myriad interactions that appear and influence it over time. Because the subject of their concern is extraordinarily complex, individual futurists see different things happening and wind up with very different views about what is likely to happen in the future.

The notion that futurists are mainly concerned with predicting the future is one of the persistent myths that futurists have to live with. A corollary myth is that their predictions are usually wrong. The latter myth arises partly from the hilarious blunders made mainly by nonfuturists, prominent amateurs who, through the ages, have attempted to anticipate the future. At the turn of the century, for instance, many distinguished scientists went on record as stating that no successful flying machine would ever be built.

Another myth is that futurists are technocrats, who believe that technology will solve every human problem. This myth is countered by the fact that futurists led the movement to establish the U.S. Office of Technology Assessment, which serves as a kind of check on technology by advising Congress on both the pros and cons of new technologies now being developed.

Yet another myth is that futurists are neophiles—lovers of gee-whiz gizmos—who have little concern for either the natural environment or the treasures of antiquity. In fact, futurists as a group are extremely concerned about the environment, constantly sounding the alarm about such dangers as acid rain and the greenhouse effect; they also want to preserve the human heritage so that future generations can benefit from it. As editor of *The Futurist* magazine, I well remember the outraged protests that erupted when we published an item suggesting that earth might someday solve its waste-disposal problem by rocketing the stuff out into space. Using space as a dumping ground for earth's wastes aroused extraordinary fury among futurists: It's bad enough to turn our own planet into a wasteland, they suggested; making the universe our dumping ground would be totally unthinkable. Futurists want to be good citizens of the universe as well as of the earth; preservers of nature as well as creators of technological wonders; custodians of the past as well as advocates of the future.

This book goes far toward explaining what futurists are by describing what some of them think. The great value of this study is that (1) it presents systematically the views of 17 unusually thoughtful futurists on a variety of important issues, and (2) it analyzes their views in various useful ways so that a reader can pick up incisive new insights into the issues under discussion. The authors, futurists themselves, have contributed their own views of the future which adds to the liveliness of this book. It should make an unusually effective textbook, practically guaranteeing lively classroom discussion.

The futurists whose views are presented here are not "average" futurists (assuming it is possible to find such an animal), but rather an outstanding selection of thinkers tackling the great issues. Any one of these futurists would be a guest of honor wherever the future is being thoughtfully discussed. To have their ideas brought together in this unique way is an outstanding achievement for which we owe a debt of gratitude to futurists Joseph F. Coates and Jennifer Jarratt.

I am delighted that the World Future Society has been able to collaborate with Lomond Publications, Inc. (through the offices of its President, Lowell H. Hattery) and J.F. Coates, Inc. in the publishing of this volume.

PREFACE

More and greater pressures on organizations, the development of more reliable tools for anticipation, and the build-up of a credible body of futurist works are promoting a positive attitude toward the study of the future. Systematic attempts to identify the factors which are shaping the future and to anticipate their consequences as an aid to decisionmaking have steadily grown over the last 35 years.

The military interest in strategic planning and profound need to better understand the implications of atomic power in the immediate post-World War II period led to a proliferation of organizations committed to strategic planning. One outcome of that passion for planning was the rise to prominence of Herman Kahn and his approach to the future. He strongly influenced the military, and to a lesser extent, corporate and other planners. Central to Kahn's thinking were: First, the concept of alternative futures, that the future is not a single inevitable state, but change can evolve in strikingly different ways. Second is the notion that stable, long-term trends can be identified and used in probing the future. Third was his extensive use of scenarios as a tool for understanding and presenting complex situations.

In the military and the commercial sectors, technological forecasting flourished in the 1950s and 1960s, along with shorter term futures studies tied to market research.

Commonly one finds the engineer offering scientific or technically grounded speculations about what could or ought to be, in the form of new structures, materials, gadgets, devices, systems, or other technological wonders. Related but distinct and usually sharply dissociated from the realities of our current world is science fiction. From the point of view of futures studies, sci-fi is of little, or no, value. Science-fiction is usually so barren of plausible psychological, social, or institutional sophistication as to fall into one of three categories: entertainment, fantasy, or cautionary tales.

Science-fiction, however, does reveal one important feature of the exploration of the future, and that is the intellectual difficulty in identifying and describing plausible *positive futures* in contrast to the relative ease with which *negative, hostile,* and *destructive futures* may be generated.

The academic community continually rediscovers the future. One branch of futures studies often flourishes in departments of sociology, where there are recurrent attempts to develop grand theories of human affairs.

Within the corporation, the adoption of a futures perspective makes its clearest mark in strategic planning, which a generation ago often took a 15- to 20-year look ahead. In recent decades, under pressures of market competition, international developments, and a volatile stock market, corporate planning has tended to be foreshortened.

The greatest stimulus in the corporate world for concern for the future comes from the awareness that the two mainstays of earlier corporate strategic planning—market research and technological forecasting—have become less reliable as the corporate external environment has become increasingly complex. The result is the revival of interest in the corporation in methods or techniques which will help in understanding and interpreting the world in which the firm is embedded, the so-called corporate external environment. Reflecting that interest in its environment is the rise of issues management in the past decade as a tool for anticipating short- or mid-range, i.e., one- to five-year, developments.

Against that background of expanding concern, interest, and awareness of the benefits the systematic study of the future may have for the corporation and other organizations, the project which led to this book was begun. The project, subscribed to by eight American corporations and two corporate service organizations, identified a group of prominent primarily American futurists. Through a process described more fully in the Introduction (Chapter 1), the authors analyzed the published works of the seventeen futurists, interviewed all but two of them, and prepared a profile of each. Review and feedback on the profiles was sought and received from all but one of the futurists. The authors then undertook to compare the futurists' beliefs and to critique the present state of futures studies as represented by their panel. Finally, the authors present their own view of forces and factors shaping the next decades.

The authors' statement (Chapter 22) is offered neither as synthesis of nor counterview to those of the panel of futurists. It is an independent piece reflecting another view of forces influencing and shaping the future of American and global society which have strong implications for the corporation and other institutions.

The present volume, while in the main following the text of the original project report, has been updated and reorganized somewhat as a result of the reception and use by the corporate sponsors and continuing study by the authors.

To increase the timeliness of this book, each of the seventeen futurists was invited to prepare a 500-word commentary, expansion, supplement, or other kind of statement appropriate to the theme and objectives of the material. For those who found the time and interest their statements are appended.

We anticipate that this book will not only be of interest to corporate readers but should find merit and use in meeting the planning challenges of government agencies, non-profit organizations, and other large public institutions such as churches and universities. It may also find an indeterminately large audience of professionals and lay people concerned about the future of the U.S., global society, our precious institutions, and their personal and our collective descendants.

The sponsors of the project were: ARCO, Bell Communications Research, DOW Chemical Company, DuPont Company, Electric Power Research Institute, Monsanto Company, NYNEX, Raytheon Corporation, SUN Company, Inc., and United Technologies.

At J.F. Coates, Inc., Dixie Lynn Griffin, Lydia Perry, John Mahaffie, Robert Connolly and Lara L. Higgins assisted us in the collection and preparation of materials. Diana Clark, Beverly Goldberg, and Janet Reid were responsible for the preparation of the manuscript.

The generous cooperation of the futurists whose work we have analyzed is acknowledged as indispensable to this project. Their willingness to be interviewed and to comment on our profile chapters gives a unique degree of reliability to what is intrinsically a difficult and chancy enterprise: organizing and describing another person's beliefs. The authors, of course, remain solely responsible for the accuracy, completeness, and reliability of the profiles and are alone responsible for the comparative and critical material.

Joseph F. Coates

Jennifer Jarratt

PART ONE

ROLE OF THE FUTURIST

CHAPTER 1

THE FUTURIST AND THE CORPORATION

For the corporation, the futurist can be a valuable general purpose means for planning, strategic direction, and insight into and interpretation of the corporate external environment. Futures studies can offer at least six distinct benefits to the corporation, or to any other organization. These are:

- Serving as a framework for interpreting present events.
- Identifying factors with which the corporation must cope, whether or not it has power to influence them.
- Providing a sorting rule among corporate choices. Usually it is best to go with the flow rather than to fight the long-term tide.
- Revealing opportunities.
- Forcing those in positions of responsibility to examine their own assumptions about the future.
- Setting up guideposts to mark the clear (and warn of the dangerous) path into the future.

The generally longer range view of the futurist may be particularly rich and helpful on scientific and technological developments which have long maturation periods, and with regard to other structural changes.

Structural change is the reordering of basic, traditional relationships. For example, is Hong Kong going to be different in the next century? What are the possibilities for mass marketing in the Soviet Union over the next twenty years? These questions require a structural analysis of the future to develop some possible answers.

Another valuable product from the futurist is the specific topical study, done generally on a shorter time horizon—five to fifteen years—and related more to products, processes, markets, labor force, locations, or issues. Topical studies of the future can generally be produced on demand and are often richly textured and detailed in their implications and applications. They reflect the craft side of the futurist's art.

The futurist is a potential antidote to the myopia that may result from coping with rapid and turbulent change. Corporations are focusing ever more sharply on short-range forces, considerations and actions. By becoming mean and lean, more efficient and effective, cutting costs, raising productivity and quality, all certainly desirable objectives, they are also taking destructive action, such as cutting strategic planning and basic and long-range research.

The corporation is weakest now in planning, and the futurist can help bolster that function and perspective by:

- Heightening an awareness of the power and sometimes near inevitability of long-term forces and trends.
- Creating positive and negative visions of the corporate future.
- Helping to formulate policy choices and the selection among them.
- Identifying radical, new, or strikingly different strategies along any dimension of corporate concern or activity.

The longer range benefits of the study of the future should not be confused with many of the bread and butter studies in market research and technological forecasting that are widespread and of varying use and value. Economic forecasting, particularly the application of econometric modeling, can be useful as a short-term tool, since its effectiveness depends upon marginal analysis. Marginal analysis applies most successfully, however, to complex stable systems in which there are only slight disturbances in one or another direction.

Issues management is a widespread new anticipatory tool focusing on the next one to five years. In fact, if not in principle, it tends to be a negative, conflict-oriented defensive approach. While itself a positive development towards the future-oriented organization, again, it is far from the whole story.

Studies of the emerging corporate environment can alert the corporation to the need for and the possibility of new modes of doing business. For example, a study that led to a heightening of the awareness of pernicious implications of the volatility of the stock market and the foreshortening of planning as a result, should alert the corporation to search for alternatives. Similarly, a look to the future may help to yield more stable long range planning and more durable structures less subject to the uncertainty and vagaries of short-term economic pressures.

How to Interpret What Futurists Believe About the Future

It is natural to look for consensus among futurists. Finding a consensus has strength and value for decisionmaking about the future, particularly in the short run and when dealing with relatively stable systems. This is the essence of what market research and econometric forecasting deliver. However, consensus can mislead when society or its systems are in rapid change or subject to new and powerful forces. In this case there is a *powerful role for the outlier: the deviant thinker, the unusual and the radical.*

The outlier is most valuable as a stimulus when the goal is the longer range, the strategic issue, the potential scientific and technological development and its impacts. The organization can be alerted to discontinuities by studying the outlier, and may benefit from an opening up of the possibility of radically new, different and better strategies. Finally, the outlier can stimulate attention to innovations in products, processes, services, and organizations.

Whether looking for a consensus or studying outliers, whether working with the common or the unusual, one must be willing to play. One must commit the time and the intellectual work to understanding, assimilating and mentally playing with what the futurist has to say. A futurist with anything significant to say is in the position of a delphic oracle, arguing points that are often two-edged, ambiguous, and subtle. While it is not necessarily the intention of the futurist to confuse, it is often the reality. Furthermore, since the study of the future is fundamentally a commitment to the unknown, one must *cultivate the art of conjecture.* The art of conjecture, like all other arts, requires attention, skill, aptitude, and, most of all, practice and play.

The corporation would be wise to adopt a more positive approach toward the study of the future, and to push its organizations such as the Conference Board and the National Association of Manufacturers, to a more thorough-going futures orientation. The individual corporation can legitimate for these organizations the look to the new, the different, the unfamiliar and the bold.

The corporate executive risks confusing opportunities with good news. One of the lessons coming from the study of the future is that there is no purely good news. There is a down side, a negative side, a risk to everything. Furthermore, not all good news is the equivalent of opportunities. Many of the most substantial opportunities for the corporation will lie in disruptive change for their industry, their business, for their market, or for their clients and customers. If one is to get at the real opportunities, one must take a thoroughly open and exploratory approach to futures information.

The strength of the specific topical futures study mentioned earlier is that it is tailored and crafted to the client, and the particular product, process, and context. The broader, general, and longer term views of the future such as those analyzed in this project are unlikely to be tailored to any organization's specific needs. The organization must provide the skill, craft, and intelligence to interpret the significant pieces of information. Hence, intellectual play is valuable.

This is not to say that the search for consensus, credibility, and accuracy, are not desirable; indeed in many situations, credibility and accuracy are the dominant criteria. For example, in an engineering diagram, accuracy is paramount. In the choice of a design, consensus might be the critical factor. And in terms of market analysis, credibility dominates. However, overemphasizing these criteria can be risky in approaching the future because insisting on them does not necessarily lead to the most important insights. Credible or not, consensus or not, close attention to what futurists are saying may force fresh and more explicit assumptions about the future of great value to the organization's business plans and goals.

How to Use This Book

This book is presented in three parts. Part I summarizes, compares and contrasts the beliefs about the future of 17 prominent futurists. Part II discusses each futurist in turn. Part III presents the authors' overview and precepts.

In Part I the process of summarizing has led to the appearance of consensus on some topics. The 17 futurists frequently cluster in one general aspect of their thinking about the future, but the range of their views is often extremely wide and diverse. We have attempted to show the range and the similarities of their views. In Part II, where each futurist is discussed separately, it is possible to explore the assumptions and ideas underlying their diverging views.

What We Did to Build This book

We recruited ten business subscribers to the project. At the first meeting with their representatives, we offered them a list of 125 futurists for possible inclusion. The most important criterion for selection was that the futurists have something to say about the future relevant to the corporation. It was somewhat important that the futurists have prominence and recognition within the futures community. Their visibility to the business clientele was of less significance, since many of the most substantial futurists have low name recognition in the corporate world. Another consideration was that they represent a diversity of points of view. Specifically, they were not to be selected solely because they celebrated the corporation, the market system, or an ideology.

The 17 futurists eventually selected are overwhelmingly American. First, most futurists are North Americans and many of those who are not are less well-known to U.S. futurists. The 17 futurists are briefly introduced and described in Chapter 2.

Conflicting schedules and other commitments precluded some candidates' participation. They had to be willing to be interviewed and to review a profile of themselves. Consequently, two possible choices dropped out and replacements were found. With the profile as background, we contacted the individual to arrange an interview. In the interview, we raised additional points that were not covered in published material, and explored open and uncertain areas. Each interviewee was not asked all the same questions. We did not urge them to talk about topics that were unfamiliar, uncongenial, or uninteresting (to them).

Many points came out of the interviews which were not apparent in the literature. These were often matters of intellectual origins and personal biography. The content of the interviews overlaps, but not in any uniform way. Based on the interview, we revised each profile into a chapter and sent it to the individual futurist, asking for review, comments, and clarification. In some cases, when we were unable to interview the subject face to face, we used the telephone, correspondence, or both. Arthur Clarke, for example, was generous in providing written commentary from Sri Lanka on our questions and on our profile of him.

In the course of the project we met with the subscribers' representatives several times. Profiles already prepared became a basis for discussion at those meetings. A preliminary version of Part I was discussed.

When the profiles were nearly all in hand, the authors compared the futurists to identify subjects of frequent and overlapping interests, concepts, and beliefs, and divergences in opinions, conclusions, and so on. This analysis is presented in Chapter 3, where the authors compare the 17 futurists' beliefs about the future with minimum evaluation. A critique of their views and beliefs is in Chapter 4. Part II contains a chapter on each of the 17 members of the futurist panel. Additional comments from several members of the panel are included in Part III, after the authors' comments and a brief guide to the futures literature. An index arranged by name and key words, ends the book.

CHAPTER 2

CHARACTERISTICS OF THE SELECTED FUTURISTS

The Panel of Futurists

Roy Amara
Robert U. Ayres
Daniel Bell
Kenneth E. Boulding
Arthur C. Clarke
Peter Drucker
Victor C. Ferkiss
Barry B. Hughes
Alexander King
Richard D. Lamm
Michael Marien
Dennis L. Meadows
James A. Ogilvy
Gerard K. O'Neill
John R. Pierce
Peter Schwartz
Robert Theobald

The most striking feature of the group is that they are all aging white males. The average age is 58; the youngest is 42, the oldest, 76. The age distribution may be relatively easily explained. The insightful, comprehensive study of the future, like the study of history, may require a degree of maturity and the assimilation of a large body of material, which can come only with age. A perspective on the future is more likely to come out of a relatively mature mind, unlike other fields of study where important contributions may be made by young thinkers. In mathematics, for example, it is widely recognized that the most brilliant of mathematicians are often in their late teens or early twenties.

The Caucasian aspect is striking and reflects the reality that the study of the future in the United States has not yet drawn the attention of racial minorities.

More difficult to understand and for the casual reader to appreciate, is the absence of women. One excellent woman candidate futurist refused our invitation. In the search for other women futurists, we were unable to identify any in the U.S. equivalent in stature, scope, and breadth of interest to those futurists already selected. Several candidate women futurists were narrowly focused or ideologically oriented toward women's issues only. Others, while relatively well-known, were reportorial or derivative in their interest in the future, not either primary thinkers or active practitioners. Two prominent women futurists were ruled out because one is married to one of the futurists already chosen and the other is married to one of the authors.

In the remainder of this chapter we briefly characterize the approach and style of each of the 17 futurists, adding our opinion on the relative importance of each individual's work to corporate interests.

Roy Amara

Roy Amara's views and his work as President of the Institute for the Future have evolved from optimism to a more conservative view of the potential for change. His early concern with methodology has broadened into a larger concern for communicating about the future with decisionmakers.

The quintessential applied analyst, he is capable of undertaking virtually any futures problem systematically, credibly and comprehensively. By laying out the forces at play and working with clients, he unfolds and organizes the implications and the implied actions open to them. He is among the half-dozen best and most effective practitioners of applied futures research. Intellectually his interests lie less in grand theories and more in matters of scope, comprehensiveness, effectiveness, and quality control. He is committed to making the study of the future a practical, useful enterprise.

Robert U. Ayres

Robert Ayres has a strong interest in science and technology's influence on economic growth and on the relationship between technology and social change. He is Professor of Engineering and Public Policy at Carnegie Mellon University, and has just completed a year at the International Institute for Applied Systems Analysis (IIASA) in Austria. Trained as a physicist, Ayres has one of the most comprehensive and diverse perspectives among the futurists. His strong commitment to systems, to quantitation, and toward scientific and technologically grounded analysis gives great credibility to the details and specifics of his work. Technical excellence is combined with great imagination. On the other hand he seems less interested in the institutional, organizational, and stakeholder aspects of forces shaping the future.

Daniel Bell

Daniel Bell is the paramount futurist in the U.S. despite his rejection of that label in favor of social theorist. As Henry Ford Professor of Social Sciences at Harvard University, his work for the last twenty years has become the centerpiece of thinking in the interpretation of economic, technological, social, cultural and political change in the emerging post-industrial society. He is concerned primarily with large changes and transitions in our society. While having identified and labeled the present transition to the post-industrial society and defined the core changes associated with that transition, Bell is reluctant to speculate about the routes technology may take, or its impacts on society, its polity, or its culture. He does see the polity and the culture as factors shaping technology and technological choices. He is reluctant to be prescriptive although he often approaches that when he deplores the expansion of entitlements or the decline of religion. His thinking is context and framework for corporate planning but presents few or no guideposts or detailed directions.

Kenneth E. Boulding

Kenneth Boulding is an internationally known social scientist, author, interdisciplinary thinker, peace researcher and distinguished Professor Emeritus at the University of Colorado. Boulding sparkles. He is the intellectual perpetually at play—serious, earnest play; playing off ideas against other intellects, playing off past against future, playing off economics against the world, playing off synthesis against analysis. While offering no sharp, clear, theoretical framework or ideology he does bring striking analytical and creative powers to the future. He offers no particular guidance or role to the corporation, but as with many broad-gauged intellectuals, almost everything he says has implications that others can profitably mine.

Arthur C. Clarke

Arthur Clarke is Chancellor of the University of Moratuwa and patron of the Arthur C. Clarke Center for Modern Technology in Sri Lanka. Clarke is the great celebrant of humankind's potential for understanding and eventually acquiring mastery over the universe by the application of human intelligence through science and technology. Ranging out 10,000 or more years, he has little interest in the short term per se, and little care or concern for our current institutions. Clarke is a powerful antidote to prosaic thinking as he relentlessly explores the limits on the potential developments and applications of science and technology. His futures work should be read not for details or specifics but for implicit strategies for probing limits. He has little direct, immediate relevance to corporate interests aside from space and telecommunications applications where his thinking is at the leading edge.

Peter Drucker

Peter Drucker is Clarke Professor of Social Science at Claremont Graduate School, in California. He is a writer, consultant, and educator. As the world's most distinguished and best known management guru, Drucker's strength does not lie in creativity or theory, but in the sorting of concepts, the highlighting of issues and the legitimation of strategies. His boundless commitment to the human enterprise and to our ability to muddle through, provides great encouragement to others and opens up an experimental positive attitude toward change. His strategy of at all costs being commonsensical is simultaneously a leavening on corporate thought and a damper on excessive exuberance or inflated expectations. Drucker's leadership lies in identifying which way the crowd is moving and getting out in front. His commitment to incrementalism, his enthusiasm for internationalization, and his strong advocacy for cross-learning fit well into these times of corporate change and turbulence.

Victor C. Ferkiss

Victor Ferkiss is Professor of Government at Georgetown University, in Washington, DC. He is by far the most academic of our futurists. His concerns about technology, the environment, possible ecological disasters, political freedom, and the future of government and the political process unfortunately do not motivate him with any passion to get the message out, to deliver it to the public in cogent, easy to assimilate terms. He is far from being a publicist and has no particular interest in the corporation or in the individual institutions of technology. For him society and the managers of society need to be replaced by "technological man" who understands the powers and risks of technology. Currently "bourgeois man" unfortunately sees market forces as the only constraint on future development. As a deep and deliberative thinker Ferkiss has great value in developing context, long term themes and foundation issues that must be dealt with eventually. While the least accessible of our futurists, the trip is well worth the time and effort.

Barry B. Hughes

Barry Hughes is Professor at the Graduate School of International Studies, University of Denver. His personal commitment to a global perspective and to integrating the divergent views of other futurists, when added to his skills and experience as a quantitative modeler makes him unusual if not unique among futurists. His modeling makes him aware of subtleties, downstream effects and interactions. His commitment to integration alerts him to the ifs, ands, and buts of any emerging situation. His self-imposed neutrality should continue to free him from ideological preconceptions. He has much to say as analyst and integrator to the corporation on the longer term global context and the consequences of alternative actions. His tools are macro, his perspective long term. Detail and implications must be left up to his readers.

Alexander King

Alexander King is President of the Club of Rome and an international civil servant of wide experience. He would say he is neither a futurist nor an ideologue. His objective, and his strength, is to promote mechanisms for problem identification and analysis and then to lay them before his constituency, which includes all major institutions of the world and its citizens-at-large. A neutral, even-handed, analysis of problems is his aim so that others, from their varied ideological and political perspectives, will be alerted to the magnitude of the problems and be free to explore solutions according to their own convictions. He is at the center of a global network of public and private leaders, thinkers and decisionmakers which any corporation would be wise to tie onto. He is neither the composer nor the lyricist, neither the player nor the conductor. His role is impresario and producer. He can pull the pieces together to make the magic possible.

Richard D. Lamm

The only recent U.S. politician to explore the future in a systematic and substantial manner, Governor Lamm sees a more controlled, restricted, and regulated environment for the U.S. He completed his third and last term as governor of Colorado in 1987. He taught at Dartmouth College and has now returned to Denver to practice law.

Often affectionately and ironically known as "Governor Gloom," Lamm tends always to see the "bottle as half empty." He is addicted to and respectful of data and good at analyzing emerging problems and outcomes, including those that comprise the corporate and business context. He has a strong sense of the limitations on public policy. His special strength is understanding how public policy may respond, mostly negatively and out of fear and, in the short run, to emerging and impending crises. While indifferent to the corporation as an institution, he offers many practical insights on how things might go wrong in the corporate environment.

Michael Marien

Michael Marien is the outstanding bibliographer of the futures field. He reads, reviews, and abstracts for *Future Survey* and edits *Future Survey Annual.* He provides the wealth of material in these journals. He is one of the foremost critics of futures thinking and of its practitioners. His awareness of who has written, said, thought, or conjectured on any subject seems to be inexhaustible and comprehensive. His ability to collate and organize that material is limitless and clever. For the corporation, Marien is a broad, deep reservoir of knowledge and information. He is the knowledge gatekeeper in contemporary futures thinking. His choice is to know everything rather than to create the new; to integrate what is available rather than to push to new boundaries.

Dennis L. Meadows

Dennis Meadows is a global modeler, simulation gaming expert, engineer, and practitioner of a lifestyle of voluntary simplicity. He is Professor of Engineering at Dartmouth College. He is co-author of *The Limits to Growth,* 1972, a report for the Club of Rome, a widely distributed, disputed, and controversial book. Precise, quantitative, global, and comprehensive in outlook, Meadows' tools are clear; their use is teachable and broadly applicable to corporate concerns. Modeling, for which Meadows is best known, is useful in exploring relationships and in creating explicit mental maps of what individuals believe. Modeling can identify and lay bare implicit issues, risks, and opportunities. Complemented by other techniques it can get at the strategic implications of products, processes, services, and policy. Modeling requires a substantial investment in time to acquire the skills, or even the understanding of its power, and that experience is likely to imprint an ineradicable pattern of thinking on the individual.

James A. Ogilvy

Jay Ogilvy is a futurist with a formal background in philosophy and a professional focus on the study of human values. He is Director of the Revisioning Philosophy Program at Esalen Institute, Big Sur, California. Prior to that he directed research at SRI International's Values and Lifestyles Program (VALS). Oglivy has unusual credentials, coming from a background in philosophy and a professional concern for human values. He emphasizes these factors as shaping and shaped by forces at play. He can throw a line deep and far back into western intellectual traditions, and often ends up with an unusual and unexpected perspective or twist to the implications of a trend. Having spent several years closely tied to business and corporate concerns at SRI International and being involved with their VALS project, he is a rich source and excellent communicator of interesting and informed analysis and speculation on the interplay of values and new developments.

Gerard K. O'Neill

Gerard O'Neill is a distinguished physicist and, as President of the Space Studies Institute, advocate for space development and space colonization. He has a time horizon of a century or more, a strong technological optimism, a belief in human ability to solve problems and make a better future. He emphasizes technology in shaping the future and defining our choices. O'Neill pursues the implications of space and the application of high technology to human affairs with uncommon passion, scientific and technological elegance, and an imposing degree of formal analysis. Implicit in his work is the potential for commercial and business applications. While it is unlikely that one can expect the detailed implications for the business enterprise to spring forth from O'Neill's work, one can expect his ideas to be pregnant with practical applications. For example, his notion of bringing potential space applications down to earth suggests that the basic mental set we have toward design and construction for the terrestrial environment could be altered to our benefit.

John R. Pierce

John Pierce is a distinguished electrical engineer. He is Emeritus Professor of Engineering at the California Institute of Technology and is associated with the Center for Computer Research in Music and Acoustics at Stanford. He is an expert looking at the future of telecommunications and computers. Pierce came late in life to a systematic look at the implications of technology. He has a strong, positive orientation toward the corporation, toward corporate research, and a thorough commitment to the expanding range of benefits which telecommunications and computer technology will bring to humankind. While in no way a systematic futurist, he has an imaginative and engaging mind, concentrating on the emerging applications of computer and telecommunications technology to every aspect of the human enterprise. His thoughts are lively, fresh, and unpretentious.

Peter Schwartz

Peter Schwartz specializes in the future environment for business, looking at corporations in many countries and business climates. His current projects include strategic planning for the London Stock Exchange. He is starting a futures research institute in Palo Alto. In his futures career he has made the transition from being a transformationalist to an enthusiast for the positive and central role of the corporation in influencing the future. After working intensively in corporate long-range planning, he has acquired depth, understanding, and sensitivity to the factors influencing the present actions and viability of the multinational. He is always bold, imaginative, and coherent in his thinking. Skilled in the formal tools of futurism, scenario building, and data manipulation, and able in communicating complexities in dealing with the future, Schwartz would be neck-and-neck with Drucker in his enthusiasm and positive orientation toward the corporation, but edge him out in commitment to the formal study of the future as an aid to planning and understanding.

Robert Theobald

Robert Theobald is Chairman of Knowledge Systems, Inc., which publishes works of social entrepreneurship and develops a knowledge base for social action. He believes we have to work at the grass roots. He is unique in combining broad scale analysis with cogent argument for the ability of individuals to instigate change. Theobald is unique in being the only major futurist simultaneously committed to macro-analysis of national and global problems and to carrying them down to the level of actions open to ordinary people. His work has gradually moved toward process as a way of unfolding factors, alternatives, actions, and options and moved away from any grand theoretical framework or even specific programmatic goals. With his powerful emphasis on the role of the individual in shaping the future, an interesting opportunity may lie in bringing Theobald inside the corporate framework to help the individuals in the corporation ask the normally unexamined question, "What can *I* do?"

CHAPTER 3

WHAT FUTURISTS BELIEVE: COMPARISONS AMONG 17

This chapter compares the views and beliefs of a panel of 17 contemporary futurists. As was noted earlier, the group are all male, almost all are American, with an average age of 58. We assume the panel represents the landscape of current futurist thinking in advanced nations such as those of North America and Europe, without claiming to have covered the entire range of futurists or beliefs about the future.

The futurists are interested primarily in the economy and society of the advanced nations, especially the U.S., and in the more sophisticated aspects of the emerging global society. Their attention to the Third World and to development issues in general is in much less depth. Rather than demonstrating any individual preference, this may reflect the origins and evolution of futures thinking in the First World from military, national, and commercial interests. Not until *The Limits to Growth,* in 1972, did a broad constituency develop for exploring the global future in terms of a growing population's demands on the physical resources of the planet.

In this chapter, the futurists' individual views are dissected, sorted, compared, and summarized to produce a composite set of beliefs about the future. As one might expect of this process, some of the finer details and shades of meaning are lost. The futurist panel may agree, for example, as they do, that the future price of energy is important to the health of the global economy, but disagree on timing, ameliorating influences, the role of energy policy, and so on. For more detail and depth on individual beliefs of special interest to the reader, read the chapters on individual futurists in Part II.

What 17 Futurists Strongly Agreed On

- **Complexity:** The futurists believe almost all human endeavors, institutions and systems are becoming more complex, because greater numbers of people are involved and because new layers of technology and bureaucracy are being incorporated. They differ on how to manage complexity, but most would say we need new tools.

- **Governments and Institutions:** Our current institutional structures, such as government, are not the answer to managing complexity. Most are out of date, bureaucratic, sluggish, with short timeframes and attention spans and lacking a world view. We *will* have new and more flexible organization of societies to manage the emerging global issues. Corporations will increasingly play a larger role, taking over governing functions and providing more services in a privatized society. So far corporations have seemed reluctant to embrace a larger role and are perhaps unaware of such a role's possibilities and responsibilities, one of which would be communication of the corporation's explicit goals and values.
- **The Dominance of Science and Technology:** Most of the futurists see technology as a, if not the, primary driver of change. The pace of new developments appears to be increasing and the potential of several areas of technology is revolutionary. The agreement is strong that these are the most important technologies:

  —**Telematics** - including telecommunications, computers, and electronics applications and links of all kinds.
  —**Biotechnology** - most importantly for its impacts on agriculture and health.
  —**Materials** - for their revolutionary potential in manufactured products, construction, and space development.

- **The Importance of Solving the Energy Transition:** All see the end of oil as the dominant source of energy in the next 20-50 years and a transition to various other energy sources. Most agree that this transition will not be accomplished without turbulence and perhaps slowed economic growth. Most note that we cannot continue to use energy as we have been. Our sense of urgency to find new energy sources may depend on first exhausting the resources we have.
- **Slowdown of World Economic Growth:** An early increase of the cost of energy, plus world population growth and greater demand for resources and food are the drivers of this trend. Some even feel a threat of global economic collapse. If countries are not to collapse some debts will have to be written off. Population and production cannot both continue to grow unchecked.
- **Transition with Continuity:** The futurists expect great changes will occur within a framework of continuity that will keep the basic shape of society much as we have known it. We will make transitions into the information age, switch to other forms of energy, bank electronically, cope with greater numbers of people and more diverse

relationships within society, while at the same time maintaining stability in our governance, management and institutional structures. This is not to say conflicts and flareups will not occur, but these are part of the world's continuity and are not expected to disable the day-to-day life of most people. Here and there, increasing complexity may outrun our ability to manage a system, but for the most part we can muddle through.

- **The Avoidance of Nuclear War:** This is one of the most important issues of the rest of the century, and represents the major threat to our ability to manage our transitions without discontinuity. Full scale nuclear war is generally not seen to be as great a threat as that of smaller nations gaining access to nuclear weapons.
- **Interdependence of the Globe:** Some believe we may have one global system in the future, in which we will increasingly need to integrate knowledge in order to shape and manage it. As we become more interdependent economically and socially, the implications of purely nationalist strategies will become more serious. The panel distrusts even the U.S.'s willingness to act in the global interest, and implies that multinational corporations ought in their own interests to support any internationally stabilizing actions.
- **Decline of the U.S.:** Almost all of the futurists anticipate the economic, and perhaps military, decline of the U.S., although for some, the effect is more apparent than real. Greater competition from other nations, and the increasing integration of the world economy will lead to an apparent decline in U.S. influence on world affairs. From one point of view, the U.S. will merely take its place among equals.
- **Education:** The futurists agree that education requires much improvement, but doubt the capability of the U.S. educational system to improve. Some even project formal educational systems to face long term decline. Education will compete with more enticing offerings—television, radio, and recorded entertainment. Information technologies probably will not soon be used extensively inside school systems.
- **Demands of the Information Society:** The information society, however, will demand new standards of literacy and competence. Though the futurists vary on how much education is needed, they believe new skills, training and worldviews are among the requirements. Universities and corporations are seen as not doing as much as they can or must in meeting the emerging demands.
- **Aging of the U.S. Population:** Several of the panel warn that the aging of the U.S. population represents a culture shock for a nation

that has been young for most of its history. We can expect intergenerational conflict and for U.S. society to stiffen and grow less flexible and more like Europe.

The next two sections, What Futurists Strongly Disagree About, and What Futurists are Uncertain Of, or Feel Disquiet About, represent a spread of diverging views. These differences range from strong disagreement and opposite positions on a topic to a more general and diffuse set of uncertainties and concerns about some issues.

What 17 Futurists Strongly Disagree About

- **Societal Change:** The ability, or capacity, of individuals, groups, political systems and nations to adapt to change, to create new and reformed institutional structures is hotly argued. Views range from a belief that only disaster will force societal change, to faith that society can accomplish the enormous structural changes that would promote a successful colonization of space. Within this basic disagreement are many smaller disagreements on aspects of societal change, the role of religion, for example, and the contribution of personal and societal values.
- **Technological Change:** Although the futurists agree on the importance of science and technology to the U.S. and the world's future, they do not agree on its value and function in society. Some believe science and technology are autonomous forces, that cannot be controlled by social choices or political regulation. Others think technological change cannot occur unless a social need for it develops. In any event, the futurists tend to believe its effects can be only partly anticipated.
- **Images of the Future:** The futurists' explorations are colored by their differing images of the future which are, in turn, shaped by their underlying optimism or pessimism. This underlying assumption can shape a view of the future that is wholly different from that of other futurists.
- **Economic Factors:** The futurists differ in their assumptions about the effects of microelectronics on the global workforce, the stability of the international flow of money and its relative importance to world economic health, on the potential impacts of the USSR and China on world trade, and the ability of less developed nations to catch up with the industrialized nations.

What 17 Futurists are Uncertain Of, or Feel Disquiet About

- **World Population Growth:** Several of the futurists question what a world with 8-10 billion people will be like, and doubt the capacity of the world to feed, house, and clothe a larger global population. The relative speed of the demographic transition in less developed countries is an uncertain factor, although at least one of the futurists is hopeful, believing it to be underestimated. Others think the world population just cannot continue to grow.
- **Military, Defense, and Disarmament:** The U.S. cannot support its military infrastructure at present levels for much longer, especially as a debtor nation. A cutback in military spending will hit hard at the U.S. and possibly the global economy. Besides these concerns, little attention is paid to the long-term military build-up or to the potential impacts of emerging world trade in arms, the growing military interest in space, and the spillover of unwanted arms to supply wars in less developed nations.
- **Africa:** The future of Africa is generally believed to be dismal, although none of the futurists has analyzed the continent's prospects in any detail. What concerns them most is whether anyone else in the world will care, or act, or can act to head off inevitable disaster. Africa as a continent is expected to continue to be politically unstable and may redivide along tribal and religious lines. The African problem with AIDS is alarming. The economy of the continent looks bleak for at least the next two decades.
- **Values and Attitudes:** Societal values do not contribute strongly as driving forces but influence events in ways that are not fully understood and are unpredictable. One specific example in the corporation is the potential disruption that may occur if baby boomers in large numbers begin to have their mid-life crises. There may never be much visible data when a shift in values occurs, yet the waves of effects pushed by such a shift can reverberate for decades. Societal mood swings between pessimism and optimism can affect emerging revolutions in technology. Attitudes are formed and shaped by events such as wars and economic depression. Some of the futurists believe values such as the work ethic are in decline in the U.S., others think that young people are workaholics.

The following section summarizes the topics that have, in general, been only briefly mentioned, or ignored by the futurist panel.

What 17 Futurists Have, In General, Ignored

- **Foreign Affairs/Foreign Policy:** Many of the futurists are internationalists and take a broad view of the world's problems. They generally are uninterested in the mechanics of resolution, that is, in foreign policy initiatives and impacts. Further, they are not especially interested in the future of either individual countries or bilateral connections, the U.S. with the U.K., for example, or the emerging U.S.-Australia linkages. The future focus of U.S. foreign policy goals is not mentioned, nor are U.S. strategic interests much discussed except in relation to energy sources and military buildups.
- **The Infrastructure:** The futurists doubt the world's ability to build infrastructure fast enough to keep pace with population growth, and there is some mention of cities, their size, and problems, but the larger issues of rebuilding, repair, and new structures, of city and regional planning, and of major and macro-engineering undertakings are not discussed.
- **The Sociology of the Future:** Some areas of this topic are discussed—demographic impacts on society, the possibility of a change in values, for example—but large groups in society on whom some of the potential changes might depend are ignored or noted only in passing.
- **Women:** The future worldwide status of women is notably ignored and their potential contribution unmentioned except in notice of their movement into the U.S. workforce.
- **Blacks, Minorities, Immigrants, and Cultural Conflicts:** Also ignored is the societal position and potential of blacks and other minorities in the U.S. Immigrants to the U.S. or migration/immigration in general do not receive much attention. Although tribalism and fundamentalism are mentioned as threats to regional stability in the world, there is no analysis of competing racial, ethnic, and cultural interests.
- **Lifestyles:** Little attention is paid to the day-to-day aspects of future life. The futurists do not deal with family life, recreation, and housing issues. Death and the more mundane aspects of old age received little note. By implication, they do not discuss domestic markets. The potential for changes in values in the context of the future of the family and its role in preserving or changing societal value structures is ignored.
- **Crime:** Changes brought by a growing population and the societal implications are discussed, but crime comes up only briefly.
- **Nations and Nation Groups:** While the futurists do look at other nations, often it is a cursory glance and leads only to questionable generalizations.

- **Unions:** The potential role of unions is dismissed or ignored. Their impact on the workforce is assumed to be declining or unimportant to the information-based society.
- **Environment:** Potential impacts of the CO_2 induced greenhouse effect and other global environmental problems, such as environmental degradation and agricultural pollution, are of general concern but are not given much detailed attention. The futurists barely ask who will pay for cleanup costs. Little is provided on how to ensure a livable environment for the future. We are told we need technological answers on how to alleviate environmental problems before they become irreversible, but the structural and economic changes that may be necessary are not explored.
- **Religion:** Religious belief as a motivator of human action and a source of values is mentioned by several of the futurist panel, most frequently in the context of fundamentalism. However its influence over the long term is assumed to be in decline.

In the remainder of this chapter the worldviews of the futurists are compared, using matrices reflecting their corporate orientation and scope of interest, the level of their global concern and technological and sociopolitical focus, and their time horizon and relative optimism or pessimism about the future. (See Exhibits 3-1, 3-2, 3-3.) The structural elements the futurists consider important to the future are identified, as well as their beliefs about the underlying causes and inhibitors of societal change. (See Exhibits 3-4, 3-5.) Exhibit 3-6 explores those institutions and systems considered likely to be important actors in the future. Exhibit 3-7 reflects the futurist panel's responses on being asked what unexpected events, discontinuities, and wild cards could disrupt their assumptions about the future. Exhibit 3-8 lists ideal, alternative, and emerging societies glimpsed in the various snapshots of the future offered by members of the panel. Exhibit 3-9 charts intellectual influences on the futures thinking of the panelists by frequency of citation and by individual.

The Corporate Orientation of the Panel

The following three matrices show how the 17 futurists could be grouped along selected axes. The groupings are the collective judgment of the team working on this project and are merely intended to display the wide range of views, beliefs, and approaches to the future represented by this group of 17 people.

Some, but not all of the futurists on the panel expect, or anticipate, that corporations, and especially multinationals, are part of their actual, or intended, audience. Several focus on future roles for the corporation, others do not. Since this project is sponsored by businesses and business-related organizations. it is worthwhile comparing the panel's range of relative orientation to the corporate world. In Exhibit 3-1, this corporate orientation is plotted against the breadth of their interest.

Four futurists, Drucker, Schwartz, Ogilvy and Pierce, are moderately to highly interested in the corporation. These four tend towards a particular rather than a broad view of the future. The three broadest thinkers, Ferkiss, Bell and Boulding, have little or no interest directly in the corporation.

Exhibit 3-1

17 Futurists: Corporate Orientation and Scope of Interest

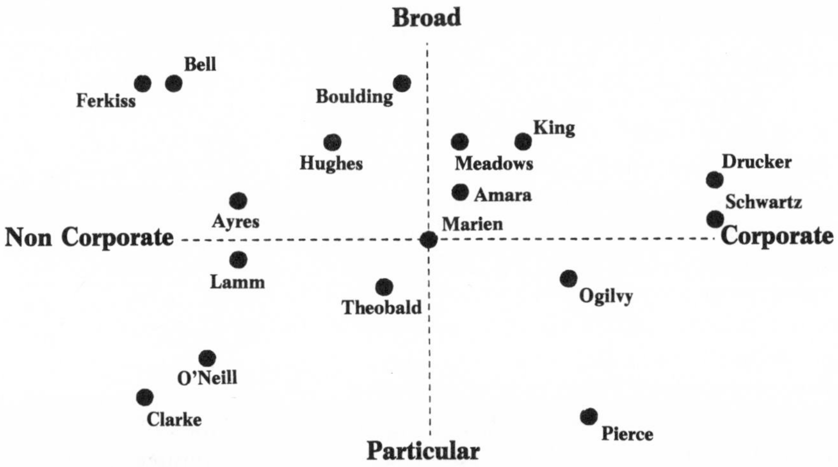

Global and Technological Orientation

Four groupings are of interest. Marien, Drucker and Amara, take a central position on the U.S. vs. the world, and science and technology against social and political factors as major drivers of change. O'Neill, Clarke and Lamm are outliers. O'Neill and Clarke are focused on technology and hold planetary and galactic perspectives, rather than just worldviews. On the other hand, Lamm's sociopolitical approach is intensely focused on the political system of the U.S. Lamm joins another grouping, with Ferkiss, Bell and Theobald, all of whom have sociopolitical approaches and low to high interest in global issues. Ayres, Ogilvy, Schwartz and Pierce, have a moderate to high technological focus. The final four, Hughes, Boulding, Meadows and King have strongly global orientations, and strike a balance between a technological and a sociopolitical emphasis.

Exhibit 3-2

17 Futurists: Global Orientation and Sociopolitical vs. Technological Emphasis

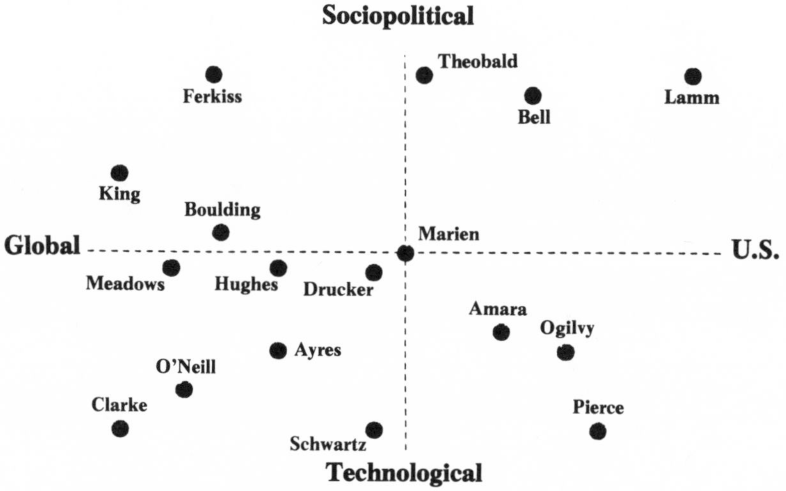

Time Horizons and Optimism

In contrasting the approximate time horizon of each futurist against his optimism and pessimism about the future, it is possible to see relationships between the two. The largest cluster—and these are among members of the group most optimistic about the future—think about periods in the 5-25 year range. Their optimism may be based, at least in part, on their anticipation of positive trends in technology based on present successes and opportunities. O'Neill and Clarke are again outliers. Their high level of optimism is based on an extremely long-range view of the future, 100-1000 years. Bell, Meadows, King, Ferkiss, Marien, Lamm, form a group moderately to highly pessimistic about the future over the next 5-50 years. Their pessimism reflects their belief that negative outcomes are likely if certain currently serious and worsening problems are not dealt with in that 5-50 year span. Boulding takes a mildly pessimistic view of the long period necessary to achieve beneficial social change, such as world peace.

Exhibit 3-3

17 Futurists: Time Horizon* and Range of Optimism and Pessimism

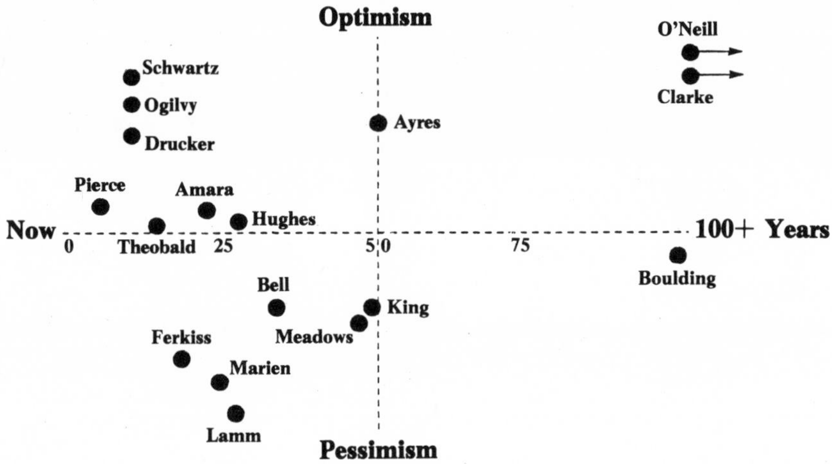

*Time Horizon years are approximations of the range of their interest in the future.

Components of the Study of the Future

The following six exhibits present a glimpse of the underlying structure of the varied approaches to thinking about the future, represented by the group of 17. These structural elements: underlying causes; drivers and inhibitors of change; major actors; events, and wild cards, and ideal alternative and emerging societies, are merely listed here to alert the reader to key concepts. More on each of these topics is available in Part II.

Structural Elements

One useful approach to the study of the future is to select a range of elements that will continue to be substantial or increase in significance and use these as a framework for building plausible alternative outcomes. Exhibit 3-4 lists structural elements the futurist panel believes to be important, and notes those members of the panel for whom a particular element appears to be significant. Names printed in boldface type indicate that this futurist emphasized this element. Lamm, for example, is the only futurist to mention immigration as important to the U.S. economy and, for him, it is a vital factor and calls for much more forethought.

Exhibit 3-4

Structural Elements Important to the Future*

A. **THE U.S. ECONOMY AND SOCIETY** (relative health, strength, etc.)	**Amara,** Ayres, Bell, Boulding, Drucker, Hughes, Lamm, Ogilvy
• Political structure and direction, role of decisionmaking and policy	Amara, Ayres, Bell, Boulding, Drucker, Ferkiss, **Lamm**, Meadows, Marien, Ogilvy, Theobald
• Societal structure, its institutions and changing balance, including a shift to an aging population	Amara, Bell, Boulding, Drucker, Ferkiss, Lamm, Theobald
• Work, jobs	Amara, Ayres, Bell, Drucker, Ferkiss, Lamm, Theobald
• Defense, outlook for spending	Amara, Boulding, Clarke, Hughes, Lamm, Marien, Meadows, Ogilvy

*Names in boldface type reflect greater emphasis given to this topic.

• Education, negative and pessimistic views of the educational system	Amara, Ayres, Bell, Clarke, Drucker, Lamm, **Marien**, Meadows, Ogilvy, **Pierce**, Schwartz, Theobald
• Health	Amara, Ayres, Clarke, Lamm, Meadows, Ogilvy, O'Neill, Theobald
• Resources, including capital and knowledge	Ayres, Boulding, Drucker, Ferkiss, Lamm
• Energy policy and potential for future shocks	Amara, Ayres, Boulding, Drucker, **Hughes**, Lamm, Marien, O'Neill, **Schwartz**
• Cities	Amara, Ayres, Lamm, Meadows, O'Neill, Pierce
• Infrastructure	Ayres, Bell
• Transportation	Bell, Clarke, Ogilvy, O'Neill, Schwartz
• Immigration	**Lamm**
B. THE GLOBAL ECONOMY	Amara, Ayres, Boulding, Drucker, **Ferkiss**, Hughes, King, Ogilvy
• Political structure	Ayres, Bell, King, Meadows, Schwartz
• Societal structure	Ayres, Bell, Drucker, Ferkiss, King, Meadows, Pierce, Schwartz
• Shifting power/trade balance	**Ayres**, Bell, Boulding, Drucker, **Ferkiss**, **Hughes**, **King**, Lamm, Ogilvy, Schwartz

• Capital, sources/availability, financial flows/international debt	**Ayres**, Boulding, Drucker, Hughes, **King**, Lamm, Meadows, Schwartz, Theobald
• Trade in weapons/disarmament	Ayres, Boulding, Ferkiss, King, O'Neill, Theobald
• Food and agriculture	Ayres, Drucker, Hughes, King, Ogilvy, O'Neill
• Industrialization/development	Bell, Boulding, Drucker, Hughes, Schwartz
• Population and cities	Boulding, Ferkiss, Hughes, King, Lamm, O'Neill, Theobald
• Energy	Amara, **Ayres**, Hughes, King, Meadows, Schwartz
C. ENVIRONMENTAL (U.S. AND GLOBAL)	Amara, Ayres, Boulding, Ferkiss, Hughes, King, Lamm, Marien, **Meadows**, Theobald
D. SCIENCE (responsibility, accountability, influence on industry)	Bell, Boulding, Clarke, Hughes, King, O'Neill, **Pierce**
• Ideas/images of the future, intellectual technologies	Amara, **Bell**, **Boulding**, Drucker, Clarke, King, **Marien**, Ogilvy, O'Neill, Theobald
E. TECHNOLOGY	**Amara**, Ayres, Bell, Clarke, Drucker, Ferkiss, Meadows, O'Neill, Schwartz
• Social innovation technologies, peace research, for example	Boulding, Drucker, King, O'Neill

• Biotechnologies	Amara, Ayres, Drucker, Hughes, Marien, Ogilvy, O'Neill, Pierce, Schwartz
• Military technologies	Ayres, Marien,
• Telecommunications	Amara, Ayres, Bell, Drucker, O'Neill, **Pierce**
• Materials	Amara, Bell, Marien, O'Neill, Schwartz
• Computers/AI/microelectronics	Amara, Ayres, Bell, Clarke, King, Lamm, Meadows
• Entertainment, video, recorded interactive, etc.	Clarke, Marien, Schwartz
• Information technologies	**Amara**, Bell, Clarke, Drucker, King, Lamm, Marien, Meadows, **Ogilvy**, **Pierce**, Schwartz
• Energy technologies	Amara, Clarke, Hughes, King, O'Neill, Pierce
• Automation/robotics	Ayres, Clarke, Drucker, King, O'Neill
• Space technologies and tech transferred, i.e., biosphere research	Clarke, O'Neill, Pierce

Beliefs About Drivers of Change

Most futurists have beliefs or implied beliefs about the drivers and inhibitors of change and the underlying causes of long-term societal shifts. All except Amara, Clarke, and O'Neill, who tend to see science, technology and innovation as autonomous drivers, believe values and attitudes drive and sometimes inhibit change. Ayres, especially, believes traditional attitudes and values are often paralyzing inhibitors.

Theobald, on the other hand, counts individual values as the primary catalysts of social change.

Most of the futurist panel considers political factors, technology, innovation, and economic conditions as other primary drivers. Bell, Pierce, and Schwartz, especially, believe increasing complexity is a new factor shaping decisions about how to run organizations and manage systems and nations. The other items are important to smaller groups of the futurist panel.

Exhibit 3-5

Underlying Causes, Drivers, and Inhibitors of Change

A. **VALUES AND ATTITUDES** - as inhibitors and drivers of change	**Ayres**, Bell, Boulding, Drucker, Ferkiss, Hughes, King, Lamm, Marien, **Meadows**, **Ogilvy**, Pierce, Schwartz, **Theobald**
• Crime	King, Lamm, O'Neill, Schwartz, Theobald
• Fundamentalism	Ayres, Bell, Boulding, Ferkiss, Ogilvy
• Declining values	Bell, Ferkiss, Lamm, Meadows
• Influence of past events	Bell, **Boulding**, Schwartz
B. **POLITICAL FACTORS** - decision-making practices and limitations	Amara, Ayres, Bell, Drucker, Ferkiss, Hughes, King, Lamm, Marien, Meadows, Schwartz
• Institutional rigidity and vulnerability	Amara, **Ayres**, Drucker, King, **Lamm**, Marien, O'Neill, Schwartz, **Theobald**
• Regulation	Amara, Lamm, Pierce, Schwartz

• Leadership	Drucker, Ferkiss, **Lamm**, Theobald
• Individual action	Ayres, Ferkiss, Theobald
• Social needs, producing action, policy, technology, etc.	**Ayres**, Bell, Drucker, King, Lamm, Meadows, Ogilvy, Pierce
C. **TECHNOLOGY AND INNOVATION**	Amara, **Ayres**, Bell, **Clarke**, Hughes, **King**, **Marien**, **O'Neill**, Pierce, Schwartz, Theobald
• Information technologies as drivers of individual, societal, and organizational change	**Amara**, Clarke, Drucker, King, Lamm, Marien, **Ogilvy**, **Pierce**, Schwartz Theobald
• Scale	Amara, **Bell**, Drucker
D. **ECONOMIC CONDITIONS** - occasionally disastrous, that spur change	Amara, Ayres, Bell, Drucker, Ferkiss, King, **Lamm**, Meadows, Ogilvy, Schwartz
• Debt	Boulding, Hughes, Ogilvy, Theobald
E. **COMPLEXITY** - in society and organizations	Amara, Ayres, **Bell**, Ferkiss, King, Marien, Ogilvy, **Pierce**, **Schwartz**
• Social experimentation and innovation	Ayres, Drucker, Hughes, King, Meadows, **Ogilvy**, O'Neill, Theobald
• Human error/competence, etc.	Ayres, Ferkiss, King, Pierce
F. **STRUCTURAL CHANGE** - larger changes not directly attributed to other factors	Bell, Boulding, Drucker, Lamm, Marien, Ogilvy, Pierce, Schwartz

G. CONFLICTING SOCIETAL DRIVES	Amara, Ayres, Bell, Ferkiss, Lamm, Schwartz
• Population growth	Hughes, King, Lamm, Meadows, O'Neill, Theobald
• Resource demand and scarcity	**Ferkiss**, Hughes, **Lamm**, Meadows, O'Neill, Theobald
• Threat/conflict	Bell, Boulding, Ferkiss, Lamm, Marien, Theobald
H. SYSTEMS THEORIES OF CHANGE	Bell, Boulding, Hughes, Meadows, Theobald
• Kondratieff, etc. cyclical theory	Ayres, Meadows, Theobald
• Ecological niche building	Boulding, O'Neill
I. OTHER DRIVERS AND INHIBITORS	
• Ideas	Boulding, Marien, O'Neill
• Indeterminate, random factors	**Bell**, Marien, O'Neill
• Gravity	Clarke, O'Neill

Casting the Lead Roles for the Future

Corporations and multinationals may be leading actors in the future, according to at least eight members of the panel. Exhibit 3-6 lists these and other likely players. This list includes some specific organizations such as the U.S. government. Other and more loosely defined, but influential, systems are expected to be actors, such as the workforce, the international financial system, language, tradition, and technology transfer. Individuals or groups of individuals, such as women and scientists appear as actors with a new or special role to play in the future. Some groups, such as unions, are considered in decline and likely to have a smaller role.

Exhibit 3-6

Major Actors, Institutions, and Systems

A. PUBLIC SECTOR	
• U.S. government	Amara, Drucker, Ferkiss, Hughes, Lamm, Meadows, Ogilvy, Pierce, Schwartz
• Nations and nation groups	Amara, Ayres, **Bell**, Boulding, Ferkiss, Hughes, **King**, Ogilvy, O'Neill Schwartz
—Soviet Union	Ayres, Boulding, Hughes, King, Meadows, O'Neill
—Europe (EEC)	Amara, Ayres, Drucker, King, Pierce, Schwartz
—Africa, in the sense of being in desperate case, not as an influential force	Ayres, Boulding, King, Meadows, O'Neill, Schwartz
—Latin America	Amara, Ayres, Lamm
—China	Amara, Ayres, Boulding, Hughes
—Asia/Japan	**Amara**, Ayres, **Drucker**, Hughes, King, **Lamm**, Ogilvy
B. PRIVATE SECTOR	**Amara**, Ogilvy
• Corporations	Boulding, **Drucker,** Ferkiss, Marien, Meadows, **Ogilvy**, Schwartz

—Industries	Drucker, Schwartz
—Telecommunications industry	Drucker, Pierce
• Multinationals	Bell, **Drucker**, **Hughes**, King, Meadows, Ogilvy, Schwartz
C. **NEW ORGANIZATIONAL STRUCTURES**, including emerging non-governmental, international, and informal structures	Amara, Bell, Ferkiss, Hughes, King, **Meadows**, Ogilvy, Schwartz
• Interest groups	Amara, Bell, Ferkiss, Meadows, Theobald
• International financial systems	Drucker, **Schwartz**
• Language (English)	Ayres, Clarke, O'Neill
D. **OTHER ACTORS**	
• Unions	Amara, Hughes, Drucker
• Religion	Ayres, Bell, **Ferkiss**, King, Ogilvy
• Workers/workforce	Amara, Bell, Drucker, Hughes, King, Pierce
• Women	Bell, Boulding, Ferkiss, Lamm
• Scientists	Boulding, Marien, Meadows, O'Neill
• Individual actors, important because of a decisive act, or in grass roots change	Amara, Ferkiss, Lamm, **Theobald**
• Technology as an independent actor	Amara, Bell, O'Neill

• Quantity/quality of information	**Bell**, Drucker, Marien, Pierce, Schwartz, Theobald
• Education	King, Marien
• Tradition	Ayres, Ferkiss
• Tech transfer, especially in the Third World	Bell, Hughes, King, Schwartz
• Death, and the right to die	Lamm

Wild Cards

Exhibit 3-7 lists possible events that may disrupt or enhance the future in the short- or long-range perspective. Some of these are wild cards, or discontinuities, and most of these are the unanticipated negative event. The futurist panel tends to believe most wild cards are bad news. Some events, such as large scale workforce transitions, may balance out and be seen as neutral in their effects over time.

Exhibit 3-7

Events, Discontinuities, and Wild Cards

A. LONG-TERM POSITIVE SHIFTS

• Biotech—agricultural revolution	Drucker, Hughes, Theobald
• Space exploration	Ayres, Marien, O'Neill
• Peace/disarmament	**Boulding**

B. LONG-TERM NEGATIVE SHIFTS

• Population overshoot	Bell, Boulding, Ferkiss, Hughes, King, Marien, Theobald
• Global polarization, into the haves and have-nots	Amara, **King**, Marien

• Massive global unemployment	Bell, Hughes, King, Theobald
• Greenhouse effects (CFCs and CO_2)	Amara, King, Lamm, O'Neill, Theobald
• Long-term U.S. economic decline	Ayres, Ferkiss, Hughes, **Lamm**, Marien

C. POSITIVE EVENTS

• Technological breakthroughs	Hughes, Meadows

D. NEGATIVE EVENTS

• Nuclear wars (LDCs)	Amara, Ayres, Boulding, **Clarke**, Hughes, Marien, Ogilvy
• Increase in terrorism	Lamm, O'Neill, Theobald
• Economic collapse (global)	**Marien**, Meadows, Theobald
• Nuclear accident	Marien
• AIDS and epidemic diseases	Boulding, Marien, Meadows, Schwartz
• Revolution in Mexico	Ayres, Schwartz
• Asian Ring war	Schwartz
• Systems breakdown	**Lamm**, Meadows, Theobald

E. NEUTRAL EVENTS

• Development of information networks globally	Clarke, **Meadows**, Ogilvy, Schwartz, Theobald
• Workforce transitions, (e.g., from mechanical to knowledge-based)	Bell, Drucker, King

• Millennial fever	Ogilvy
• Intensive computer use	Ayres, Pierce
• ETs, antigravity, and other advanced technologies	Clarke, O'Neill

Glimpses of Emerging Societies

Exhibit 3-8 opens an interesting window on the kind of societies emerging in advanced nations at the end of the industrial age. Several of the futurist panel agree the emerging society will be knowledge or information-based. A few expect and hope for a science-based society, either as a superculture supported by advanced technologies, or one supported by a sea-change in our scientific and political priorities. These priorities will shift towards solving social and physical problems of the global society.

Social change drives other reconstructions of society towards an active peace and in the direction of a more cooperative and participative political and social structure. In the U.S., Drucker and Ogilvy believe we are shifting towards a society in which most former government services are provided by the private sector.

Exhibit 3-8

Ideal, Alternative, and Emerging Societies

A. **INFORMATION SOCIETIES**	Amara, Ayres, Bell, Ogilvy, O'Neill, Pierce, **Schwartz**
• Post-industrial societies	**Bell**, Drucker
• Knowledge-based society	**Bell**, Boulding, Drucker, **King**, Marien, Ogilvy, Theobald
B. **SCIENCE-BASED SOCIETIES**	
• Scientific superculture	Boulding, Ferkiss, O'Neill
• A new scientific order with different priorities for science	Ferkiss, Marien

• Space colonies	**O'Neill**
• Robot society	**Clarke**

C. NEW SOCIAL ORDER SOCIETIES

• Peaceful society	**Boulding**
• Ecological humanist society	**Ferkiss**, Meadows, O'Neill
• A more cooperative society	**Pierce**, Theobald
• Participatory society	Amara

D. OTHER SOCIETIES

• Privatized society, run and serviced by the private sector, primarily U.S.	Drucker, Ogilvy
• Global homogeneity—all societies and communities much the same	Boulding

Antecedents to the Futurist Panel's Thinking About the Future

Panel members were asked to name the intellectual antecedents to their thinking about the future. Among those who responded to this question, few of their citations overlapped, although several of the group have influenced each other. Exhibit 3-9 shows those names cited by at least two futurists, and on the following page, other cited influences.

In the next chapter, the strengths, weaknesses, and gaps in the panel's approach to the future are addressed.

Exhibit 3-9

Cited Influences on the Futurist Thinking of 17 Futurists

Harrison Brown	Ayres, Lamm, Marien
Herman Kahn	Ayres, Hughes, Marien
Joseph Schumpeter	Boulding, Drucker, Theobald
Lester Brown	Ayres, Lamm
Arthur C. Clarke	Ayres, O'Neill
Willis Harman	Amara, Lamm
Don Michael	Marien, Schwartz
John Naisbitt	Lamm, Marien
William Ogburn	Ayres, Marien
Eduard Pestel	Hughes, King
C.P. Snow	Ayres, Lamm
Jules Verne	Clarke, O'Neill
H.G. Wells	Boulding, Clarke
Gregory Bateson	Ogilvy, Theobald
John M. Keynes	Boulding, Theobald

Exhibit 3-9 (continued)
Additional Citations by Futurists

Roy Amara
Paul Baran
Kan Chen
Olaf Helmer
William Linvill

Robert U. Ayres
Dennis Gabor
S.C. Gilfillan
Ted Gordon
Allen V. Kneese
Norman McCrae
Ron Ridker
T.B. Taylor

Daniel Bell
Colin Clark
Karl Mannheim
Karl Marx
Robert McIver
Max Weber

Kenneth E. Boulding
Elise Boulding
Teilhard de Chardin
Charles Darwin
Methodism
Fred Polak
Quakerism
Lewis F. Richardson
Adam Smith
D'Arcy Thompson

Arthur C. Clarke
Hugo Gernsback
Herman Melville
Olaf Stapledon

Peter Drucker
Thomas Watson, Sr.

Barry B. Hughes
Bariloche Foundation
Globus Project (Berlin)
Wassily Leontief
Donella Meadows
Dennis Meadows
Mihajlo D. Mesarovic

Alexander King
Julian Huxley
Aurelio Peccei

Governor Richard Lamm
David Brower
Sir John Clubb
Will and Ariel Durant
David Halberstam
Garrett Hardin
John McPhee
Peter Peterson
Arnold Toynbee

Michael Marien
Daniel Bell
Yehezkel Dror
Peter Drucker
Buckminster Fuller
John W. Gardner
Bertram Gross
Betrand de Jouvenel
Henry Marien
John Platt

Dennis Meadows
T.S. Kuhn
Richard Duke
Jay Forrester

James A. Ogilvy
Roland Barthes
Jacques Derrida
Michel Foucault
G.W.F. Hegel
Martin Heidegger
James Hillman
Herbert Marcuse
Arnold Mitchell
F.W. Nietzsche
Peter Schwartz

Gerard K. O'Neill
J.P. Bernal
Robert Goddard
J.B.S. Haldane
Rudyard Kipling
Konstantin Tsiolkowsky

Peter Schwartz
Stewart Brand
Fernand Braudel
Paul Hawken
Lewis Mumford
James Ogilvy
Paul Valery
Pierre Wack

Robert Theobald
William Blake
St. Francis
J. W. von Goethe
E.F. Schumacher

CHAPTER 4

STRENGTHS, WEAKNESSES, AND GAPS IN CURRENT FUTURES THINKING

The relative strengths and weaknesses of futures thinking as exemplified by the 17 members of the futurist panel are explored in this chapter. This exploration sets out to answer the question: from the user's point of view what is substantial, coherent, and thoroughly studied in these views of the future, and what is less well covered or ignored?

Not surprisingly, the business user reasonably is interested in the future of the large, publicly owned or privately held multinational corporation. Beyond this corporate concern, however, and a need to know more about the external corporate environment, business users are aware of and concerned about implications for society as a whole.

Facts, data and sources used by the panel members are not disputed here. These, although they may support a futurist's sense of the direction of a trend and the strength of a shaping force, are not necessarily the basis for their assessment of the future. In any event, most of the panel members approach the future qualitatively, rather than quantitatively. Even when they use numbers their choice of data appears to be driven by underlying qualitative assumptions and arguments.

Since we do not intend to quarrel with figures, we offer alternative criteria for assessing our panel.

What Makes a Good Futurist? How Do You Know?

A good, well-rounded, futurist must:

- characterize the society, or situation being studied and recognize, outline, and account for the present situation,
- generate at a minimum, a coherent image(s) of the future, and,
- provide a road map or a description of how to get there.

These are minimum requirements. Beyond these, the exceptional futurist may also have a thorough sense of history, a unique approach, the ability to show us rich visions of the future that leap off the page, to catch our imagination with images we can connect to our own lives, and to be willing to work with us on developing strategies and in planning action steps.

The futurist's depth of field, breadth, range, and time horizon are also important if we are to have our spirits enlivened and our actions galvanized. What tools and techniques they may use is interesting but not essential. The potential of their vision to drive action and policy may be acutely appropriate especially for someone with a vested interest in the survival and health of an institution or a cause.

All of the futurist panel meet these essential criteria to varying degrees. Some do generate powerful images and the long term vision that can effect change. What about the whole picture, however? Are there gaps, blurred depictions, grainy places, distorted perspectives? This chapter explores the beliefs about the future included in this project, and looks at where there may be weaknesses and gaps.

It ought to be interesting to look at how those who think about the future change their beliefs as time passes and events occur. However, most futurists are structuralists whose interest is in long term shifts and not in quickly changing fashions and enthusiasms. For this reason, futurists tend to embellish rather than change their beliefs. More changes in thinking about the future can be expected from younger futurists, whose ideas about the future are still being developed.

What Are Their Strengths?

The strengths of futurist thinking are more fully discussed in Chapter 1, Chapter 2 and Chapter 3. Here we merely review two points about their work that ought to be kept in mind in our discussion of gaps and weaknesses.

- As a whole, the futurists present a broad sweep of the future that can inform and guide an institution in placing itself and its role in time and place.
- The strengths of futurists are like those of the Delphic oracle. She listened to the questions, paused a long time before speaking, and then spoke in a manner somewhat beside the point but pregnant with many meanings. Her message was not to be taken literally but as an indicator of plausible possibilities. The panelists converge on some topics, diverge or disagree on others, but as students of the future they are exceptionally alert to, and generously announce, signals, warnings and portents of change.

What Are Their Weaknesses?

- Their emphasis is on driving forces rather than outcomes. At the same time, there is little agreement on trends, no general statement of a trend that several futurists share. This leads to their talking beside each other's points, rather than building toward a substantial discussion of a topic.
- In general they have nothing to say at the prescriptive level, no ideology, no intellectual worldview.
- Their relatively thin use of quantitative techniques results in their description of the future being less accessible and meaningful to those for whom a numerical analysis based on a specific algorithm is an important tool for understanding concepts and trends.
- Although effective and powerful images and insights about the future arise from the panel, especially of the extremely far future, there are no visionaries with an integrated and compelling view of the journey to a great society in this group. Nor are any of them utopians. These are mostly practical men, grounded in present day issues, assessing trends and problems, and seeking reasonable solutions in the near term, or they are academics addressing similar concerns at some middle distance.
- The study of the future does not appear to be governed by any ethical or moral principles, or to generate any ideology. The panel members, of course, have ethical values, but work to keep them subdued and invisible to avoid contaminating their thoughts about the future. This results in a curiously neutral and passionless analysis. Here and there, moral passion can be inferred, but on the whole the futurists avoid its expression. One reason for this may be that in advanced industrial societies like the U.S., and in sophisticated academic communities, ideology and moral concern are suspect, distrusted and discounted.
- Although one might expect to, one cannot draw a grand theory of social change from these studies of the future. The panel gives weight to various and different underlying causes of societal shifts, but have not moved far toward solving the most critical problems of modern social science.
- One would seek in vain for common ground in the futures landscape of the panel. Rarely do panel members refer to, or cite each other, or indeed any other cogent body of thought. It is as if each vision of the future existed independently. More overlap occurs than is apparent from our study, but it is plain that futurists do not seem to talk to one another or debate each other's views of the future. Unlike artists

and musicians who frequently pick up themes from one another and refine and elaborate them, sometimes over centuries, there are schools of thought in futures thinking but little elaboration or development from one to another. This may be a characteristic of a new field and reflect among some futurists the absence of any large number of predecessors.

- On the whole, the panel is oriented to problems rather than opportunities. Those who have a more resolutely positive approach are also those futurists with most interest in the corporate future. This may appear to make them highly acceptable from a business point of view, but a stronger, more tightly woven fabric would combine all strands and hues of problem and possibility.

Have the Panel Left Gaps in the Look to the Future?

- There are gaps in the time horizons—the panel does not have the next 100 years fully covered. Most of the group have flexible, but short ranges, of from 5-25 years. Almost no one looks at the 30 to 100 year future. The long term thinkers have little interest in the immediate or the short range.
- It was noted earlier that women are left out of the panel's view of the present and of the future. So also are minorities, family life, domestic and day-to-day concerns, and so on. These may seem to be petty omissions against the grand sweep of events, and obviously no individual can be expected to study everything, but they raise some of the same concerns about the study of the future that have been raised about the study of the past. As a result, we have no clear indication of whether the futurists believe these aspects are important, of no consequence, overlooked in the interests of brevity and clarity, or covered in the futurist's mind under some other heading.
- We do not know, from the panel, what the agenda for further future studies ought to be. From their collected work, we might decide what ought to be explored and build an agenda, but the panel members themselves have not raised this issue.
- Except for the work of one member of the panel, Governor Lamm, the contribution of the political system, as an actor, or as an element, is largely unconsidered.

Other Considerations?

- Many of the panel's assumptions about the future are not made explicit, and remain hidden, or obscure. It is not obvious that the futurists recognize any obligation to scour their thinking for hidden or unexamined assumptions and acknowledge them. Frequently it is difficult to sort assumptions from conclusions because the whole is one fabric. No hierarchical order exists to make their conclusions more accessible.

The Panel on Several Topics

From all the topics covered in the panel's studies of the future several were selected in this discussion as exemplary of strength and weakness in treating important topics.

Energy

The panel agrees energy is a key factor for the future. Summarized, their views include the following:

Amara: Energy costs will increase. We will be dependent on foreign oil into the next century. Crises and shocks will force us to new technologies, but these will not be fully effective before 2000. Nuclear fission is wounded. If we began R&D now, we could operate a fusion reactor by the early 21st century. Other technologicâl possibilities are coal, with better combustion; fuel cells for decentralized uses; and photovoltaics, a limited role.

Ayres: The oil age will end in the next 30-40 years. The next fuels may be gas or coal. Nuclear power will be limited. Photovoltaics and solar technologies will be prominent after 2050. The world energy system is unstable, subject to crises, and we may come to a fight over supplies. Much non-productive activity will occur in adapting to greenhouse warming effects. Energy scarcity may cut down travel, expand electronic communication, and make us all farmers.

Boulding: We will run out of oil slowly, conserving, substituting, bringing in new technology. We may be pushed off planet for new sources. Our real problem is management, because unless we can maintain what we have built, our energy driven society will collapse. Utilities are too rigid for these changes.

Clarke: "The age of cheap energy is over, the age of free energy still lies 50 years ahead."

Drucker: Oil prices and energy demand will remain low because we have already shifted our manufacturing and technology away from the energy intensive to the information intensive.

Hughes: We are in an energy transition likely to produce economic shocks to the global economy and requiring collective social choices to complete it. By the next century, oil and gas will fall from 70% of our energy budget to 30-40%. Of three alternative choices, nuclear implies a strong governmental regulatory role; solar implies small-scale industries, decentralization, and reduced corporate role; and coal implies new industries, needs for capital, new technologies, and government support.

King: Nuclear or coal based energy systems cannot meet the need because of their potential high risk and high environmental costs. Any new energy system is 40 years ahead. More could be done with nuclear energy. Photovoltaics is attractive. Fusion is a long term strategy with problems in development and potential side effects. Bioresources promises food and energy for LDCs in Asia, Latin America and Africa.

Lamm: Expect new energy crises, with political outcomes being energy rationing and mandatory conservation.

Marien: We have many future energy choices but these are being obscured by subsidized cost accounting. If we counted all the costs it would discourage use of nuclear power.

Meadows: By the mid-1990s, as cheaper oil stocks are depleted, the world will experience serious oil shocks. Meadows believes Japan is preparing for the next shock while the U.S. does little. Hopeful assumptions about new energy technologies that will permit an easy transition from rising oil prices to an abundance of cheap power are not justified.

O'Neill: Conservation and increased efficiency will work for a while, but the U.S. cannot easily tolerate more than a 10-20% reduction in energy use. Environmental effects will be more important. Current sources will persist. Of the new, ocean thermal and solar satellite are promising. Fusion power and solar, less so.

Schwartz: We can and will manage our energy problems. Improvements in efficiency will exert leverage. LDCs will leapfrog to less energy use through advanced technology. Oil demand in the U.S. could fall 50% by 2000 if prices can be held above $20 a barrel.

Theobald: We ought to expect at least one energy crunch in the near future. Coal is too environmentally damaging, so we will have to look again at nuclear fission and explore fusion.

One has an urge to bring this group into a discussion because they talk beside each other's points. Certain critical assumptions are unstated but implicit. Schwartz' optimism, for example, is based on current fall in demand, but tends to ignore growing global population and the lack of capital among many poor nations for advanced technological solutions. O'Neill is committed to technological solutions to global resource problems. Except for King, this view of the energy future tends to be from the position of the large user, rather than the moderate, or small consumer. Their outlook is circumscribed by the search for a technological solution, although they mention some implications for structural change if these solutions are not found. Hughes exemplifies a more integrative approach by taking into consideration other views and by bringing in questions of social, political, and structural choice. Together, they fail to engage in useful terms who should do what, when, and why.

Education

Amara: Educational institutions will not be major players in the future. Their use of new information technologies is likely to be slight, and slow to increase. More corporate-sponsored technical and skill-based training will be needed.

Ayres: Problems in education may result from educational experiments of the 1960s and 1970s. These experiments shook up a rigid system. We will return to a more intellectually competent approach to education in the U.S. Expect longer schooling in advanced nations requiring more education for skilled jobs, and full participation in the society and its culture.

Boulding: The solution to all human problems lies in passing on the store of human knowledge, and creating new applications of the knowledge. The development and use of new educational technology is worthwhile to improve the learning process. The educational potential of art is neglected.

Clarke: Communications and computers will be network and core. The school will burst out of the schoolhouse walls. Children will be brought up best friends with the computer. We need training to cope with complexity, but this may make people passive. AI will tailor education to the individual.

Drucker: Education in the U.S. will improve. When or how is not clear. New requirements for quality are increasing. High wages paid for blue-collar work devalued knowledge and skill and discouraged school performance. Workers are switching to jobs requiring knowledge, and skill. They will demand a higher quality of education for their children.

King: We overlook the potential of education for bringing about social change. However, universities have poor potential for change. Information technology will give the Third World access to the world's knowledge, limited only by the ability to select what is useful out of the enormous mass.

Lamm: As the educational system declines, computers and related technologies will replace teachers. However the rate of college dropping out will increase as students find a degree does not often produce a well paid job. As a wealth-creating institution, our educational system performs indifferently.

Marien: The information society will have less effect on schools than many expect because these institutions have more purposes than learning: day care, for example. Although access to the world's storehouse of intellectual wealth is an appealing idea, educational offerings will compete against more enticing entertainments.

Meadows: Educational technology can be and is available, but the educational content will be simplified and trivialized. More education is already being done by businesses than by colleges. This however, is frequently narrowly focused on commercial interests.

Ogilvy: The educational system is in deep trouble. Three issues are important: declining demand, greater diversity and range of quality, and new educational needs. Children learn more about the "American experience" from television and radio than from school. People cannot compete with computers in accuracy—therefore creativity and how to learn from error will be more important.

Pierce: Changes are occurring in education with the implementation of information technologies. Technologies create opportunities for education out of school. Air travel has brought the educational opportunity of world travel for many people.

Theobald: We can cut schooling and teach people what they need to know, when they need to know it, rather than laying up a store of knowledge. People are likely to hold a variety of jobs, to need new skills, and to know how to use unemployed times productively. Community colleges are a more useful model than four-year universities. We should permit parents to send their children to their choice of school, allow more people to teach, and not force parents to send their children to high schools that have become destructive environments.

There is agreement on a disastrous decline in the quality of education, but little said about how it came about. Most of the panel write off our educational institutions as rigid, weak and ineffective. Amara expects them to lag other rapidly evolving systems and organizations, such as the corporation. Others believe the educational system can make little effective use of information technologies, and has no internal momentum for reform.

There is a tendency to impute what may be other failures in society to education, rather than to see the system as a reflection of societal will and societal choice. Ayres and Drucker, two of the few optimists about education, believe the system will respond to the new demands for knowledge. In fact the futurists generally deplore the state of education, but have not developed their concepts of it and its place in a complex society.

Technology

Amara: Always an actor in, but not a driver of, social change, technology is overestimated in its rate of diffusion and underestimated in its long term impacts.
Ayres: The long term trends are towards greater efficiency, the limits of performance and greater complexity. Complexity is the price of approaching the limits of performance. Large corporations are tending to become managers of complexity.
Bell: Part of the new family of technologies will be intellectual technologies, framed around management of complexity. Decision-making tools are likely to expand and improve. Our emerging technologies will be more dependent on our theoretical knowledge and ability to specify the performance and outcomes of what we design and build.
Clarke: Technology will increasingly shape the future. Factories will automate in the next 100 years, but by then we will be forced to consider the rights of advanced machines with capabilities similar to our own and to design them to function ethically.
Drucker: Social innovation is as important as technological innovation, especially to large organizations.
Ferkiss: People can take control of technology, but they need a more thorough technological education and understanding. Technology's capacity to monitor, to alter biology and degrade or destroy the environment threatens our political freedom.
Hughes: Technology drives, but is moved or shaped by social and political forces. Most important technologies of the future are semiconductors, the newer energy technologies, and biotechnology.
King: Technology molds society, but the most prosperous societies benefit most. After initial unrest and social and institutional change, microelectronics will be globally beneficial in its effects over the long term.
Marien: The moods of a nation can affect technological development as people alternately fear its effects, or hope for its solutions to

problems. Information technologies, biotechnology and materials technologies have revolutionary potential.

Meadows: Technology cannot outstrip its cultural support. New technologies need an infrastructure on which to build. Among those technologies that promise revolutionary effects are microelectronics, voice-activated computers, superconductors, expert systems and biotechnology.

Ogilvy: Biotechnology is not likely to be commercially significant before the end of the 1990s. Information technologies are moving through the "age of incompatibility." When that is over, they will expand enormously. Faster transport technologies are now possible, and will impact the economy.

O'Neill: Technology can solve those problems of human society that arise from the dilemma of finite resources and unlimited population growth.

Pierce: Science and technology are creative and revolutionary factors in our world, and likely to be emphasized more strongly in the future in all areas. The need for standardization is an inhibitor to the fast development of some technologies and this creates a social problem for us between our desire to compete and our need to cooperate.

Schwartz: Technology drives, social and political forces hold the status quo. Nanotechnology will be one of the most important technologies to human life.

Theobald: Technology will continue to drive society, especially U.S. society. But we continue to underestimate its effects and lag in controlling and shaping it. We need new social mechanisms to do so.

These views demonstrate clearly that members of advanced nations thinking about the future must account for the forces of technological change acting on their own, and on other societies. Almost all of the group except Lamm are gripped by the need to account for technology's impacts on society, the realization that no effective technique yet exists for doing so, and the suspicion that in promoting new technologies, we are riding a runaway horse. O'Neill and Clarke have greater faith in the benign influence of technologies than do the others. Ferkiss is especially gloomy about impacts. Learning to anticipate, adapt, manage and control emerging technologies seems to be a major societal task in the next few decades. The futurists give us no help in how to do it.

The Threat of Nuclear War

Most futurists would agree the threat of nuclear war is one of the greatest horrors ever faced by humankind. As a present difficulty, it is one that ought to be faced and analyzed. The panel members worry about the threat but ignore it in their views of the future, like the typical Californian functionally indifferent to the impending earthquake. Except for Boulding, who explores peace research and the activist approach to peace as a long term strategy for shifting societal attitudes, the panel does not advance our thinking on this issue.

Work and Jobs

There is much interesting material in the panel's analysis of work, workers, and the workforce. Drucker, King, and Bell, especially, describe workforce transitions to information and knowledge-based work in scenarios that emphasize the effects on global competition, on institutions, on organizational management and the structure of the workforce. For the most part, the futurists approach work from the economic point of view of the employer, the large corporation, and the government. They are out of touch with potential impacts on the individual and on the individual's workplace. We lack an image of what an ideal worklife and workplace would be like in a knowledge based society and the panel does not provide one, or even hint at the value of such an image as a driver of change.

Africa

We are alarmed about Africa by the panel's concern for its future. Those of the group who commented on the continent see it as bleak. This is a thoughtful surfacing of the concern many people have felt but by no means an analysis of what must be a complex future, with a highly uncertain long term outcome. We want to know more, but the implication is that disaster seems inevitable, and cannot be averted even by the combined (and hypothetical) efforts of the rest of the world. Therefore nothing much can or will be done, and therefore it is not worth exploring. As noted earlier, most of the panel avoid moral passion in the interests of neutrality and objectivity. Here, however, is where neutrality may be morally disturbing.

Summary

This chapter reviewed the futurist panel's beliefs about a few selected topics. For details on their beliefs about many other topics, the reader should look to the individual chapters which follow. What we see to be each futurist's key beliefs about the future are summarized at the beginning of each chapter.

A summary comment is in order, however. The sources of strength that each of the futurists brings to his studies are also the bases for weakness. The conscious or unconscious desire to be neutral works against the creation of positive, goal-driven images and visions of the future. Neutrality also works against the definition of what must ultimately be a political agenda for making the transition to an envisioned world. On the other hand, to move into the ideological and political arena might subvert other desirable functions of these futurists. There are exceptions. O'Neill and Clarke do have long-term visions, although they are extremely weak on the transition question. On the other hand, Governor Lamm is powerful in his passion for promoting change in the immediate future. But that passion has made him a special pleader and probably, to some degree isolated him, as reflected in the label, "Governor Gloom."

A regrettable shortcoming throughout the futures movement is the relative reluctance to engage in direct head-to-head encounters. Consequently, at the superficial level there is much talking beside the point. But at the substantive level are the missed opportunities to force the exposition of latent or tacit assumptions, and to force the exposition of clearer visions of the future and the implications for a healthy transition to those futures.

Again, these weaknesses are the reverse side of the strengths that the panel of seventeen brings to the future. Theirs are self-assigned pursuits where they each feel they have strength and presumably the highest likelihood of influencing change.

Let us now turn to our individual futurists in all their stimulating, provocative diversity.

PART TWO

FUTURIST PROFILES

INTRODUCTION TO PART TWO

Part Two reviews and analyzes the beliefs about the future of each of the 17 members of the futurist panel. Some members of the panel, while willing to have their beliefs about the future explored, do not describe themselves as futurists and do not wish anyone else to do so. Therefore the term, futurist, is used here only for convenience in describing a group of people prominent, among other things for their deliberations about the future.

Each chapter deals with one futurist. They are ordered alphabetically. The first page includes a brief characterization of the futurist and a summary of his key views on the future. This is followed by a more detailed biographical note.

Each futurist's worldview is introduced and followed by an extended discussion of his beliefs about more specific issues, such as the future of telecommunications. Toward the end of the chapter we look briefly at causes the futurist believes underlie change.

Each of the futurists was asked who had influenced his thinking about the future. Their responses are reported in an influence diagram at the end of each chapter. One or two of the futurists did not supply any names and, therefore, for them the diagram is omitted. References round out each chapter.

The chapters follow the same general format, and cover many of the same subjects. No attempt was made, however, to make the chapters, the analysis, the interviews, or the subjects covered, mechanically uniform. The chapters consist of an analysis of published (and in some cases, unpublished) work, modified and enlarged by interviews with the individuals, then further modified by review comments by each panel member on his own chapter.

CHAPTER 5

ROY AMARA

Roy Amara is well recognized as an experienced futurist. His views and his work at the Institute for the Future evolved with its clients as they moved from optimism about the potential for broadsweeping and beneficial changes in society in the 1960s—anything is possible—to a more conservative and circumscribed view of the potential for change. His early concern with methodology which reflected his engineering background has broadened into a larger concern for involving and communicating with decisionmakers. Excellence in method is not enough to carry a message, he believes.

KEY VIEWS ABOUT THE FUTURE

1. The U.S. economy will grow 2-3% a year over the next 20 years.
2. The world's nations will shake down into the haves, the have-somes and the have-nots.
3. Technology brings us up against our limits to growth and challenges us with the obsolescence of our institutions and an ever faster pace of evolution into complexity.
4. We need an image of the future that will enable us to survive within our global limits.
5. The interactions and synergy between emerging technologies such as biotechnology and information will spur new and better products and applications.
6. The future structure of (the U.S.) government hangs on the outcome of a ten year experiment in redefining the role of government against that of the private sector.
7. In the next 10-15 years we will reset out political and social and economic directions to adapt to a more technological and global society.
8. Worldwide, participatory movements of all kinds are likely to become one of the dominant transforming forces of the rest of the 20th century.

BIOGRAPHICAL NOTE:

Roy Amara is president of the Institute for the Future, in Menlo Park, CA, which he has headed for 16 years. The Institute worked for government, then about ten years ago began introducing more private sector projects. Today, its major emphasis is on its work for corporations, including a substantial amount of research on telecommunications and its impacts. In its evolution, the Institute reflected the changing views of its clients, moving from optimism and expectations that radical changes would occur in society, to a more balanced interest in trends affecting the future, then to analysis of structural change as it might affect the marketplace.

In the 1950s and 1960s Amara held executive positions at Stanford Research Institute, where his interest in the future was triggered by an assignment to write a 5-10 year plan. SRI acquired its first contract to do futures research, in education, when Amara brought his former professors at Stanford, Willis Harman and William Linvill, into the SRI proposal.

Amara had a five-star education, at MIT, Harvard and Stanford. He is widely known for his studies of the future corporate environment, of emerging social and technological issues, and forecasting and planning methodologies. His early interest in the future was on the analytical, methodological and technical side. In this he was influenced by Paul Baran, at the Rand Corporation, with whom he worked on a joint project for the Department of Defense, and by Olaf Helmer, also at Rand. William Linvill is credited with interesting him in systems thinking. (See the influence diagram at the end of the chapter.)

Amara wrote ***Business Planning for an Uncertain Future,*** (Pergamon, 1983) with Andrew J. Lipinski, and many reports and articles. In 1981 he published five articles in *The Futurist,* examining the futures field, its origins and directions, and establishing criteria by which futures research could be judged. For this chapter, we read a selection of his publications over the last 10-12 years and interviewed him in California. The interview and his writings reinforce each other. Amara writes precisely, with a consistent view of the future which has shifted only marginally over time.

WORLDVIEW

Roy Amara is guardedly optimistic about the future. Some things are working fine—others are not and promise trouble ahead. The pace of change, especially technologically, is accelerating and many emerging technologies offer new benefits for human wellbeing. His worldview emphasizes continuity rather than abrupt change. The complexity, inertia and homeostatic responses of society combine to resist sudden and radical change. He characterizes the emerging society (in the U.S.) in these four terms:

1. more limits—slower economic growth and personal consumption.
2. more participation—individuals and groups wanting access into political and economic systems.
3. greater complexity—everything nudging everything else, creating interdependency and new connections.
4. change at an accelerating pace, making history a less useful guide.[1]

In 1981, Amara segmented the closing decades of the 20th century into two chunks, 1980-1990 and 1991-2000. The first he describes as a period of "laying pipe" in which we set new directions and in which the economy runs in place while adjustments are made to adapt to change. The second segment is likely to be driven by rapidly emerging technologies, for example in computer communications, energy and biotechnology, by changing demographics and by the rise of new institutions and new societal mechanisms.[2]

The increasing use of technology faces us with limits, with the penalties for growth and with interdependence. Technology increases the choices available to us but in many cases our old institutions are inadequate to the task of choosing. Most of our stress is of our own making. We are being forced to live within our means and to deal with the social divisiveness setting limits will create. We need to develop a science and an art of complexity and change and to recreate our society on a human scale.

This notion of returning to the human scale in our institutions and our international relationships recurs frequently, but Amara does not seem especially hopeful of achieving it. However he does believe that participatory movements of all kinds, worldwide, are likely to become one of the dominant transforming forces of the rest of the 20th century. What is occurring is:

- Citizens are bypassing traditional institutions because these have become ineffective or are providing insufficient choices.
- New processes are being created in society (he is primarily referring to the U.S. here) with greater opportunities for individuals to act, i.e., decentralization in the public sector, autonomous workgroups in the private sector.[3]

We are seeing the breakup of major institutions, unions, for example, the use of initiatives and the growth of public interest groups. If these are to be effective at more than local levels, Amara believes they will need good information which, presumably, technology can supply.

The argument has been made (by Polak) that we have little capacity for imaging our preferred future. Amara argues that we, on the contrary, are experiencing an overload of imagery—we have too much sensation and information to achieve consensus. We are experiencing a fragmentation and a regionalization of society.

In discussing the futurist's role in creating a vision of the future, or a guiding image, he notes that an image of human dominance over a limitless planet may have helped industrialize the world. A new image of a more holistic relationship with nature may now be the means of our global survival.

SPECIFIC ISSUES

Telecommunications and Computers

Distinctions between telecommunications and computers are disappearing.

"• The diffusion of gallium arsenide devices may become the biggest technological surprise of the next decade.
- It is likely that erasable optical disks with associated hardware and software will be commercially available by the end of the decade.
- It is possible that practical light switching systems able to handle as many as 1,000-10,000 addresses or outgoing lines will be commercially available in the early 1990s."[4]

Future Information Societies

According to Amara, information technology is one of the most powerful shapers of U.S. society. The intersection of information technology with other emerging technologies is likely to prove revolutionary. For example, information technologies connected with energy are producing 'smart' houses and will result in 'smart' cars. The use of CAD is boosting the exploration of new materials. The intersection of information technologies with biotechnology is creating biosensors, and so on.

At least 50% of the economy will be information related and the revolutionary technologies will begin to break down boundaries between work, education and leisure.[5] One outcome is a dwindling work week and increasing productivity of the workforce, 2-2.5% a year. Rapidly rising energy costs may lead to greater substitution of communications for transportation.

Defense and Disarmament

The defense budget is newly visible and the competing demands within it more apparent. Cutbacks in defense budgets are not likely before the 1990s, however, when the availability of new technologies could reduce the need for ground based conventional forces and weapons. Amara foresees a swing back to and more demand for social programs at the expense of defense as the nation copes with rising divisiveness over social benefits driven by the demographics of a middle-aged bulge and an aging population.

International and World Regions and Populations

Beyond 1990 we are likely to see a new world, one in which global polarization is inevitable. Amara divides it into three, the independents, the interdependents and the dependents. Nuclear proliferation, the struggle for energy, increasing fragmentation along tribal, ethnic, and linguistic divisions will reshape the existing conflict towards less East vs. West and more West vs. West (the U.S. and Japan), East vs. East (the USSR and China), North vs. South (the Haves vs. the Have-nots).

The U.S. will still be dependent on foreign oil, maintain its strengths in agriculture and high technology and face increasing competition for world trade. The three groups of nations Amara identifies as:

1. Independent by reason of resources, agriculture, industrial base, etc.—U.S., USSR, Mexico, Brazil, Australia, Canada:

    - These nations will tend to dominate,
    - tend to isolate themselves, and
    - become self-sufficient.

2. Interdependent nations by reason of fewer resources and uneven development will develop closer foreign ties, have back-up relationships and partnerships and will be a new world influence and intermediary—EEC and Mediterranean North Africa; Japan and the People's Republic of China; and Colombia, Venezuela, Ecuador, Peru, Bolivia, and Chile.
3. Dependent nations with few resources, high fertility, poor agricultural and industrial sectors—Bangladesh, India, Chad, Burma, Uganda, etc.

- These nations are unattractive to others,
- they need strong government to make any progress, and
- are likely to have chronic wars and revolutions.

U.S. Political Directions

The future structure of government hangs on the outcome of a ten year experiment in redefining the role of government against that of the private sector. Current cutbacks in social programs are a part of that experiment, testing the private sector's ability to cope with social needs and social justice. If the experiment succeeds it will be prolonged. If not, the 1990s and the 2000s will bring social upheaval reasserting government's role.

Intergenerational conflict developing between the huge middle-aged population (40+) and the newly old (the active 60s+) over benefits and pensions may drive a reassessment of government. The increasing conservatism of the judicial system, especially the Supreme Court, may also provoke dissension. The need to cut personal consumption that Amara anticipates, and the sense of limits to growth pressing on new expectations and aspirations, may also be divisive.

Our institutions are not good prospects for adapting to rapid change and are generally distrusted because:

- new institutions are created without dismantling the old,
- the structure of many institutions conflicts with their aims and functions,
- institutions grow and become unwieldly and inefficient,
- their internal incentives favor short-term approaches,
- they have few measures of social accountability.[6]

This distrust and dissatisfaction increases the need for new methods for dealing with emerging social problems; for example, the distribution of opportunities for growth over the whole society is being moved from the economic to the political arena—as the environmental movement has done.

Information technologies are creating new relationships for politicians with citizens.

Environment

Amara sees that considerable progress has been made on many environmental issues. He does note, however, that the growth-limiting factors of environmental clean-up costs have been moved into the political arena from the economic as a part of a larger debate on how limits to growth will be achieved.

Environmental regulation is in a volatile phase leading over the long run to a more pragmatic regulatory environment but offering new opportunities for corporations to act as change agents.

The Economy

Amara is optimistic on the economy, expecting 2-3% growth over the next 20 years. He does *not* subscribe to the various theories of long term economic cycles (as described by Kuznets or Kondratieff, for example). He does believe societies hang on too long to obsolescent practices before price mechanisms redirect the flows of capital and research into new frontiers.

Amara expects laborforce shortages as the rate of entering workers drops and growth of women's participation slows. Crucial problems of a prosperous economy are the distribution of wealth and work to avoid a two-class, polarized society. As an aging society, however, we may be less risk-taking, more interested in health and the quality of older people's lives.

Problems of resource availability can be managed within a concept of limitations. High oil prices would be a blessing, acting as a spur to emerging energy technologies. Given reasonable energy prices the long term prospects for materials can be considered inexhaustible, e.g., for iron, aluminum, magnesium, titanium, wood, glass, cement and plastic. Water supplies can be managed.

Financial resources should be more heavily invested in U.S. strengths in agriculture and chemicals; computer/communications systems; aircraft: control systems; optical, dental, and medical equipment; as well as in infrastructure and modernization. Science and technology comprise our most cost effective investment. The role of government in international competition and domestic regulation may be important, especially as government has stepped back from regulation and direction of private enterprise.

Education

Educational institutions are not among the major players in the future, their evolution lagging other sectors of society. More corporate-sponsored education is likely to meet technical and skill needs. The use of new information technologies in the educational system is likely to be slight, and slow to increase.

Health

With sufficient economic growth, the U.S. can afford a high level of expenditure for health care. There is the risk that people will have only the health care they can afford. Universal health insurance is more likely to evolve at state than at national levels.

Technology

Technology is almost never the driver of social change but it is almost always a major actor. Although society generally has a dismal record in forecasting the diffusion and effect of new technology, one generalization does seem to apply: we consistently overestimate the rate of diffusion and the impacts of technology in the short run but underestimate diffusion and impact in the long run.

Automation

The piecemeal approach to automation is being discarded. As costs are driven down, and the speed, size and reliability of equipment are more attractive, new needs and expectations begin to make themselves felt.

Restructuring of office hierarchies and management functions will occur slowly as employees acquire sophisticated replacement technology to orchestrate their enormous needs for face to face, intergroup and interpersonal communication.

Creating a nurturing, exploratory environment for workers by exploiting the potential of the technology is possible, and most likely to be used to stimulate scientists in R&D areas. The call will be for database systems, conferencing, model-building systems, and verbal, conceptual or graphic tools.

For management, the managing of human resources may be the critical factor in the new, more participatory environment. The new technologies will redefine where work is done, when, and in what style; and may be used to fill needs for more external contracts, with groups and customers. The quality of choice and judgment will be crucial as abilities to collect and process data increase.

Energy

- Energy costs will increase. We will remain dependent on foreign oil, well into the next century.

- Energy crises will return, demanding another look at alternative technologies.
- The effect of new energy technologies will not be felt until well into the 1990s.

How electric power is generated, and what the size and rate of demand for electricity will be, will remain controversial to the end of the century, with effects on the structure of the electrical industry. Nuclear fission is a wounded technology. Its output will likely decrease in the early 1990s. Technology from countries with a lead in nuclear energy, France, for example, may provide a comeback in the next century. (Note that the airship offers a parallel case of being dangerous, abandoned and then brought back with new and safer technology.) A potentially revolutionary technology is fusion. A fusion reactor could be operating in 2000—if the R&D were begun now. It is a likely possibility for the early part of the 21st century. Other important energy technologies are:

- Coal—improved combustion methods.
- Fuel cells—for cogeneration units in decentralization strategies and in small commercial uses—the sleeper of the 1990s.
- Photovoltaics—an important but circumscribed role in the next 10-15 years in electricity generation, especially in remote areas.[7]

Other Technologies of Importance

The interactions and synergy between emerging technologies such as biotechnology and information will spur new and better products and applications.

- Biotechnology—a wide variety of applications in chemical processes and products, agriculture and health care.
- Materials, ceramics, alloys, composites.

In his 1986 report, *Twelve Emerging Technologies for the 1990s,* Amara discusses the significant opportunities existing at the intersections of new technologies. These interactions create new and more powerful and complex uses and products. For example:

- Energy + information leads to the "smart car, house," etc.,
- Energy + materials leads to weight reduction and higher temperature operation of composites,
- Energy + biotechnology leads to coal desulphurization by bacteria,

- Information + materials leads to the use of computer assisted design (CAD) for stress analysis,
- Information + biotechnology leads to biosensors,
- Materials + biotechnology leads to protein engineering.

Typical examples of future synergistic technologies would be a ceramic gas turbine auto engine operating at greater efficiency at higher temperatures, and the use of genetically engineered microbes to extract metals from ores.

Cities

Cities are on the rise with a new role and function, of processing people. Allied with this is a growth in regionalism emphasizing social, ethnic, and lifestyle differences, and based on population, economics, and opportunities. These regional differences may favor some cities, such as Boston, over others.

Other Topics

On several subjects Amara has less to say—housing and religion, for example,—and he describes some topics as less critical, such as food production (but not distribution) and changing lifestyles and values, which he sees as critically important but derivative of other trends.

UNDERLYING CAUSES

Amara is neutral to causes, and indisposed to attributing blame. He sees changing attitudes as lagging social changes and events and he sees societal values deriving from conditions rather than determining them. There is little evidence for a resurgence of traditional family structures although there is reason to believe that our values will favor less risk, more conservatism in the sense of preserving wealth, and be less innovative. The role of a futurist may be to promote better choices, among those who need to make choices. As he notes above, Amara believes modern decisionmakers may have too much, rather than too little, information to reach consensus.

Creative tension exists in the U.S. system between public and private sectors pushing the balance of power back and forth to achieve a balance. For example, deregulation of telecommunications may have swung the balance over too far, opening the possibility of re-regulation.

Although he would not predict any discontinuities, Amara suggests where to look—to biotechnology and its effects on agriculture which could be highly beneficial to the U.S. economy, and to potentially revolutionary benefits of emerging materials sciences. Environmental effects of ozone and increasing concentrations of fluorocarbons in the atmosphere may produce a negative discontinuity, as may the proliferation of nuclear weapons to developing countries.

EXHIBIT 5-1

FORCES INFLUENCING THE FUTURIST THINKING OF

ROY AMARA

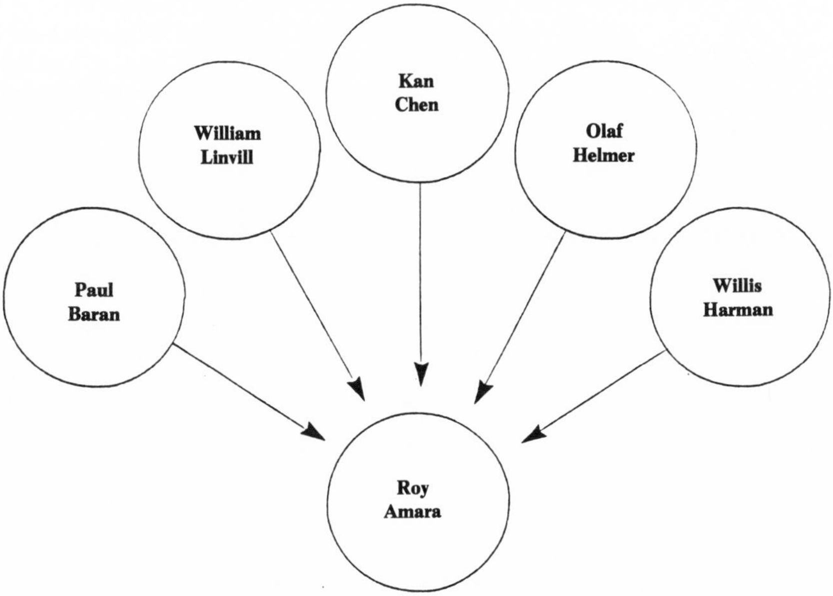

REFERENCES

1. Roy Amara and Andrew J. Lipinski, *Business Planning for an Uncertain Future,* Pergamon, 1983, Chapter 11.
2. Roy Amara, "Points of Departure," *Executive,* Cornell University, Spring 1981, p. 15.
3. Also the formation of citizen groups identifying with the future, Iowa 2000, etc., in Roy Amara, "Toward the Year 2,000, National Priorities," Institute for the Future, Menlo Park, CA, January 1981.
4. Roy Amara, *Twelve Emerging Technologies for the 1990s,* Institute for the Future, Menlo Park, CA, April 1986, p. 10.

5. Roy Amara, "Points of Departure," *Executive,* Cornell University, Spring 1981.
6. Roy Amara, "Imperatives for Tomorrow," *World Futures Society Bulletin,* November/December 1981.
7. Roy Amara, *Twelve Emerging Technologies for the 1990s,* Institute for the Future, Menlo Park, CA, April 1986.

CHAPTER 6

ROBERT U. AYRES

Robert Ayres brings a worldview to his futures thinking. He has a strong interest in, if not a bias towards, scientific and technological developments as the primary drivers of economic growth, but he also presents a sophisticated understanding of complex relationships between technology and social change.

KEY VIEWS ABOUT THE FUTURE

1. In technology, there are long term trends towards greater efficiency and higher performance, towards the limits of performance, and toward greater complexity. Coping with complexity is the major driving force behind the spread of computers.
2. People: their values, customs, habits and institutions, provide both driving forces and constraints on change. One key constraint is the inborn human propensity to make errors.
3. Complex systems tend to become rigid, requiring extreme pressure to change them. Most institutions and nations can be seen as systems and their future deduced in many respects from their behavior. However, the future is not by any means fully determined by the past.
4. The management of complexity is a key problem for all bureaucracies and institutions, as well as for industries.
5. Dynamic systems such as the domestic and international economies respond to pressure by short- and long-term cycles of growth and shrinkage, due mainly to shifts in macro-technologies such as electrification or computerization.
6. The U.S. is in the middle stage of decline in its role as a center of power. Still powerful, it is more fragile than politicians and the public seem to think.
7. World economic growth will slow down over the next century because of needed diversions of resources for maintenance and repair of the environment, the infrastructure and the energy system. The coming end of the age of oil will require staggering investments in its substitute, whatever it may be. Energy in the next century will be far more expensive than it has been in our lifetimes.

BIOGRAPHICAL NOTE

Robert Ayres is a professor of engineering and public policy at Carnegie-Mellon University. He is currently on assignment as deputy leader of the Technology-Economy-Society Program of the International Institute for Applied Systems Analysis, in Laxenburg, Austria.

He is the author of two recent books on trends in technology and their socio-economic impacts: *The Next Industrial Revolution,* 1984, and *Robotics: Applications and Social Implications*, 1982, with Steven M. Miller. He is as well the author of many articles and several books on various aspects of technological forecasting and social change. He has been a consultant on private and public sector technology and social impacts issues. He is a member of the American Economic Association, a fellow of the AAAS and a member of the World Futures Studies Federation, the World Future Society, and the International Institute of Forecasters. His book, *Uncertain Futures: Challenges for Decision-Makers,* 1979, expounds many of his views on the future, and is the key source, along with an extensive interview, for this chapter.

In the middle 1960s, Professor Ayres was doing technological forecasting at the Hudson Institute. He and Herman Kahn influenced each other's thinking about the future. Work at the Hudson Institute resulted in Ayres' first book, *Technological Forecasting and Long Range Planning*, 1969. As a visiting scholar at Resources for the Future in Washington, DC, his thinking was influenced by Allen V. Kneese, Ron Ridker and other associates. Other early influences were Arthur C. Clarke, Harrison Brown, sociologists William Ogburn and S.C. Gilfillan, and then later, T.B. Taylor, Lester Brown, Dennis Gabor, and Norman McCrae. Ayres draws on Brown's work at Worldwatch for his scenario of world food crisis.

WORLDVIEW

Professor Ayres describes two extreme approaches to forecasting the future as "alpha" and "omega."[1] Alpha futurists believe either that the future is positive and improving steadily, all growth is exponential and trends continue, or alternatively, that the future is headed towards disaster, all decline is exponential and downward trends continue. The Omegas leap ahead to assume an ideal future already accomplished by a transformation, the impacts and form of which are not usually described in any detail.

Ayres is alpha about some trends and prospects but almost never omega, although he carefully makes the point that unpredictable events may upset predicted trends, causing crisis and radical change.

The common use of exponential growth functions as a way of describing future change is limited, he believes, although it has been useful in forecasting the rapid growth of a specific technology such as the number of long distance telephone messages.

People are slow to change. Their values, beliefs, and customs—evolving out of prior experiences and circumstances—frequently delay and obstruct the development of new policies and social innovations. People get in the way of implementation of new technology which could improve their lives; the values they hold may work against the improvement of their societies; and their groups and institutions become rigid over time, requiring massive pressures to reform them. Personal decisions, however, can be important to the future. In some circumstances an individual with special qualities can 'tip' a country or even a region from one possible path to another, such as the Ayatollah Khomeini and Deng Xiaoping.

In Ayres' view, innovation occurs when science and technology make it possible to respond in a new way to a social need. Policy and economics control the rate and direction of the subsequent developments.

Political systems compete to reach a conflicting set of socially desirable goals that he characterizes as equity, economic efficiency, personal freedom and stability. Several of these goals, while desirable in themselves, tend to be incompatible with each other. For this reason, almost any political system tends to develop great internal strains.

Economic efficiency is not readily achievable unless a large number of people in the nation's population hold and act on values which Ayres believes create wealth. The six wealth-creating values are:

- Motivation—life is felt to be meaningful, have purpose.
- Positive Attitude to Work—an urge to achieve, pride in skills.
- Integrity—dependable, can be trusted.
- Reality Orientation—able to attack problems, seek solutions, control emotions.
- Concern with Future—willing to sacrifice, responsible for self and children.
- Optimism—hopeful for the future, confident improvements can be made.

He believes these values are in decline in the Western world and are not strongly held in other regions, Africa, for example, or Moslem countries.

In *Uncertain Futures*, Ayres acknowledges Herman Kahn's idea of "trained incapacity" reflected in the assumptions of some scientists and technological forecasters that growth in a technology, or an industry, must continue because it is technically feasible, regardless of need, preference, or economics.

EXHIBIT 6-1

WEALTH CREATING VALUES: BY COUNTRY

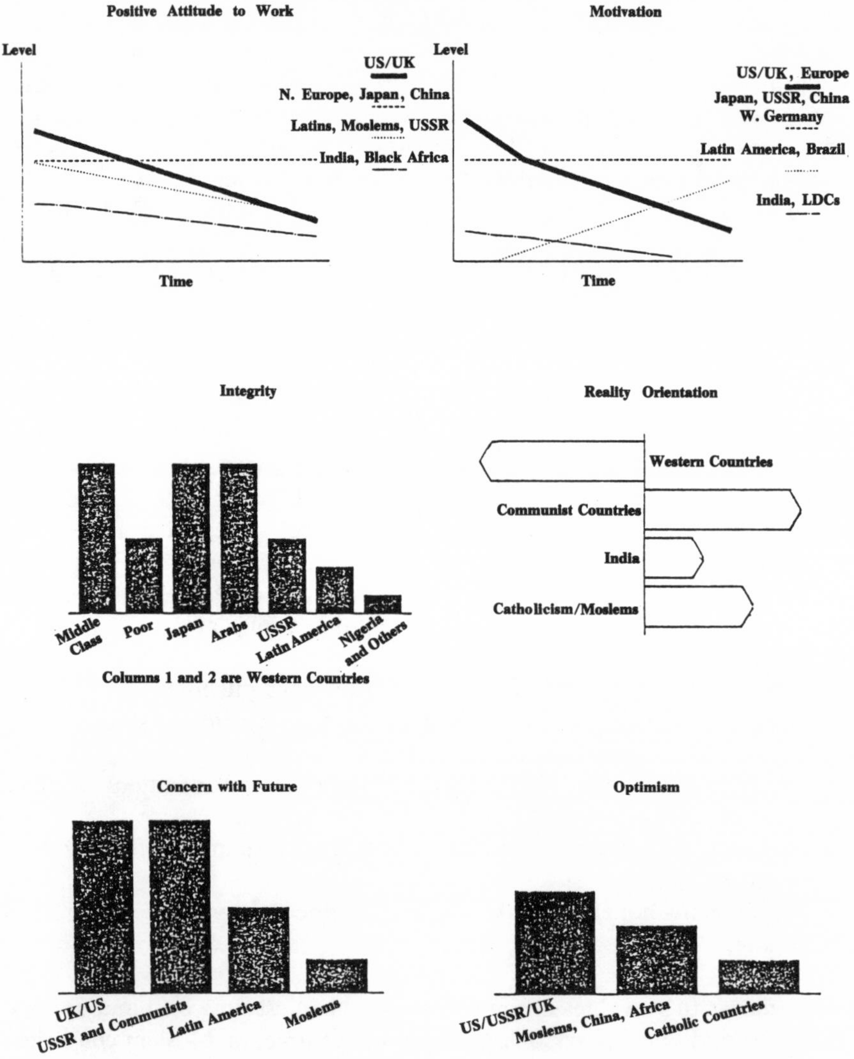

J.F. Coates, after Ayres, **Uncertain Futures,** 1979

SPECIFIC ISSUES

Technology

In technology, there are long term trends towards higher efficiency in the use of resources, towards the limits of performance, and toward greater complexity. There are examples in transportation, in the control of the environment, in biology, in the design and manipulation of microscopic objects, in composite materials, in chemicals, and so on. Complexity is the price of approaching performance limits in all technologies, guns, clocks, cars, or computers. Large multinational firms tend to become 'managers of complexity.' The Caterpillar Corporation has 25,000 worldwide subcontractors, for example.

Biotechnology will bring greater complexity to the chemical industry, making possible methods and processes that will be more effective and conserving of energy and materials.

Automation and Robots

An important driver of automation is our society's obsession with quality, driven in part by product liability concerns and antipathy towards risk. Complex systems are intolerant of defects—as exemplified by recent problems with the space shuttle. Although training, motivation, and human factors research attempt to minimize human error, humans will continue to make mistakes. Therefore eventually removing people from the direct handling of processes and products is the only route toward a zero-defect world. We now have smart sensors making 100,000 or 1,000,000 fewer errors (per opportunity) than people do. It is therefore likely that computers will eventually replace people in *all* routine tasks, especially in manufacturing.

One transition effect of factory automation will be to remove from the market certain work skills, such as drafting, welding, painting, machining and assembly. These will no longer be marketable. The range of blue-collar jobs in factory production will be far smaller, ultimately limited to model-making, tool-making and maintenance, but craft skills may persist in small shops and specialized production.

Telecommunications and Computers

The U.S. and Japan

If video communications begin to be substituted for voice-alone, the growth of voice transmissions should begin to saturate and then decline in the 1980s and 1990s. A big demand for links between computers is likely, with more and more larger computers being used to supervise and coordinate the linkages. Networks of linked computers will create true automation of the factory, the automobile, and the home.

The Rest of the World

Europe is behind in the most advanced developments because of an inadequate telephone system, but is likely to play catch-up as France has done. The USSR may follow worldwide trends in industry, but lag in consumer applications. In less developed countries the new technologies will initially take root only in some larger cities.

International Economics

Certain countries are destined to be major actors, by reason of having advantages such as large populations/land area, access to resources, advanced technology and internal discipline and cohesion. On the other hand the nationalism of small countries tends to break the cooperative bonds which might be formed by larger nations to manage major world issues, such as food, monetary stability, etc. Ayres believes nationalism is a deep-rooted force acting against peace and world cohesion; however he does see trends towards the sacrifice of sovereignty for a greater good in the European Economic Community. Such institutions as are being formed by the EEC are of the kind that will be needed for international negotiations on global issues, the allocation of resources, for example.

Ayres believes that regrettably by the mid-1990s, the U.S. will be internationally competitive only in military technology. Japan will assault and erode all other U.S. competitive advantages in high technology. Japanese economic, political and military pre-eminence will lead to a more unstable world. The Japanese hold on democracy is tenuous. Because they admired U.S. power, they admired and adopted its institutions. When this power declines, admiration and imitation will turn to scorn.

The following table summarizes Ayres' views of the economic future for several nations and regions as of 1978, with additional and more recent comments. These projections are, at best, mixed, except for a positive outlook for France based on its promotion of high technology. Ayres is less positive about France's future today.

The Economic Future of Several Nations and National Groups

West Germany	slower economic growth, difficulties with institutionalizing innovation.

France could have been the wealthiest nation in Europe by 2000; a high technology leader, slowed by political difficulties.

Italy reduced economic growth, environmental degradation, and over-dependence on foreign oil, but with political stability could improve its position.

Benelux smallness becomes an advantage, trade prospers, ethnic troubles continue.

U.K. continued economic crisis, especially after the North Sea oil starts to run out and industrial, political incompetency continues. [This is probably Ayres' best example of rigid system which small pressures, i.e., those of government, cannot affect.]

Europe perhaps a U.S. pullout would help. Europe is in good shape socially and politically, but it has problems of slow economic growth and limited incentives for entrepreneurship.

U.S. a new period of significant economic growth is possible but less likely, providing capital investment is available. Strength in areas needed to improve productivity, automation, chemical processes and computers, is available.

Canada linked to the future of the U.S. Could grow rapidly if separatism does not cause crisis.

Japan Japanese business interests spread across the world, encountering the unfamiliar and the undisciplined workforce. Resistance to its export policies will restrain its economy somewhat. Japan faces a crisis: it must stimulate domestic growth by giving consumers a better deal, but will not find that easy, given the nature of the Japanese political system.

Soviet Union satellites will stay ahead of the USSR economically. Economic crisis may force decentralization of the Soviet bloc; down-the-road troubles are likely for Gorbachev.

Africa	a total disaster area that will require vast amounts of resources.
Brazil	it seems to have gotten a new but somewhat shaky grasp on democratic processes, and its prospects are very good. An ecological disaster could result from deforestation.
Argentina, Venezuela	in fairly good shape for the moment, but Argentina could slip back into military dictatorship if economic troubles deepen.
India	a potential industrial powerhouse in the urban portion but the deadweight of the bureaucracy and primitive customs are preventing development.
Nigeria	unstable, uneven development.
China	economic success likely—the current leader is a political genius, but the country has a problem of succession.

World economic growth will slow down over the next century because of great needs for maintenance and repair of the environment, the infrastructure, the energy system and other major functions.

World Regions and Nations

Ayres takes a systems approach in considering the stability and potential for unrest in nations. The USSR, for example, appears stable, but is maintained so with the help of intense internal surveillance. As a rigid system, it is probably unaffected by small pressures, such as those of the dissidents. Ayres argues, however, that suppression of intellectuals may also suppress new scientific discovery and new technology, leading to economic stagnation. Such stagnation, if combined with ethnic unrest, could conceivably provide a large enough hammer to break the Soviet system. The shock waves will be very hard to control, however.

Tourism is likely to develop in new directions, to North and Northwest-Africa, the west coast of South America, the Polynesian islands and perhaps the coast of Brazil.

Japan has already lost a large share of its exports of iron and steel products and moved to high technology manufacturing in telecommunications, satellites, electronics, computers and high quality consumer goods. Neither Japan, nor West Germany, which is following a similar path, will make much impact on business or entertainment services because of an inherent language difficulty.

The U.S. Economy

Ayres tentatively subscribed to the theory of long term (Kondratieff-Schumpeter) economic boom and bust cycles superimposed on shorter cycles, known as inventory adjustment cycles.

He believed (in 1978) the 50-year (Kondratieff) cycle will repeat itself at least one more time in the U.S., from 1975-2025. In such a scenario, there would be gradually increasing prosperity from 1977 to 1982—with short term boom and bust cycles superimposed on the longer term trend—a major crash in 1983-1984, with potential for a worldwide economic crisis, a glut of oil in the early 1980s as a result of OPEC's collapse, and depression in the energy industry. So far this scenario has assumed a Democratic administration, but this switches in 1984 to a Republican, with a platform of aid to struggling cities and public works programs. Economic recovery begins after 1986 but it is feeble and set back by short term recessions in 1987 and 1991. Interest rates and commodity prices will bottom out about 2005 and stay low until a new long term upswing of consumer spending and industrial expansion begins to compete with government borrowing and push up energy prices.[2]

The "Post Industrial" society (as described by Daniel Bell), Ayres characterizes as one in which appetites for non-material services rise faster than demand for material goods. Quality becomes more important than quantity. Using these criteria, the U.S., Canada, all of Western Europe, Japan and probably the USSR will be post industrial by 2000. No other country, except perhaps Brazil, has the potential to join this club even by 2025.

Resources issues are all manageable. Even if the U.S. experiences acute shortages, in the long pull it would find substitutes, and in the short run, could manage the crisis. So, for example, if cobalt from Zaire or platinum from South Africa were cut off, the U.S. would manage easily.

There are several possible discontinuities which would affect the economy positively—a more intensive use of computers aimed at productivity, for example. Space could be an important turnaround in terms of resources. War, instability in the Middle East, a revival of protectionism, famine, and financial collapse, are disruptive possibilities, although not considered highly probable.

U.S. Political Directions

The U.S. is in the middle stages of decline as a center of power. The decline is accelerated by political premises which are based on several popular illusions. Among these are: the illusion that the U.S. has unlimited technological resources; the illusion that it can afford Star Wars; the illusion that it can be the only free market in the world; the illusion that military confrontation with the USSR, rather than economic confrontation with Japan is the critical issue.

Ayres believed in 1978 that the U.S. might be dismantling its capitalist system for a form of "soft" socialism. Business cycles of boom and recession, while entirely natural and to be accepted in a capitalist society, tend to provoke cries to relieve the suffering of the unemployed. Over the long term the protective legislation enacted—unemployment insurance, pensions, injury compensation and so on—begins to rigidify the system, taking people away from work involved with production and moving them into work involved with the redistribution of wealth. In 1986 he had modified this view and now believes that the trend toward socialism is stalled and may even be in reverse, at least for now.

New political directions are needed, with the Democrats shaking free of their commitment to central government and organized labor, and Republicans pulling away from the ultra-conservative right.

Future Information Societies

English speaking countries have, and will continue to have, an advantage in the development of service industries because English is likely to remain the dominant language of most of the information industries, including finance, insurance, business services and, incidentally, of computers, nuclear energy, aviation and space travel. This does not apply in manufacturing or the engineering of hardware.

Defense and Disarmament

Ayres explores the possibility of some sort of second Russian revolution, brought on by the increasing rigidity of the system, its inability to adapt to increasing pressures for change and therefore the likelihood of radical change. He couples a crisis, or a coup in the USSR, with a scenario of nuclear proliferation, the explosion of bombs in Africa, Latin America and Asia, and the growth of tighter controls on individual freedom to attempt to maintain world stability.

Two other scenarios, a world energy crisis and a world food crisis, present consequences for world stability and the likelihood of military action. The use of nuclear weapons by any of the larger nations he believes unlikely, but a nuclear war would be the end of civilization, especially if all or a large share of the available weapons (about 50,000) are fired. Non-nuclear spats and squabbles around the world are probable with the principal consequence for larger nations being an effort to contain them. The increasing dependence of the U.S. on exports of military hardware is an extremely dangerous trend.

Energy

The key issue is not whether there will be new energy technologies, but rather the problem of choosing correctly and not acting too soon. Over the next 30-40 years we will see the end of the age of oil and entry into an age of alternative fuels, perhaps gas or coal. The end of oil will stimulate new investments in gas and coal that are less efficient and, to some extent, sterile in terms of increased overall production. Nuclear power will replace only a small portion of the oil. Solar energy and photovoltaics should become prominent after 2050.

It is extremely unlikely the world could agree to cut back on carbon dioxide-producing fuels. In consequence there will be a lot of non-productive economic activity relocating people and business to avoid greenhouse impacts.

The world energy system is unstable, driven by demands resulting from increasing prosperity and drawing from a limited supply. In one scenario, Ayres suggests that the world will come to a fight over the remaining supplies. The long term consequences of an energy crisis would shift society in the developed world towards more use of electronic communication, less travel, more labor intensive agriculture, and less use of private transportation.

Environment

Temperature rise as a result of the greenhouse effect will be a significant environmental problem in the next century. Resource substitution and the effort to reclaim the environment will involve us in higher performance, technological innovation and enormous investment, including shifting the population away from threatened low-lying areas or protecting them by means of dikes and sea-walls.

Health

Growth in the current health care system seems implausible if only because it would eat up an improbable amount of the U.S. Gross

Domestic Product. To this point, the U.S. health care system appears to benefit mainly doctors and hospitals, although reforms by the current administration are improving the picture. The aging population will increasingly concern the health care system. Here we might learn from the Japanese who are intelligent leaders in caring for the elderly.

Around the world including the U.S., infant mortality continues to be a health care problem.

Education

Some of the problems in education today may be the result of educational experiments of the 1960s and 1970s. These experiments shook up a rigid educational system, creating change and what some see as decline. When the dust settles, we will return to a more intellectually competent approach to education in the U.S. The trends are towards longer schooling, at least in technologically developed nations which will require more education for skilled jobs and to participate in the customs and mores of society—an appreciation of the arts, for example.

Food and Agriculture

In 1978 Ayres thought that during the next 25 years the U.S. could continue to dominate the world in agricultural production, providing about 75% of exportable agricultural commodities. However in the last decade Argentina and Brazil have become low cost producers. Ayres is now less concerned than he used to be about the probabilities of major famine.

Cities

Cities in the U.S. will experience a renaissance except for a few—the Bronx, Detroit, Cleveland. Nothing will make the city disappear, although offices may become smaller, with more work done at home, or at alternative sites. Small and diversified families as well as singles will influence housing to more condominiums, high rises, and townhouses. As blacks migrate to the older suburbs, spreading out and diluting poverty, the well-to-do will return to cities. This will have a favorable effect on city schools.

The Sunbelt growth is not over. The Snowbelt's growth is slowing down but will continue, with the biggest growth area in the Rockies.

Religion

Religion—it's hard to kill. In 1978 Ayres saw a growth of fundamentalism coming out of a sense of hopelessness from inability to deal with forces beyond one's control. Those forces are not going to be more readily controlled, and therefore, fundamentalism is likely to continue to prosper. Fundamentalism will peak as a rural movement, but there could be an urban mutation.

Other Topics

On several topics, Ayres has little comment, except to note that they are important issues—civil and criminal justice, for example, a mess which may provoke reform in the next ten years.

UNDERLYING CAUSES

The understanding of underlying societal structures that govern behavior should be a first step towards reforming organizations and institutions. Organizations, such as corporations and unions, function according to the rules laid down by the underlying structure of law, which often promotes shortsighted behavior. Rather than seeking to do the near-impossible, and change behavior within the current rules by exhortation, organizations should press for structural changes, Ayres believes.

Ayres deplores values and customs he sees as obstacles to improvement of the human condition. The example of millions of sacred cows in India is frequently mentioned. Waste and wasteful practices of all kinds are to be abhorred, especially when these lead to the design of inefficient technologies such as those which resulted from cheap energy in the U.S.

EXHIBIT 6-2

FORCES INFLUENCING THE FUTURIST THINKING OF ROBERT U. AYRES

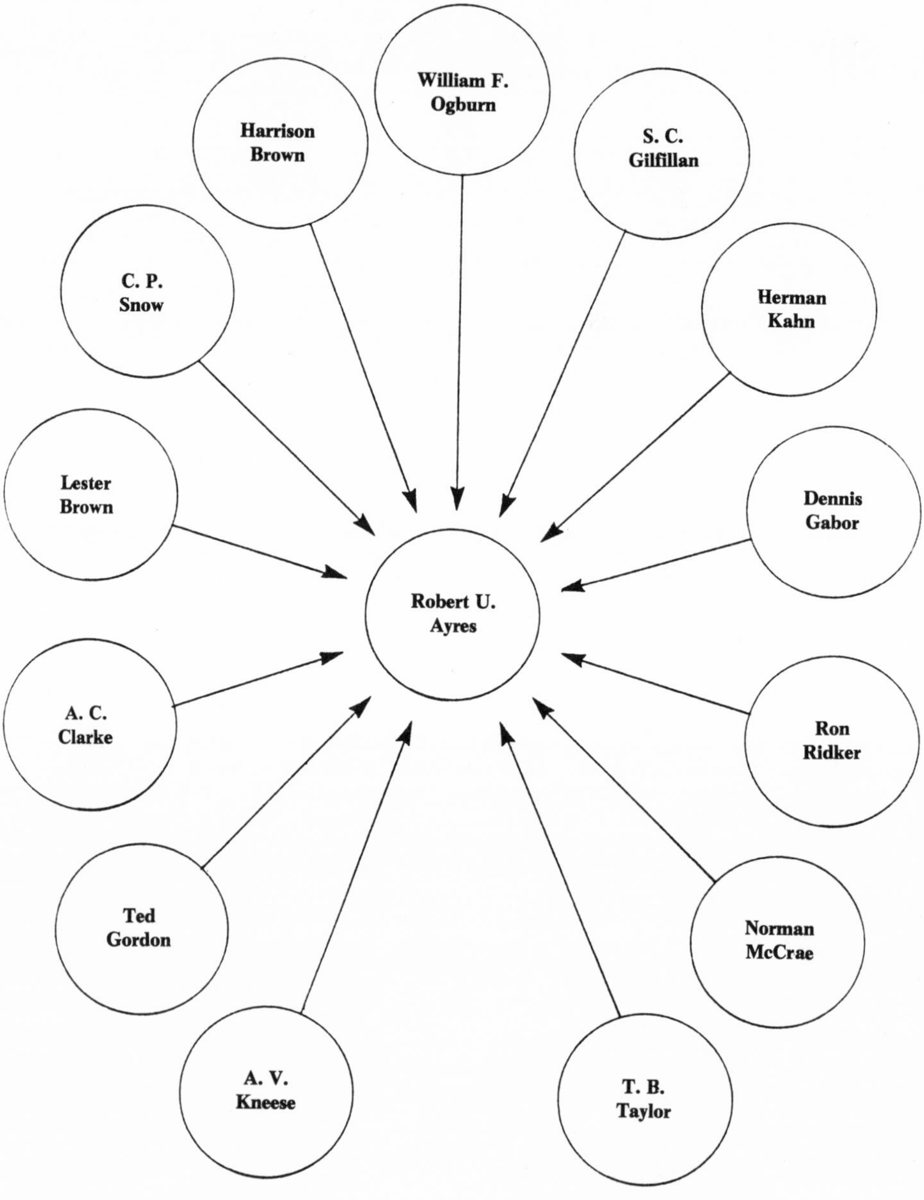

REFERENCES

1. Robert U. Ayres, *Uncertain Futures: Challenges for Decision Makers,* Wiley, 1979.
2. This scenario is described in more detail on pages 144-146 of *Uncertain Futures.*

CHAPTER 7

DANIEL BELL

Daniel Bell is one of the foremost American sociologists and social theorists. His work for the last twenty years, framed around the concept of the emerging post-industrial society, has become the conceptual and intellectual centerpiece of thinking in the U.S. and among the other advanced industrialized nations in the interpretation of the broad sweep of economic, technological, social, cultural and political change in which we are enmeshed. While Bell is universally seen as a premier futurist, he prefers to see himself as a student of long term and fundamental social and institutional change.

KEY VIEWS ABOUT THE FUTURE

1. The post-industrial society will be increasingly dependent on information, especially on scientifically-grounded theoretical knowledge. Information and service jobs will predominate.
2. The success of capitalism grounded in a Protestant ethic contains the seed of its own decline. Prosperity and education move successive generations to self-centered gratification, and away from deferred gratification and a sense of *civitas*, i.e., a collective or community-oriented set of values.
3. The nation-state is too small for the big problems of life, and too big for the small problems.
4. Accompanying the central role of theoretical knowledge are new technologies which reflect: broad application of electronics, miniaturization, digitalization, and an expanding competence to design to specifications.
5. Intellectual technologies will be increasingly crucial to the management of complexity.
6. Human capital is appreciating.
7. The three realms of society, the technoeconomic, the polity, and the culture, are only loosely coupled, so that changes in one do not necessarily have direct anticipatible effects on the other. Each realm is also a boundary constraint and an influence on change in the other realms.

BIOGRAPHICAL NOTE

Daniel Bell, Henry Ford Professor of Social Sciences at Harvard University, graduated from the College of the City of New York in 1938 and earned his doctorate at Columbia. He was a staff writer and later managing editor of the *New Leader* (1939-44). He then became managing editor of *Common Sense* (1945) and took his first academic assignment as assistant professor of social sciences at the University of Chicago (1945-48). He was labor editor for *Fortune* magazine for a decade. He started lecturing in sociology at Columbia in 1942, and was made professor in 1958. In 1969 he migrated to Harvard. Bell has served on numerous commissions. He was the U.S. representative to the Organization for Economic Cooperation and Development (OECD) Interfutures Project (1976-79) and a member of the President's Commission on Technology, Automation, and Economic Progress.

Bell was chairman of the American Academy of Arts and Sciences Commission on the Year 2000, which in 1968 resulted in *Toward the Year 2000: Work in Progress* and stimulated a distinguished cadre of thinkers, including Herman Kahn, to turn their attention to what was then the last third of a century.

He is a prolific author. The present chapter draws from *The Coming of the Post Industrial Society: A Venture in Social Forecasting* (1973), and its complement, *The Cultural Contradictions of Capitalism* (1976).

We have also drawn on a 1977 paper, "The Future World Disorder: A Structural Context for Crises," prepared for the OECD and reprinted in *The Winding Passage.*

Bell pointed out the significance of his chapter, "The Social Framework of the Information Society," which appears in *The Computer Age: A Twenty Year View*, edited by Michael Dertouzos and Joel Moses. We have also found Bell's introductory essay, "The Year 2000—The Trajectory of an Idea" in *Toward the Year 2000*, valuable in highlighting the origins of his interest in the future. Bell has generously supplied us with unpublished notes and charts, and we had the advantage of hearing his engaging and informal lecture at the Congressional Office of Technology Assessment, September 15, 1986.

As a student of both Marxist and non-Marxist socialism of the 19th century, he has characterized himself as a post-Marxist thinker, presumably by way of satisfying the demands of those who would push us each into labeled boxes. He is indebted to scores of other 19th century thinkers and draws on a panorama of contemporary analysts and social thinkers, extracting, interpreting, re-interpreting, and integrating concepts and ideas into his own comprehensive framework. Karl

Mannheim and Max Weber rank with Marx in influence. His own teacher at Columbia, Robert McIver, was also an influence. Bell acknowledges the contributions of the Australian economist, Colin Clark, for his pathbreaking conceptualization of economic activity in three sectors, the primary sector of extractive industry, the secondary sector, manufacturing and transportation, and the tertiary or services sector.

WORLDVIEW

The Realms of Modern Society

Bell rejects the notion that society is an integrated whole, a complex system. Rather, for him, it is an amalgam of three realms; the social structure, including the techno-economic structure, the polity, and the culture. His concept of the post-industrial society refers primarily to the first realm, the techno-economic. In Bell's view, changes in that realm do not determine either the polity or the culture. He is inclined to the contrary view that the cultural and political orders dominate—or at least constrain—technological choices. Exhibit 7-1 outlines this general social schema. One can find and interpret many conflicts within our society in terms of this three-part division of society into distinctive realms. For example, under the first column of axial principles, the economic criteria of functional rationality, efficiency, and effectiveness, characteristic of business decisions, is at odds with the political pressure for equality. Each of these in turn is at cross purposes with a cultural characteristic, the drive toward self-realization with its intense focus on the individual. The concerns of the individual work against a requirement for political stability, shared beliefs, and a willingness to compromise.

Next, consider the column on the relation of the individual to society. The traditional industrial society has segmented people's roles. One is professionally a lawyer or a physician or an assembly line operator. On the other hand the polity emphasizes participation in decisions affecting one's interests while the cultural realm celebrates the whole person.

The Post-Industrial Society

Exhibit 7-2 summarizes Bell's concept of the post-industrial society. A key feature is the shift in the labor force from predominantly fabrication, material production, and manufacturing to post-industrial society's emphasis on service sector employment. More subtle, less visible, and in the long pull, more important, is the shift to dependence on codified theoretical knowledge as a directing force for change. Every

Exhibit 7-1

The Disjunctive Realms of Modern Society

1. **Realms**	**Techno-Economic**	**Polity**	**Culture**
2. Axial Principles	Functional Rationality	Equality	Self-Realization
3. Axial Structures	Bureaucracy	Representation	"The Democratization of Genius"
4. Central Value Orientation	Material Growth	Government by Consent of Governed	The Value of the "New"
5. Relations of Individual to Society	Segmentation into Roles	Participation in Decision	The Emphasis on the Whole Person
6. Basic Processes	Specialization	Negotiation-Conflict	Break-up of Genres and Distinctions
7. Structural Problematics	Reification of Institutions and Persons	Entitlements	The Question Judgements of What is Value

General Schema of Society

1. **Realms**	**Techno-Economic**	**Polity**	**Culture**
2. Axial Principles	Tools for Increase of Resources	Stipulation of Power	Existential Meanings
3. Axial Structures	Organization of Production	Legal or Customary Institutions	Sacral and Esthetic Authorities

4. Central Value Orientation	Control over Nature	Justice	Transcendence
5. Relations Individual to Society	Instrumental — Labor as Means	Jural Standing	Self to an Ultimate
6. Basic Processes	Differentiation	Definitions of Actors and Arenas	Syncretism
7. Structural Problematics	Disruption of Custom Scarcities	Legitimacy	Dialectic of Release and Restraint
8. Patterns of Social Change	Linear	Alternation	Ricorsi

society has operated on the basis of knowledge. The critical difference between the industrial and the post-industrial society is the switch from experimental, empirical knowledge and know-how, to theoretical knowledge. The great society-shaping technologies of the 19th century were created by amateurs, by tinkerers, by empirical geniuses. Theoretical knowledge either followed or was ignored by the developers of the 19th century technologies. Today, theoretical knowledge dominates in electronics and in material science. Coming out of the post-industrial transformation is the new class, the knowledge and information workers.

A stream of new conflicts accompanies the transformation from the industrial to the post-industrial society. For example, the ownership of intellectual property will become more important because theoretical knowledge does not fit the traditional property categories of the industrial society. Theoretical knowledge must be protected and rewarded if we are to have incentives for its effective development. The concept of "technology" itself must expand, since technology has historically meant the physical, and more recently, the physical and biological. One must embrace institutional and intellectual technology inventions, since these will become more important factors in shaping, organizing, and managing our world.

Exhibit 7-2

The Postindustrial Society: A Comparative Schema [1]

Mode of Production	**Preindustrial Extractive**	**Industrial Fabrication**	**Postindustrial Processing; Recycling Services**
Economic sector	**Primary** Agriculture Mining Fishing Timber Oil and gas	**Secondary** Goods-producing Manufacturing Durables Nondurables Heavy construction	**Tertiary** Transportation Utilities **Quarternary** Trade Finance Insurance Real estate **Quinary** Health Education Research Government Recreation
Transforming resource	**Natural power** Wind, water, draft animal, human muscle	**Created energy** Electricity—oil gas, coal, nuclear power	**Information** Computer and data-transmission systems
Strategic resource	Raw materials	Financial capital	Knowledge
Technology	Craft	Machine technology	Intellectual technology
Skill base	Artisan, manual worker, farmer	Engineer, semi-skilled worker	Scientist, technical and professional occupations

Methodology	Commonsense, trial and error experience	Empiricism, experimentation	Abstract theory, Models, Simulations, Decision theory Systems analysis
Time perspective	Orientation to the past	Ad hoc adaptiveness, Experimentation	Future orientation: Forecasting and planning
Design	Game against nature	Game against fabricated future	Game between persons
Axial principle	Traditionalism	Economic growth	Codification of theoretical knowledge

Another emerging conflict will frame itself around those workers whose incomes rise rapidly because they are backed by new theoretical knowledge and those other workers in our society such as nurses, policemen, and teachers whose work is more or less inelastic to technology driven productivity gains. The labor conflicts will be over closing the wage gaps.

Education for the new world will create its own problems as will the rise of the adversarial culture and the resistances of bureaucracy to change.

Bell has a metaphor for his trichotomy of societies:

> *. . .pre-industrial society is a 'game against nature'. . . .industrial society is a 'game against fabricated nature'. . . . a post-industrial society is a 'game between persons'. . . .*[2]

Cultural Contradictions

"Irony" is a term not extensively used by Bell but is implicit to his analysis of many problems. In Bell's cultural realm, one of the consequences of the success of the industrial era has been an extraordinary degree of personal freedom and opportunity as well as the development of strong attention to the self, self-realization, self-fulfillment, or "self-actualization." This concentration on the self is reflected in the way we in the U.S. ransack the world to acquire its benefits in a helter-skelter, self-engorging way. A further mark of modernity is that there is a shift from the old, including our roots, to a concentration on the new and the future. The epitome of this is the bourgeois entrepreneur and his relentless search for the new, the sensational, the stimulating. This ubiquitous self-centeredness undercuts the very values of hard work and deferred gratification which made it all possible. For Bell, "modernism has thus been the seducer."[3]

The Changing Market System

From the point of view of the polity, Bell sees five forces or elements together structurally transforming the old market system:

- The institutionalization of expectations in the form of entitlements has led Bell to coin a phrase, "a revolution of rising entitlements," to describe the situation. We have moved away from the concept of earning, saving, husbanding, and preparing for the future with this new sense of entitlements. At the low end of the economic scale the expectation is welfare. In the middle class it is free or heavily subsidized public education.
- The incompatibility of our numerous wants and diverse values is breeding inescapable problems of choice.
- The rise of spillover or secondary effects of economic growth are important factors in our collective concerns.
- Worldwide inflation reflects expanding demand and lagging capacity.
- The shift in many crucial decisionmaking processes is from the marketplace to the political domain.

Put in a different way, the West has lost a sense of *civitas*, the willingness to make sacrifices for the collective good. In the absence of of *civitas* we are adrift in setting our priorities.

Bell argues strongly the need for a "public household" but tells us nearly nothing about who, how, when, or by what means we might achieve that objective. He celebrates the value of religion and hopes that its restoration will help provide that public value. On the other hand, it would be hard to believe that he sees the current prominence of religious fundamentalism as a positive step in the direction of a renewed *civitas*.

SPECIFIC ISSUES

Values

A key value for Bell is lost in the decline of a strong Protestant ethic, presumably including the Protestant work ethic. He encapsulates his harsh judgment in terms of installment buying and the credit card, which pushes us to excessive consumption, eroding a traditional Protestant commitment to saving for the future.

Women

Bell's structural analysis sheds light on the status of women and their emergence as a major segment of the workforce. Two conditions were necessary for this emerging role of women. First was the now decades old shift in cultural attitudes and second was the more recent institutionalization of a market. The cultural attitudes changed decades ago but only recently has there been the rise of the human services sector which has led to the institutionalization of a market for women's employment.

Emerging Technologies

Bell is working on a book, tentatively entitled, *The Next Technological Revolution*, developing his notion that we are moving to a knowledge based society, dependent increasingly on theoretical knowledge. The characteristic example of his concept is seen in the shift in the way materials are handled. Until quite recently, there were a small number of relatively standardized materials, a variety of iron and steels, copper, brass, aluminum, polyethylene, polyvinyl-chloride, etc. If we chose to build or make something, we had to work within the boundaries of the capabilities of those materials, thereby limiting our ability to meet our goals. A radical, if not revolutionary, change has transformed our approach to selection and use of materials. We now can literally specify the performance characteristics of the material we want and most likely create that material in the laboratory and introduce it successfully into commerce. For Bell the new capability is both revolutionary in the materials domain itself and in the paradigm of our emerging technological capabilities across the board.

Information and Telecommunications

In the post-industrial society,

> *A new social framework based on telecommunications may be decisive in the way in which economic and social exchanges are conducted, the way knowledge is created and retrieved, and the character of occupations and work in which men engage.*[4]

Closely tied to this central role of telecommunications or more properly, "compunications" (a somewhat awkward term conceived by Anthony Oettinger of Harvard and more euphoniously captured by "telematics"), is the shift from goods-producing to a service society. The second is the strong role of theoretical knowledge and third is the emergence of intellectual technologies as key tools for social management, where the intellectual technologies include such things as systems analysis and decision theory. The key to the intellectual technology is the substitution of knowledge, wisdom, experience and intuitive judgment by some formal algorithm. A big problem in the information society is the virtual absence of any economic theory of information. Information obviously is not a commodity or an article of commerce in the traditional sense. For example, when sold or given away it still remains. It has characteristics which will take time to understand and codify. In terms of information technology, Bell sees five emerging problem areas:

- The meshing of telephone and computer systems.
- The substitution of electronic media for paper processing.
- The expansion of television through cable.
- The reorganization of storage and retrieval to allow for interaction.
- The expansion of the education system through computer aided instruction.

Coming out of these transformational technological changes are numerous emerging issues. Consider, for example, the infrastructure.

Transportation, Energy, and Communication

Society has three basic clusters of infrastructure. The first is transportation, the second is energy, and third is communication. Bell sees little likelihood of radical developments in transportation. On the other hand, should a ballistic airplane be developed which would link New York to Tokyo in 3 to 5 hours or London to Sydney, etc., the increased banding together of the world surely would be a change.

There may be some significant new developments in the energy infrastructure but the really big actions will be in the communications infrastructure. The communications infrastructure will raise the crucial question of the best techno-economic organization to achieve the most efficient and effective use of the technology. Do we go competitive or integrated? Do we create monopolies or promote competition? Bell sees unregulated competition rather than government regulated spheres as being far more productive.[5]

How the third infrastructure develops depends on some issues of the polity such as:

- The location of cities.
- The possibility of more centralized or national planning.
- The roles of centralization and privacy.
- The possible divisions of society between the elite and the masses.
- The international organization of telematics.

World Disorders

Bell is pessimistic about the global situation. He has epitomized it in the observation that "the national state is too small for the big problems of life and too big for the small problems."[6] The scope and urgency of problems arising from this mismatch must drive us to seek new political arrangements to preserve freedom and peace in our shrinking world.

His international analysis done in 1977 is as cogent and applicable today as it was then, primarily because Bell chooses to address issues at the structural level and structure changes slowly. That structural situation is as follows:

There have been two major sociological and geopolitical transformations in the Western world:

- The rise of the welfare state, especially "the revolution of rising entitlements" and the greater freedom in culture and morals.
- The end of the old international order and the emergence of a large number of heterogeneous, diverse states.
- Separate and distinct but interacting with the above are the technological revolutions in transportation and communication, tying the world together in real time and the rise of the science based industries of the post-industrial era, the associated global integration of manufacturing, and displacement of jobs in manufacturing from the advanced to the less developed nations.

Coming out of these structural changes is a new class struggle not between labor and management or owner and worker as in the 19th century, but between larger interest groups. Associated with this is the rise of more political intervention in the economic sector.

Four structural problems will affect the advanced nations:

- Growing interconnectedness and interdependence creates a double bind in the advanced economies; the need for someone to think about the system as a whole, since everything is systemic, conflicting with the rise of special, legitimate, powerful, individual interests.
- Data and protectionism.
- The demographic tidal wave.
- The rich and poor nations. While that difference will always exist, we have run into new problems with international industrialization. For example, international manufacturing will lead to an international labor base.

Bell sees situations among the advanced nations similar to the crisis in the 1920s and 1930s arising, in which there will be many insoluble problems, a parliamentary impasse with little or no likelihood of any group commanding a majority, growth of an unemployed, an educated intelligentsia, and the spread of private violence, which regimes are unable to check.

The Multinational Corporation

For Bell, the multinational corporation is a primary instrument for the transfer of technology to the developing nations. As part of the long-term integration and shift to a global economy, the U.S. is likely to move more toward a "headquarters economy" as more regularized, standardized processes migrate overseas.[7] That division of labor between rich and poor nations is one of the factors pushing the U.S. toward a more service based economy and a high technology service based economy at that.

Intellectual Technologies

Technology is a broad concept for Bell, going well beyond traditional, physical, and biological technologies, to embrace almost the full range of notions associated with Jacques Ellul, for whom technology is virtually equivalent to technique. An emerging critical part of the new family of technologies will be intellectual technologies, framed primarily around the management of complexity. Among the new intellectual technologies are the techniques for rationalizing our decisionmaking such as operations research, the techniques for the formalization of judgment, and the application of empirical and mathematical rules. Along with the rise of intellectual technologies is the observation that the period of great scientific achievement based on specialization is now being overtaken by growing cross relationships among theories. We are beginning to reintegrate our knowledge of the world.

Among the intellectual technologies are Markov chain applications, the Monte Carlo technique, information theory, cybernetics, and game theory.

Modeling Society

Bell is pessimistic about the ability to model society. We do not have the knowledge or the theory, although from the technological point of view we do have some insights into how society changes. Adding futher difficulty to the modeling of society is its increasing openness. The strength of models is in closed systems.

Bell also makes a sharp distinction between prediction and forecasting and has relatively little interest in prediction, that is, in statements about the probabilities of particular events. Forecasting requires a basic understanding of structural forces at play as a route to anticipating some of their potential consequences. Bell does, however, see that an approach through multiple "social frameworks" can be the basis of insight into social forecasting. His seven frameworks are:

1. The geopolitical relationships and the strategic variables assumed to be associated with each of them. So, for example, in the dimensions of conflict between East versus West, West versus West, North versus South, East versus East, each one has these strategic variables to consider: demographic transitions, energy dependency, minerals and metal resources, agricultural status, industrial status, science and technology capabilities, and military capabilities.
2. The post-industrial framework.
3. The infrastructure. As already noted, the basic infrastructure variables are transportation, energy, and communications.
4. The matching of scale. Many issues arise from the fact that the nation states are too small for the big problems and too big for the small problems.
5. Centripetal and centrifugal tendencies including possible political and economic integration in Europe, the Mediterranean basin, and the Mideast. At the same time we have sub-national fragmentation working vigorously in the U.K., France, Spain, Yugoslavia, and the Soviet Union. There are emergent world structures in finance,

science, and health. There are trans-national organizations, and there is the growing recognition of vulnerabilities and societal susceptibilities to shock and economic maladjustments and adjustments, terrorism, and so on.

6. New technological changes.
7. The new belief systems, including the revival of traditional religions, especially fundamentalism in Islam and in Christianity, the rise of cults, new "primordial attachments" such as ethnicity, the rise of irrationalism, and the decay of Communist ideologies.

Limits to Forecasting

Several central concepts in Bell's views set a severe limit on the expectations which he or others may have about social forecasting. First with regard to his concept of realms discussed earlier, he sees that they change in different ways; the techno-economic sectors do not change in the ways that culture changes. There is no single general principle which acts in determinant fashion and which one can use as a guide to isolate the leading and lagging elements of change. A second limiting factor is clear in his book on post-industrial society. That whole activity is conducted in the spirit of "as if" in the sense that he draws out social science fictions as logical constructs trying to identify dimensions and then see how the future would come out with and without interventions. Put differently, the idea of an industrial society is a principle. Whether societies can or cannot move in that direction is an empirical, not a logical issue for Bell.

Bell also rejects the concept of the pace of change as not useful. He is more comfortable with using scale as the metric with regard to what is changing. An example of the mismatch of scale is the international economy which has greatly expanded, multiplied in the number of actors, and increased in volatility and velocity of actions, yet its political management is on a totally inadequate scale.

Finally, it should be noted that in his current research and work not yet published, Bell is developing methodologies for tracking technology and for using the social frameworks discussed above to see how technologies may change our ways of acting.

UNDERLYING CAUSES

From the point of view of day-to-day life, life in the year 2000 is more likely to be similar than it is to be different from that in the previous decades. However, the changes that will occur will be driven by four major forces:

- Technological change. Bell notes in the area of technological change that among the critical developments are a move toward

  — miniaturization,
  — the intrusion of electronics into all kinds of devices and services,
  — the application of theoretical knowledge, and,
  — digitalization of all information.

- Diffusion of goods and social claims throughout the economy.
- Structural developments in society, such as the centralization of the political economy, the shift to the service sector, the rise of the university as gatekeeper, and the increasing importance of human capital.
- The relationship of the U.S. and the rest of the world, which could in some sense be the most important of these basic factors.

EXHIBIT 7-3

FORCES INFLUENCING THE FUTURIST THINKING OF

DANIEL BELL

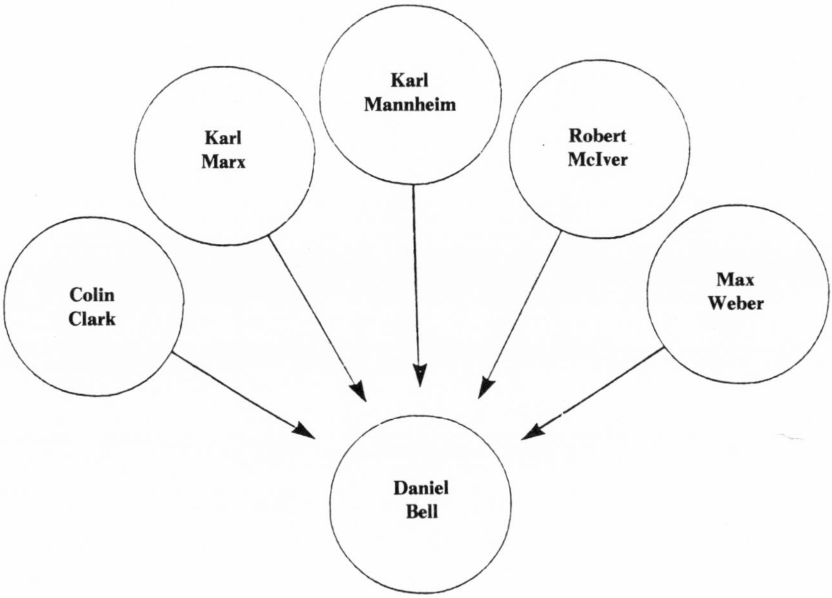

REFERENCES

1. Daniel Bell, "The Social Framework of the Information Society," in Michael L. Dertouzos and Joel Moses, eds., *The Computer Age: A Twenty Year View,* The MIT Press, Cambridge, MA 1979, pp. 166-167.
2. Daniel Bell, *The Coming of Post-Industrial Society,* Basic Books, Inc., New York, 1976, p. 116.
3. *The Cultural Contradictions of Capitalism,* Basic Books, Inc., New York, 1976, p. 19.
4. "The Social Framework," p. 163.
5. "The Social Framework," p. 196.
6. "The World Future Disorders: The Structural Context of Crisis" (1977), reprinted in Daniel Bell's *The Winding Passage,* Basic Books, Inc., New York, 1980, p. 227.
7. *The Coming of Post-Industrial Society,* p. 485.

Additional Readings:

Daniel Bell, "The World and the United States in 2013," *Daedalus,* Journal of the American Academy of Arts and Sciences, 116:3, Summer 1987.

CHAPTER 8

KENNETH E. BOULDING

Kenneth Boulding is an internationally known social scientist, author, interdisciplinary thinker, peace researcher and university professor. He is a former president of the American Association for the Advancement of Science (AAAS) and of the Society for General Systems Research.

KEY VIEWS ABOUT THE FUTURE

1. Peace is a continuing evolutionary process. War interrupts this process, sometimes catastrophically. In the long term, however, we are evolving towards a more peaceful global social structure.
2. The great era of change was from about 1860 to the 1920s. The present period shows not so much an increase in the pace and rate of change as the emergence of a world system.
3. Science is the greatest hope of humanity and also its greatest threat of annihilation.
4. The position of science in society is regulated to a great extent by the image of science in the minds of non-scientists, especially decisionmakers. Non-scientists are increasingly fearful of products science has helped make possible.
5. Knowledge, and know-how, energy and materials are crucial factors for the future, as they have been of the past.
6. Deterrence is an illusion, limited nuclear war is an absurdity, arms control is an hypocrisy. Stable peace is the only national security now available.[1]
7. In any situation there is some optimum level or range of variety. Some trends, such as that toward worldwide homogeneity are not necessarily positive, stabilizing, or safe for the human future.

BIOGRAPHICAL NOTE

Born in 1910, in England, Kenneth Boulding came to the U.S. in 1932 as a Commonwealth Fellow at the University of Chicago. He has taught economics at a variety of institutions, including Colgate, Iowa State and McGill Universities. From 1949 to 1968 he was professor of economics at the University of Michigan where he was also, for two years, director of research at the University's Center for Conflict Resolution. He later moved to Colorado, where he now lives and is distinguished professor emeritus at the University of Colorado. From 1967-1981 he directed the university's program on general social and economic dynamics at the Institute of Behavioral Science. Professor Boulding has held many visiting professorships overseas, for example at International Christian University, Tokyo, the University of Melbourne, the University of Edinburgh, and, in the U.S., at Dartmouth, Cornell and the University of Texas at Austin, among others.

Boulding describes his interest in the future as springing from his religious and social origins. As a Wesleyan Methodist, a chapel goer from a working-class family, he was the first of his family to go to college and did well at Oxford University in chemistry, then in economics. Yet he was not socially accepted there as a fellow and instead won a fellowship at the University of Chicago. As a 14-year-old child he had been fascinated by H.G. Wells' *Outline of History*; as a young economist, he was influenced by John Maynard Keynes. Then in 1954, at Stanford's Center for Advanced Studies in the Behavioral Sciences, he met the Dutch futurist, Fred Polak, who affected Boulding and his wife Elise strongly. Polak's effect on the Bouldings was so profound that Elise Boulding learned Dutch in order to translate Polak's book, *Image of the Future.* Boulding's year in Japan in 1963 was also formative, introducing him to a non-Western outlook with its own distinctive approach to education and to culture. Many of his students were Marxists, but he saw that, as a whole, the society was taking great strides in learning. These factors influenced his ideas on social dynamics and led to his book, *Ecodynamics, A New Theory of Societal Evolution*, in 1978.

This chapter draws on a selection of his many books and articles and an interview. He says about his own field:

> *The social sciences are a quantum mechanics from the very beginning, full of Heisenberg principles, in which the attempt to get information out of a system changes it. Human knowledge is itself an essential part of the social system which we are trying to learn about. We cannot learn about it without changing it. This often means that the immediate past is a very poor guide to the future.*[2]

WORLDVIEW

We may be passing into a new region of time in which the world's future fans out across five possible directions ranging from the wipe-out of civilization through nuclear war to an almost unimaginable realization of all our most optimistic hopes.

The fivefold fan of the future:[3]

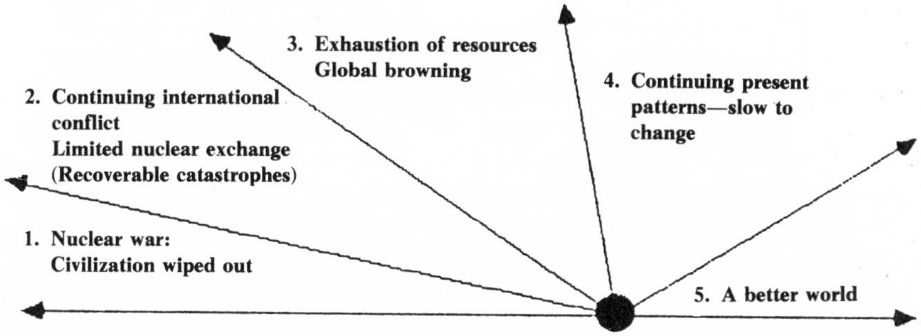

Panel 2 of the fan is more likely to be in our future than Panel 1. Panel 3 is based on the Club of Rome's model in *The Limits to Growth*, in which the resources of the earth are exhausted and the planet's carrying capacity exceeded, with a corresponding deterioration in environment and lifestyle for everyone. New energy technologies, such as photovoltaics, which shift to new sources of supply, and the concept of human intelligence as an inexhaustible resource that can create new technological solutions, go some way towards mitigating the bleakness of the third panel future, in Boulding's view. In Panel 4, we go on as we are, incorporating slow, evolutionary change. Panel 5 represents a better world, which also has some positive probability. This would involve the rapid spread of human knowledge and learning sufficient to control population growth; increased productivity, especially of the poorest quarter of the human race, to eliminate destitution and crippling poverty; the development of increased skills of government, the detection and reversal of movement away from human betterment; the abolition of war; better intervention into pathological criminal subcultures; improvements in child-rearing; and so on.

The great era of change which created the modern world began with the so-called agricultural and industrial revolution, especially in Britain, in the 18th century. It accelerated with the application of science to productive technology after 1860 with the chemical and electrical industries, and so on. Interrupted by the world wars and the Depression, it resumed after about 1950 with the control of disease, the expansion of education, a population explosion mostly in the poor countries, a six-fold increase in international trade between 1950 and 1980, and an enormous expansion of communications and inter-cultural penetration. Clouded with the nuclear threat and the arms race, the world is increasingly becoming a total system in trade, culture, communication, and military threat, but still retains much that is local.

Boulding's view of the future includes many dilemmas, many choice points, many forces that could bring the greatest good, or the greatest destruction. Knowledge, and know-how, energy and materials are crucial factors for the future, as they have been of the past.[4] As an imaginative, creative conceptualizer, probing and testing new concepts against traditional ideas, his arguments, in consequence, are not a closely woven fabric. He uses metaphor and allegory liberally, including all species, all concepts, products, social systems and bodies of knowledge as elements fitting into their own niches in larger ecosystems. For example, a new technology takes root in the scientific and technological ecosystem if a niche is open. In the same way, an emerging new value may be taken up by a society with an unfilled need for it among its current system of values.

In a contribution to Michael Marien's survey of how futurists have changed their views over the last 20 years, *What I Have Learned, Thinking About the Future, Then and Now,* 1987, Boulding reviews what he said in *The Meaning of the Twentieth Century: The Great Transition,* 1964.[5] He believed then that we were moving from mere civilization to post-civilization, to a scientific and technologically based superculture—at least in the highly developed sections of the world. This continues to be true, with the addition of a sense of incipient crisis worldwide.

The threat of nuclear war is increasing and national defense systems have become enemies of world security. Some progress is being made in controlling fertility We are making encouraging progress in the conservation of energy and the use of alternative technologies.

Some new traps are opening before us:

- One is movement towards cultural and ecological homogeneity as we become a one-world society. Man is spreading himself, his religions, his plant and animal species, his soda and blue jeans around the world. Cultural diversity may become an issue in the next century.
- An economic problem is the erosion of profit by interest, and the unproductive use of borrowed money leading to a concatenation of debt that threatens individuals, companies, banks and nations.
- Boulding deplores the tendency of our political process to develop leaders with unrealistic views of the world who lack the skills of governing.
- The fundamentalist trap is another one the U.S. may yet fall into, by electing a leader who appeals to some earlier sense of order or

security, as Khomeini did in Iran, and Falwell might do in the U.S. Such regimes as Khomeini's seem to need scapegoats to persecute.

Boulding recognizes changes in the status of women as an important trend and would rewrite his earlier work to change what seems to him now to be sexist language.

SPECIFIC ISSUES

The U.S. Economy

The economy is a system and economics a net positive-sum game. However, the system includes a threat dynamic, one which makes us conform. We pay our taxes, for example, because we are implicitly coerced to do so. Many of these threats are internalized, guiding our behavior without our being aware of their function. On the positive side of the system are exchange and trade dynamics that are beneficial. Competition is not the equivalent of conflict, however. For Boulding, the war industry is a cancer on the economic system.

Among the capitalist societies, he notes a sense of malaise caused by worsening problems in the economic system, such as an increase in international debt. He suggests that in the aging of its population and the slowing of change, the U.S. may be a maturing society. Western civilization as a whole may be nearing its end, either by catastrophe or by being driven to create a new society by the old society's exhaustion of resources.[6]

The Future of the U.S. Corporation

A long-term political trend towards making capitalist society more economically just may involve corporations through a move to increase employee ownership plans and to develop other ways in which the ownership of captial can be more widespread, and individual net worth increased. One other related development is the growth in private pension plans.[7]

The International Economy

Inflation is a common and recurrent disease of national economies. It is now endemic worldwide. There is some evidence for a "Kondratieff" cycle of about 60 years. Inflation-unemployment is one of the greatest unsolved problems of open-market societies. International economics and politics are not a balanced system, but are a constantly changing flow, an evolutionary disequilibrium. Boulding criticizes modern economics as an attempt to balance that which should not and cannot be in balance.

He regards the current debt-heavy state of the international financial system as an area of social pathology potentially damaging to the U.S. as well as to Third World countries.

All economic models of world development have been too simple and have not addressed the question of sustainability, of redistribution of income, of who develops, and where. It is hard to be optimistic about Africa's economy, for example, over the next few decades.[8]

The Soviet Union changed little over 20 years, but may be changing now under Gorbachev. China, on the other hand, has made many changes, although both it and the USSR are described by Boulding as the last of the 19th-century empires. The rise of OPEC is the most striking economic event, one which has inconvenienced rich countries and caused hardship and economic damage to the poorer developing countries, but is now relatively weak.

Defense and Disarmament

Boulding takes a long-term, optimistic view of the prospects for peace. A meditation on the nature of peace runs as a thread through all his work on other subjects. In his view, peace is the process, the important, strong, background texture of existence. War is an event interrupting this process, sometimes catastrophically. He deplores our concentrating time, money, and the power of scientific thought on the event rather than the process. Over centuries, however, we are evolving towards a more peaceful global social structure. War and peace, like science, are learned activities. War as an institution is declining in legitimacy, but, as decaying institutions do, lingers on to threaten peace and the new order. Peace, as a new institution, or institutionalized process, is not yet fully legitimate. Nuclear war remains as the big discontinuity that could upset all our progress towards the mastery of peace. It may be that we cannot learn to avoid nuclear war without a catastrophe, such as a limited nuclear exchange, or a widespread famine, to teach us what we need to know to avoid a nuclear Armageddon.[9] Based on the outcome of recent wars, a well-managed defeat may be more economically productive over the long term, at least partly because the military influence on decisionmaking is temporarily either defeated or destroyed, enabling a nation to plan a civilian future. Victory, on the other hand, is costly, forcing a nation to rebuild without being relieved from the burden of defense and military spending.

A few years ago, Boulding noted that one of the values of peace research was its bringing together of an interdisciplinary group of individuals in an effort to develop a normative science in a specialized field. He estimated these peace researchers were political scientists (35%), sociologists (21%), lawyers (14%), general systems thinkers (8%), and about 6% apiece from the fields of economics, history, psychology and anthropology.[10] He sees peace research as becoming increasingly sophisticated in its study of the nature of threat systems.

Conflict involves the perception of changes for the better and for the worse. Decisions in conflict are based on one of several images of the future. One side believes the change leading to the conflict will reduce its welfare, the other that it will improve its welfare. If either or both sides have unrealistic images of the future, the outcome of the conflict may well be different from that expected by either side. The zero-sum outcome is a rare case, in which one side's gain is seen as equal to the other side's loss.[11]

Threat is connected to conflict and is an underlying support of all human social systems. It is useful in maintaining traffic control and tax collection, but can produce counter-threat, which leads to deterrence and arms control. Deterrence will eventually break down unless transformed into another system. Therefore, Boulding believes, there is a positive probability of the nuclear deterrent failing to deter in the next 100 years.

He believes the economic approach to defense, aiming to achieve balance in mutual deterrence, is worthless because the real conflict is between humans and the national defense organizations they have built that now threaten to destroy them.

> *Deterrence is an illusion, limited nuclear war is an absurdity, arms control is hypocrisy.*[12]

The nation state ought not to be defended by threat, because in the process its defense organization will destroy the world. It can achieve security by stable peace. Other institutions besides states support the legitimacy of the defense organizations. World religions, for example, preach peace and encourage war. Science subverts its dedication to truth by practicing lying, secrecy, and suppressing curiosity in the service of national defense. These subversions present scientists with ethical difficulties. At present, these are not widely discussed, but are likely to encourage significant change within science and among scientists when the issues are raised and debated more openly.

Science

Science is universal in the world today. According to Boulding, however, science is still a subculture living in an ecological niche of universities and laboratories, within a social ecosystem that does not support its values, although it does support it economically.[13] Tension between the two communities over values has arisen before, and may again. The position of science in society is regulated to a great extent by the image of science in the minds of non-scientists, especially decisionmakers.

Non-scientists are increasingly fearful of products science has helped produce: chemicals, DNA, nuclear power, for example. In Boulding's opinion, the greatest social cost of science is being paid in the development of weapons.

One traditional job of science is to supply political leaders with new and more destructively efficient weapons. In doing so, the knowledge of new firepower spreads and tends to make all territories indefensible. As gunpowder left the medieval castle without defenses, so the nuclear missile threatens the viability of the nation state. Citizens can no longer be protected by armies and their weapons—they are instead held hostage by them. Boulding believes it tragic that so many scientists are working on war and weaponry, and so few, on peace and improved ploughshares. Science is the greatest hope of humanity but perhaps also represents its greatest threat of annihilation. We need new peace tools, for example, a new technology of non-destructive testing in social conflict.[14]

Energy

We will run out of oil, slowly, replacing it with substitutes and conserving it with new technology and better management. To some extent, the development of breakthrough energy technologies will be dependent on exhausting our current sources. A growing population will push us to more and wider searches for sources of materials. This in turn, will force us to jump beyond our scientific and territorial boundaries in seeking solutions. One possibility is for man to move out into the solar system.[15]

Our current resource questions are problems of management rather than supply, as can be seen in water demand issues, for instance. According to Boulding, we need to pay more attention now to more thoughtful management of energy because, unless we can conserve and bring in new sources on a worldwide scale over the next 200 years to maintain the artificial environment we are creating, society will collapse.[16] Boulding is critical of energy utilities, believing them to be incapable of the flexibility and change that will be needed.

The Environment

Parts of the globe are total worldwide systems, such as the atmosphere. The ocean consists of two or three partially connected systems, the land masses each consists of a separate set of systems, and the biosphere is a mesh or network of smaller systems. Taking this as background, man is the first species to have a universal ecological niche. Man can, and has, fit into every other ecosystem.

This means the future of the human species is dependent upon decisions made in many systems and from many points of view. Boulding believes a high level of variety is ideal. Some trends, such as that toward worldwide homogeneity, are not necessarily positive, stabilizing, or safe for the human future.

As development proceeds and as human knowledge increases and spreads, class and power systems tend to become more complex, more diffuse, and more fluid. Communism concentrates power much more than capitalism does wealth, but even this is fluid and tends to diffuse. This does not preclude the likelihood that a substantial proportion of the human race will be underprivileged and in severe poverty for a considerable time to come, especially if population growth is unchecked.

It seems probable, however, that world population is overshooting its niche. What the consequences might be, Boulding does not speculate on to any extent, except in anticipating a deteriorating environment and the potential for disastrous events—nuclear war, for example—or the death of large numbers of people from a disease such as AIDS.

Education and Learning

What Boulding calls "noogenetics"—learned structures in biogenetically produced nervous systems that are transmitted from one generation to the next by a learning process—exist in pre-human evolution, but are overwhelmingly important in human history. The biogenetic (DNA) pool of the human race has changed very little in the last 50,000 years. Human knowledge, know-how, and the artifacts that proceed from such, have expanded enormously. This idea led Boulding to think about why, in the 1500s, when science and scientific thinking grew and flourished in Europe, it did not in China. The Chinese had been the source of scientific and technological inventions for thousands of years, but these ideas in their individual niches never grew together and developed into the expanding system of the scientific and technical revolution that swept Europe and much of the temperate zones from the 17th into the 20th centuries. Before that time, the niche for science was almost nonexistent in all cultures. One reason why scientific thinking found niches in Europe may have been that the cultures were becoming too diverse for tight control by any one cultural institution.

Boulding believes the solution to all human problems lies in passing on the store of human knowledge, studying what we do not know, and creating new applications of the knowledge structure. Therefore, the development and use of new educational technology and educational art is worthwhile to improve the learning process. The educational potential of art, and its methods, is a neglected approach to this task.[17] He has two general propositions:

- what is not there cannot be discovered, and,
- if something is there, it is likely to be discovered eventually.

This cuts across his concern about why knowledge is discovered, or developed, in one place or one cultural system, but not in another. In order for a discovery to occur, or a subsequent body of knowledge to be nurtured, presumably a niche must be open in the societal or cultural ecosystem.

U.S. Political Directions

Individual, group, or society's decisions are based on an evaluation of alternative futures. Boulding believes that attention given to one issue that needs a decision withdraws attention from others. Therefore there is a scarcity of decisionmaking resources, creating a moral economy that the culture must manage and share.

In politics, however, decisions for the common good are usually made on the basis of images from the past few decades projected into the future. Prohibition is an example of the consequences of a political decision made on images of the past.[18] One of the greatest expressions of the moral economy, in contrast, is the nation's move against discrimination.

Some future political decisions are likely to continue to be based on avoiding images of past evils rather than emerging future goods. The evils of the Depression and World War II remain powerful images for many legislators, encouraging their support of the military and defense systems.

UNDERLYING CAUSES

Boulding's view of underlying causes is somewhat ecological. Conditions must be favorable for change to occur. An opening in the ecological system must be available, the old must be discredited or in decline for the new to take its place, or the current system must have suffered a disaster, for a new concept to develop out of the ashes.

EXHIBIT 8-1

FORCES INFLUENCING THE FUTURIST THINKING OF KENNETH BOULDING

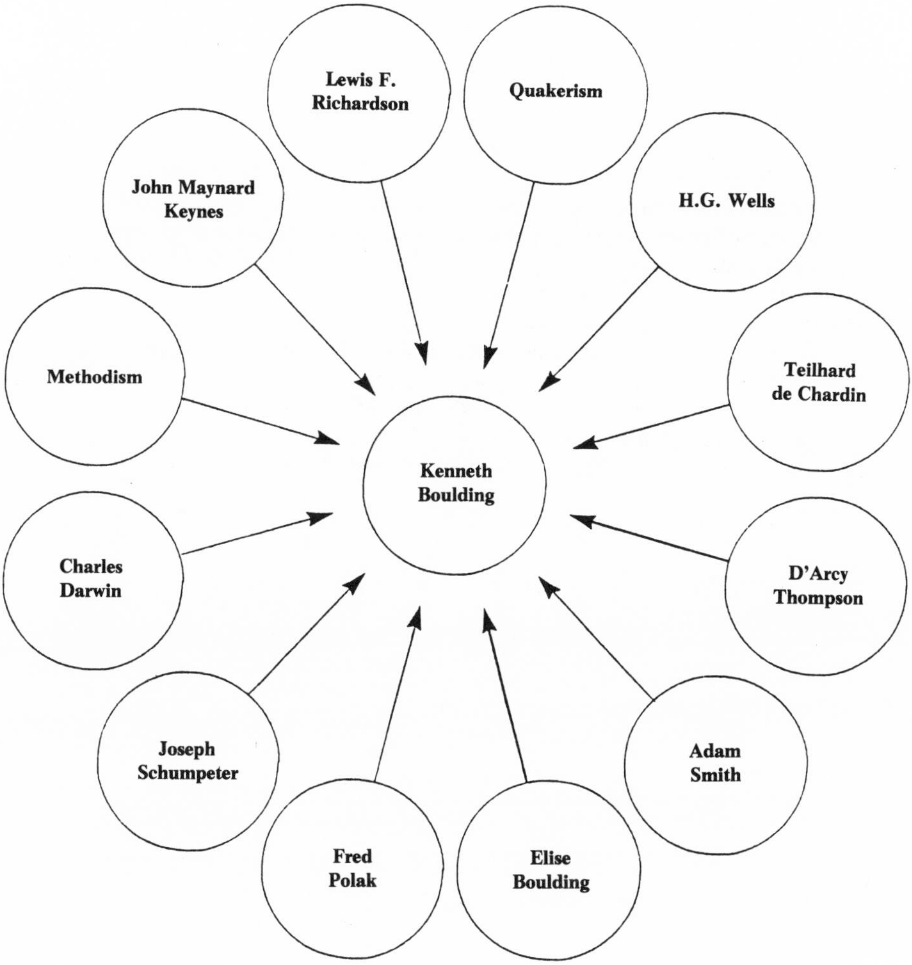

REFERENCES

1. "Pathologies of Defense," *Journal of Peace Research,* 21:2, 1984, p. 107.
2. "What Went Wrong with Economics?" *American Economist,* 30:1, Spring 1986, pp. 5-12.
3. Interview with Kenneth Boulding, Santa Cruz, CA, February 11, 1987.
4. "Fruitful Inconsistencies: The Legacy of Adam Smith," *Technology Review,* 78:5, March/April 1976, p. 3.
5. Kenneth E. Boulding, "The Meaning of the Twenty-first Century: Reexamining the Great Transition," in Michael Marien and Lane Jennings, eds., *What I Have Learned: Thinking About the Future Then and Now,* Greenwood Press, NY, 1987, pp. 23-32.
6. "The Ripening Society," *Technology Review,* 82:7, June/July 1980, p. 6.
7. "Making Capitalism Just,"*Technology Review,* 81:1, October 1978, p. 12.
8. "What Went Wrong with Economics?" pp. 5-12.
9. *Ecodynamics, A New Theory of Societal Evolution,* Sage Publications, Beverly Hills, CA, 1978. For the notion of the declining legitimacy of war see also Boulding's article, "Pathologies of Defense," *Journal of Peace Research,* 21:2, 1984, pp. 101-108.
10. "Peace Research," *International Social Science Journal,* 29:4, 1977, pp. 601-614, and "Toward a Normative Science," *Technology Review,* 19:3, January 1977, p. 8.
11. "Pathologies of Defense," p. 103.
12. "Pathologies of Defense," p. 107.
13. "Science: Our Common Heritage," *Science,* 207:4433, February 22, 1980, adapted from Boulding's presidential lecture to the AAAS in January 1980.
14. "Welding and Nondestructive Testing of Social Systems,"*Technology Review,* 81:16, May 1979, p. 8.
15. *Human Betterment,* Sage Publications, Beverly Hills, CA, 1985.
17. *Ecodynamics: A New Theory of Societal Evolution,* p. 338.
17. "A Technology for Educational Art," *Technology Review,* 77:7, June 1975, p. 5.
18. "Symbol, Substance, and the Moral Economy," *Technology Review,* 81:2, November 1978, p. 4.

CHAPTER 9

ARTHUR C. CLARKE

Arthur C. Clarke has one of the longest and most distinguished records of exploration of the implications of scientific discoveries and technological inventions. In the tradition of the great visionaries Jules Verne, H.G. Wells, and Olaf Stapledon, he has systematically explored the long term consequences of science for humankind in fiction, non-fiction, and film.[1] A landmark in his thinking was his conceptualization of the communications satellite during a stint in the Royal Air Force at the end of World War II. While developing sooner than Clarke had anticipated, geosynchronous orbital satellites have become the backbone of continental and international telecommunications.

The principle which makes Clarke so stimulating and provocative a futurist is his will to push to the limits the possibilities latent in science. The power of that principle in the hands of Clarke is beautifully revealed in the freshness of *Profiles of the Future*, **written twenty-five years ago.**

KEY VIEWS ABOUT THE FUTURE

1. Science and technology will dominate the future socially, politically, and institutionally and increase their dominance over time.
2. We can now reasonably play out some interactions of society and institutions with the technological developments over the next 50 years, and see viable choices.
3. Information technology is the dominant technology of the future.
4. Humans will ultimately be superseded by the descendants of their own creations, smart machines.
5. For the immediate future, our most important concern must be the avoidance of nuclear war.
6. Effective understanding and anticipation of the long range future requires a balance between logic, nerve and imagination.

BIOGRAPHICAL NOTE:

Arthur C. Clarke is Chancellor of the University of Moratuwa and the patron of the Arthur C. Clarke Center for Modern Technologies, in Sri Lanka.

He is the author of some 70 books and 500 articles. He was born in 1917 in Minehead, England, and raised on a farm. In his youth, he became hooked on Jules Verne and H.G. Wells and the science fiction of the period. As a young man he contributed to the British Interplanetary Society. Clarke left his employment to join the Royal Air Force, where he became an advanced radar instructor. On the basis of mathematical analysis during this period, he calculated the location and conditions for a synchronous orbit satellite and conceived of a network of communications satellites. An account of this research was published in October 1945 in *Wireless World.*

After the war, he graduated from King's College, Cambridge, with a degree in physics and mathematics. He holds at least 25 honors for his accomplishments in science and the arts.

He broke out of the limited orbit of sci-fi fame to public acclaim with the film *2001*, based on a short story, "Sentinel."

Clarke's major influences were Verne, Wells, Olaf Stapledon, and Hugo Gernsback, to whom he dedicates *Profiles of the Future* and memorializes as the man "who thought of everything." Clarke himself is nudging a global generation or two toward the celebration of the human mind and the limitless opportunities it creates for the future.

This chapter is based primarily on *Profiles of the Future*, revised in 1984. *July 20, 2019: Life in the Twenty-First Century* deals with a range of public and private concerns from robotics and transportation to the hospital and education, from recreation and psychiatry to sex, war, and crime. Clarke wrote only the introduction and epilogue and edited the contents. While he agrees with most of the material, he takes exception to the treatment of sex and war.

An interview in *Playboy* has been useful. His report to the Pontifical Academy on "The Impact of Space Exploration on Mankind," October 15, 1984, is timely.[2] A melange of personal and topical material is sprinkled through *1984: Spring: A Choice of Futures.*

Clarke now reports that he will do no more thinking about the future, aside from science fiction, except in the area of communications.

WORLDVIEW

Clarke is committed to the extrapolation and exploration of the ultimate possibilities which present or emerging scientific knowledge implies. Characteristic of the subtle mind, it is sometimes difficult to sort out the witty from the earnest; the semi-serious from the rock solid. Helpfully Clarke puts forward three rules of thumb:

- Clarke's first law: "When a distinguished and elderly scientist says that something is possible, he is almost certainly correct; when he says something is impossible, he is very probably wrong."
- Clarke's second law: The only way of discovering the limits of the possible is to venture a little bit past them into the impossible.
- Clark's third law: "Any sufficiently advanced technology is indistinguishable from magic."

He puts his second law somewhat differently in other contexts.[3]

Clarke's greatest strength and his most systematic focus is on space and communications. A great number of people have trodden over the short range—the next fifteen to fifty years. Clarke is unusual in looking at the limits of science in the hundred year, thousand year, and ten thousand year future.

His explorations of the potential limits of science do not discuss the effects on the individual, and on societies or institutions. On the other hand, he is clear that technology will increasingly shape the future. And conveniently, it is in technologies rather than in politics and economics that he sees prediction as most feasible.

Clarke regrets a growing disenchantment in the West with the potential benefits of scientific and technological development, but believes neither unlimited optimism nor unlimited pessimism is justified. As a guide to exploring the future, Clarke notes that three essential ingredients are logic, faith, and imagination. The latter two may, in a healthy sense, defy logic. The severe limitation that the failure of imagination brings is captured in his observation that the situation can arise:

> *. . . when all the available facts are appreciated* and *marshalled correctly—but when the really vital facts are still undiscovered, and the possibility of their existence is not admitted.*"[4]

SPECIFIC ISSUES

Space

Clarke is so well known for his contributions to thinking about space that he can delight in poking fun at his own prominence. He tells of his fantasy that when extraterrestrials arrive, they will cry out, "Take me to Arthur C. Clarke." And then, of course, his nightmare fantasy is that they may instead cry out, "Take me to Isaac Asimov." Not only was Clarke first to conceive and analyze a plan for synchronous orbital communication satellites, but he also, over 35 years ago, conceived of the mass driver, a system providing limitless propulsion to spacecraft.

He sees no substance to any argument that space will relieve U.S. or global population pressures, although he does see space as being a haven for the intellectually and the physically daring.

His views on extraterrestrials have changed. From recent evidence he believes extraterrestrial intelligence is less likely. Extraterrestrial life is more likely to be discovered first outside the solar system and its detection is more likely to occur through the telescope than it is through exploration by spacecraft.[5]

Clarke, of course, recognizes that there may be resource, or wealth, to be discovered in space, but the primary reason for the exploration of space lies in satisfying our passions for knowledge and beauty.

His enthusiasm for the information and communications implications of space in the next few decades is boundless. He sees personal telephones, "Talkman," as universally available. Assuming the village to be a fundamental unit of society and the model for all other settlements, Clarke expects communication links to all other communities will be routine, universal, and low cost. Throughout the world, the electronic age equivalent of the village blacksmith will be the technician responsible for servicing and maintaining a community's ground station.

Transborder data flow and related matters will not be resolved by the wisdom of politicians but by the imperatives of technology. Telecommunications obliterates borders.

With regard to the Challenger disaster, Clarke had long ago said that disaster was in the cards, since vertical take-off is risky. He recommends and anticipates future craft launching horizontally and moving to the vertical.[6]

His views on the strategic defense initiative, SDI, are more complex, uncertain, and fluid. He had expressed opinions that SDI was unworkable, but his current view would value pursuing the potentially unworkable, since it would assure a technological lead and would focus attention on the madness of Mutually Assured Destruction (MAD). The enormous cost incurred in responding to SDI will intimidate the Russians, who can less afford it than the U.S., into a more rational move to control nuclear weapons.

Engineering in Space

Clarke anticipates that engineering structures in space—the space elevator, the vertical railroad, which was conceived of by the Russian

Yuri Artsutanov and which others have either independently conceived of or further analyzed—will make movement into space commonplace and cheap.[7] Following the elevator may be the wheel surrounding the earth. On the other hand, some more modest space engineering projects seem less plausible, such as the solar power satellite to beam energy down to earth. Aside from the problems of the technology itself, it hardly seems competitive in Clarke's mind with other alternatives, such as ocean thermal energy conversion. Orbiting mirrors, another possibility, could turn night into day. A more challenging question is whether we want to, not whether we can, do it.

Transportation

Clarke exhibits great skill and imagination in taxonomies and matrices. His approach finds a place for almost every form of transportation, including the horse. He celebrates the virtue of the horse for its flexibility and intelligence and its ease of maintenance in the short range, and anticipates that we may eventually develop some "compact elephant" of comparable dexterity. The automobile will become an automated part of a complex, telemated world.[8] He has a number of interesting points to make with regard to land and sea travel, seeing a great, bright future for the machine able to travel on a pillow of air over land or sea. The submarine travels below the surface where energy demands are substantially lower. Submerged giant plastic sausages, towed by submarines, could provide low cost ocean transportation for goods and commodities.

Time, space, and gravity are the boundary concerns in many aspects of Clarke's long-term speculations. He sees no way in which gravity can be neutralized or overcome. But there is no absolute reason to foreclose the possibility. Speed is easier since there seems no reason why we cannot, in successive technological breakthroughs, asymptotically approach the speed of light. A fantasy solution to the problems of space and gravity, "teleportation," is almost, but not quite, dismissed. Clarke concludes that we do not know enough to say absolutely never. He offers as a charming analogy the travail of long distance movement for a poor, one-dimensional creature on a Mobius strip and his elation when he learns to move through a second dimension, that is, bore a hole in the strip.[9]

Energy

Concern for resources puts Clarke's technological optimism in tension. He argues cogently, if not convincingly, that there is no absolute shortage of energy or materials, although now they are not always available in the form or at the price that we prefer. And while many futurists, notably those associated with the Club of Rome, justifiably alert us to impending shortages, technology is neither doomed nor dooming. The tragedy of our period of history in Clarke's view is that we must recognize that while "the age of cheap energy is over, the age of free energy still lies 50 years ahead." Clarke's optimism is based on nuclear and solar power and the recognition that all around us—in the oceans, in the land, in the most common materials, such as granite—lie all the resources that we could ever want or need.

The Human Mind and Body

To Clarke the capabilities of the human mind are enormous and untapped, presenting an incredible potential for our development. Technologies for capturing and impressing information and memories on the human brain will surely develop. A "mechanical educator" will undoubtedly be invented to impress knowledge more quickly and reliably than we have acquired it in the past. Artificial memories are likely to develop. The body itself, especially the brain, is not limited by death as a biological inevitability. Unlike machines, our bodies continually rebuild themselves and the messages for reconstruction often become garbled. But in any case, the brain certainly could live longer than the body if we chose to pursue that line. He even anticipates, drawing from one of his own novels, that at some time the bulk of citizens could slumber in memory banks awaiting recall while only a small percentage of our descendants are awake at any one time.

The Long-Term Future of Man

Clarke makes no bones about it: in his view, we are a transitional species likely to be superseded by artifacts derivative of our own creation. As the tools man invented in turn invented man, the new tools we are inventing will invent machines superior to us. One of the great advantages of machine over man, of course, is that biological entities cannot be built with precision parts, whereas technical instruments can be. Hence, the quality control potential is greater for machines than for biological systems. Further, much of the energy used by man is used to repair and rebuild. He points out that von Neumann and Turing have long since developed general principles for the construction of self-repairing and self-reproducing machines.

Drawing on Nietzsche, Clarke sees man as a rope stretched between animal and superman, a rope across an abyss. And having served that noble purpose we will pass away. In the course of that long-term evolution Clarke sees many more of the mechanisms that nature has provided being used by us in new, different, and appropriate ways. For example, as we develop, we may employ two languages, one for thinking and one for feeling, the second reserved for us alone and the other universally understood.

Education

On education, he has little to suggest that is not already emerging, being tested and being experimented with. Assuming his views of education fit those of *July 20, 2019*, there will be an explosion of technological gimcrackery and good fellow feeling. Communications and computers will be both the network and the core. The school will burst out of the schoolhouse walls and be everywhere all the time for everyone. "Individualized instruction," to use current jargon, will be available to everyone. Career training will be everywhere. Children will be brought up best friends with the computer. He acknowledges the need for training to cope with the complexity and the diversity of our world, and yet at the same time suggests that much of the training will move workers toward passivity, docility and acceptance of boredom. Artificial intelligence will play a role in optimizing the tailoring of education to the individual.[10]

Health

The views on hospitals expressed in *July 20, 2019*, encapsulate an understanding of the emergence of information and high technology in the future of health. As one might expect, computer assisted devices, electro-mechanical gadgetry, data collection and analysis, new forms of diagnosis and manipulation and mechanics, such as the mechanized surgeon and the robot assistant, will characterize much of health practice in the hospital. Institutional change may move toward specialization, new modes of payment, and availability of care.

Mental Health

Mental health will be enormously enhanced in the future by the extended application of both chemical and electrical technologies. The present widely developing knowledge of brain chemistry, with specific locations for mental functions and with specific lesions responsible for mental incapacities, will be thoroughly understood and appropriate chemical interventions available. These interventions will correct or enhance capacities of the mind according to need or taste. Direct memory enhancement, with real or synthetic memories, will be routine. Perhaps the ultimate in applied psychiatry will be the development of the biochip, that is, the organic, chemically-based semiconductor device. When implanted in the body,

> *the next step was to make the bio-computer a God-like instrument of thought marrying the number-crunching power of electrons to the reasoning ability of the neurons.* [11]

Automation and Robots

Clarke is committed to the passage of primacy from man to machine in the future. In the next 100 years factories will automate and robotize, but towards the end of this time we will be forced to discuss the rights of machines whose capabilities approach our own and we will be confronted by questions of designing and making machines to function ethically.

Recreation and Entertainment

Clarke is an enthusiast for the movies. He anticipates that television, albeit with high resolution and with many other bells and whistles, will be the most popular mass medium but the movie theater itself will become a more dramatic, exciting and diverse place. In addition to extremely high quality and the introduction of such techniques as holography Clarke believes simulation is an important new factor. The extension of a Disney concept, the human looking robot, will provide entertainment thrills such as the "all star simulated symphony." He anticipates a resurgence of Hollywood under the pressure of competition and employing many of the new high resolution techniques which we have glimpsed in "2001," "Bladerunner" and the various displays of Walt Disney. He expects more direct stimulation of the sensorium, but the themes will remain the same—thrills, violence, love stories, westerns, etc. In sports and athletics the tools of science, whether biological, physical or material, will converge to create and select superior athletes and superior materials and promote superior high speed, more precise, effective games, contests and athletics.[12]

Home and Office

The house as seen in *July 20, 2019* will be almost alive as a consequence of the intense application of information technologies to the structure. Not only will structures be self-diagnostic and self-maintaining but the house itself will become robotized. It will not only be programmable but it will be able to sense the environment, sense the attitude of the occupants, and have a vast repertoire of capabilities.

The central office technology will be artificial intelligence. When coupled with other information technologies and automation, it will wipe out the human support structure. All routine office activities—collection, storage, filing, indexing, retrieval, etc.—will be done by information machines. Artificial intelligence, when coupled with emerging technologies of direct contact through the skin with the brain, will permit one to conjure up a staff, to create workmates and subordinates of any desired shape, temperament and demeanor. Of course there will always be reverse snobbery: for some, the apex of office prestige will be real desks, windows and a human secretary.[13]

Disarmament and Defense

> *. . . Nothing is more* fundamental *than the prevention of nuclear war. If we fail in this all else is irrelevant—science, politics, religion. . .*"[14]

Clarke's approach is to identify and reinforce the horrors of war from nuclear devastation to death rays and on the other hand, to advocate and promote the use of space for peaceful purposes. His long term view is summed up in his 1946 essay on the future of rockets in war:

> *The only defense against the weapons of the future is to prevent them from ever being used. In other words, the problem is political and not military at all. A country's armed forces can no longer defend it; the most they can promise is the destruction of the attacker. . .*"[15]

More recently, in a 1986 lecture he addressed the technical and logistical problems of "Star Wars," lasers and other attempts at global defense, noting that defensive systems could become offensive. He concludes that:

> *The real problem is not military hardware, but human software—though the right kind of hardware can certainly help. A stable peace will never be possible without mutual trust; without that, all agreements and treaties are worse than useless, because they obscure the real issue.*"[16]

UNDERLYING CAUSES

Clarke's relentless commitment is to the exploration of the outer limits of science's potential contribution to the evolution of human society. He sees science and technology as anticipatable in their direction and outcome, as well as the dominant shaping forces of the long term future. Consequently, even in the relatively short run of the next 50 years, where the surest forecasts may be made, he gives relatively little attention to the institutional, social, or cultural context of the emerging developments, and even less attention to the details by which we may get from here to there.

EXHIBIT 9-1

FORCES INFLUENCING THE FUTURIST THINKING OF

ARTHUR C. CLARKE

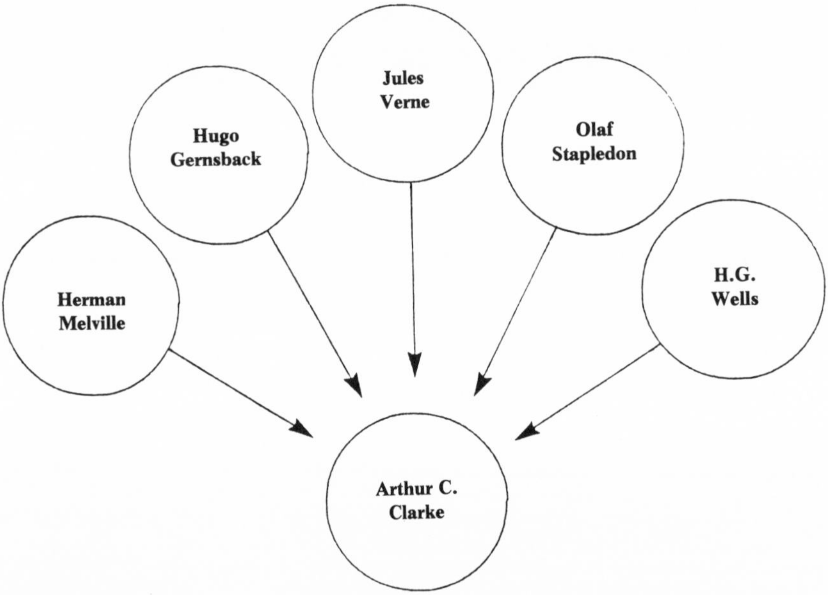

REFERENCES

1. Especially, in the films *2001* and *2010.*
2. Arthur C. Clarke, "Space Communications and the Global Family," *Study Week on The Impact of Space Exploration on Mankind.* Abstract, edited by Carlos Chagas and Vittorio Canuto, Pontificiae Academiae Scientiarvm Scripta Varia, 58, ex Aedibvs Academicis in Civitate Vaticana, MCMLXXVI.

3. *Profiles of the Future: An Inquiry Into the Limits of the Possible,* Holt, Rinehart and Winston, New York, 1962-1984, p. 36.
4. *Profiles*, p. 27.
5. "Playboy Interview: Arthur C. Clarke," *Playboy*, Vol. 33, No. 7, July 1986, pp. 49-66.
6. "Playboy Interview," p. 60.
7. *Profiles*, pp. 205-209.
8. *Profiles,* p. 50.
9. *Profiles*, pp. 82-93.
10. *July 20, 2019: Life in the 21st Century,* Macmillan Company, New York, 1986, Chapter 5.
11. *July 20, 2019*, p. 216.
12. *July 20, 2019*, Chapters 8 and 9.
13. *July 20, 2019*, Chapters 10 and 11.
14. "War and Peace in the Space Age," December 1982, reprinted in *1984: Spring, A Choice of Futures,* Ballantine Books (A Del Rey Book), New York, 1984, p. 42.
15. *1984: Spring*, p. 56.
16. Clarke, Arthur C., "Star Wars and Star Peace," the Nineteenth Jawaharlal Nehru Memorial Lecture, New Delhi, November 13, 1986, p. 12.

CHAPTER 10

PETER F. DRUCKER

Professor Peter Drucker is the leading exponent of the organization, its bright future and the opportunities and problems facing its management today. He has been writing, talking, and teaching since the 1940s about phenomena that will affect the structure of economic life in the U.S., Japan and elsewhere.

KEY VIEWS ABOUT THE FUTURE

1. The publicly owned corporation is one of the central institutions of the modern world. Management is the social invention devised to run the large enterprise.
2. We are all learning how to manage. One of the questions for the next 50 years is, what does the success of management mean for the society and the public interest?
3. The corporation's first public duty is performance. After that it may take on any public duty that lies within its competence. Its contribution may include the resolution of social problems by turning them into business opportunities.
4. Several technologies are hot prospects for development, but social innovation will be equally important to organizations, especially in the period of slow economic growth that lies ahead.
5. Information-based organizations will be more like symphony orchestras than the military, with more soloists and specialists, and control being the ability to get information.
6. A major transition for all societies will be from mechanically assisted work to knowledge work. Knowledge work requires schooling, capitalization, and continuing education.
7. The emerging world economy is developing a new monetary system and new economic relationships, demanding a more centralized management approach from the multinational corporation.

BIOGRAPHICAL NOTE

Peter Drucker is at Claremont Graduate School, in Claremont, California, where he has been professor of social science since 1971. Drucker is a writer, a consultant and an educator. He holds 14 honorary degrees, from universities in the U.S., U.K., Japan, Belgium and Switzerland.

Born in Austria in 1909, and educated in Vienna and at the University of Frankfurt, he came to the U.S. in 1937. Before that he worked as an economist for a London bank and, for a few years after he came to the U.S., continued to advise British banks and to act as American correspondent for British newspapers. He began consulting with U.S. corporations in the 1940s when he concluded that an integrating principle of Western society is the large organization. He decided to study it. Corporations were cool to his approach, as he describes it, until eventually General Motors invited him in. Between 1942-1949, he was professor of philosophy and politics at Bennington College, Vermont, and professor of management at New York University from 1950-1972, where he continues as a distinguished lecturer. He is also a professorial lecturer in Oriental art at Pomona College, California.

Professor Drucker is a fellow of the American Association for Advancement of Science, of the American and the International Academies of Management, of the American Academy of Arts and Sciences, and an honorary fellow of the British Institute of Management.

In a recent book, *The Frontiers of Management,*[1] Drucker recalls losing the job he had with a Frankfurt bank in the 1929 crash. Soon after, he wrote his first book, *The End of Economic Man*, not published until 1939. His second book, *The Future of Industrial Man*, in 1942, reflects his own turning toward the future. He notes that between the 1929 crash and the 1940s, people in business began to learn the science and art of management. At first it was a concept for large businesses, especially in the U.S. Today, management as a valuable tool and as a concept has become part of the culture. He went on to write a number of books and many articles on management and related issues, as well as to lecture in the U.S. and overseas. In *The Frontiers of Management*, he describes himself as one of the three management experts, (Juran and Deming are the others) who the Japanese believe responsible for their economic success since World War II. For 30 years, between 1950 and 1980, he taught them management and marketing in annual seminars for senior government and business people. They absorbed and turned effectively to their own business use the idea that the purpose of a business is to create a customer and to satisfy a customer.

In commenting on this chapter, Drucker spurned the title, futurist, saying he has never considered himself one. His concern is with seeing the reality of the present through clear eyes, rather than with the clouded vision of traditional—and no longer true—assumptions. This chapter, therefore, draws on that part of his work which reflects on how the future will be shaped by current reality, specifically, *The Frontiers of Management*, a compendium of his recent writing on the corporate organization. Drucker declined to be interviewed for this chapter

WORLDVIEW

Peter Drucker believes that we structure our society in terms of organizations that are created, grow, acquire power and legitimacy, decline and disappear. New styles of organization wax and wane over time as their usefulness in the structure of society shrinks. Some organizations, such as the medieval craft guilds, were strong once and have disappeared except for their ceremonial functions. Today, the newly powerful organization is the business enterprise; in the U.S., the publicly owned corporations.

Drucker frequently asks the question: as a successful organization that is wittingly or unwittingly influencing society, to what extent should a corporation pursue the public interest and the public good, as well as its own economic aims? His answers vary, but most often he says that business can work for the public good best by transforming social problems into business opportunities.

Management is a social invention devised to run the large business enterprise. Its effectiveness and sophistication have grown and its use has spread as small organizations, non-profits, universities, and government have learned the art. Business management will be drawn more into issues of public interest as the work of managing the society moves more into the private sector.

Drucker approaches the present, and the future, emphasizing a managerial style. In his general strategy we identify emerging problems, and analyze the forces and factors influencing them. We break the problems down into smaller, easier problems and search for solutions. Then we learn how to manage the emerging problems and identify business opportunities as they arise out of the process.

The mid-range, about 10-15 years, is his time horizon. But his solutions to the problems he identifies often reflect already emerging developments, and their likely direction in the near future.

He has been pessimistic about the state of the world over the past few decades, but believes we have the capacity and the potential to survive and continue to improve.

SPECIFIC ISSUES

International Economy

A number of pieces that used to be tightly connected to national and regional economies have been cut loose, are moving in opposite directions, and are reforming into a world economic system with dynamics not yet fully understood. Many effects of the new dynamics are counter-intuitive. The U.S. has been hard hit in some respects by these changes, yet has one of the lowest unemployment rates. The Japanese, on the other hand, appear to have been flexible in meeting the needs of the emerging world economy, yet their own economy is now sluggish and unresponsive.

According to Drucker, the world economy has emerged as dominant, for the following reasons:[2]

- It has been assumed that national industrial economies were dependent on the supply and price of raw materials. Some futurists assume that as resources become scarce, manufacturing costs, and thus living costs, will skyrocket. In fact, the downturn in the raw materials economy has had little effect on the industrial economy.
- Another driving force is the decoupling of manufacturing production from levels of employment. Manufacturing production in the U.S. has held steady at 23-24% of U.S. total GNP since the 1950s, while by 1980 only one in six of U.S. workers was in the blue collar laborforce and that number was dropping.
- The world economy is being fueled by the movement of capital, rather than trade in goods and services which is only about $2.5-3 trillion a year, compared with $75 trillion a year being turned over by by London market in Eurodollars.

Underlying these shifts are two more fundamental changes, a reversal of the dynamics of size from bigger is better to medium and small is more effective, and the more intensive and extensive use of knowledge and information in manufacturing and business. Drucker's examples include the shift to robotics and automation, and the use of R&D and information technology to scale down needs for materials, labor and plant size. The cost and availability of capital to make these shifts becomes an urgent factor in international trade. Automation in a highly industrialized country can lower overall manufacturing costs and thus can outweigh the advantage of low labor costs in less developed countries (LDCs). Most of the LDCs, Drucker believes, cannot leapfrog to advanced technology because they cannot afford it, nor do they have the educational and knowledge base to support such a jump. Nor can they any longer sell their raw materials at high prices, or use their labor cost advantage to upgrade their economy.

A U.S. policy emphasizing industrial employment over industrial production would be disastrous for the nation because it would favor the older, materials-based industries that cannot compete with overseas labor costs, discourage them from change, keep capital from profitable industry, and increase unemployment.

The dissociation of international money flows from goods and services trade may be the result of several factors,

- the shift from fixed to floating currency rates in 1971,
- two oil shocks,
- the U.S. deficit, and U.S. efforts to use high interest rates to attract foreign capital, and,
- other attempts by nations to manipulate the international money flow to avoid tackling domestic issues.

One outcome may be a growing lack of confidence in the U.S. dollar. Devaluation of the dollar would affect the Japanese, who hold 50% of the dollars owed by the U.S., and add to the economic suffering for raw materials producers. More likely is no particular outcome: a continuing, but reduced, U.S. deficit more or less propped up by other nations for fear of other alternatives.

Drucker notes that as competitive advantage can be wrung from international exchange rates, U.S. business must learn how to manage them.

He expects to see the formation of new development concepts, in which the LDCs learn from each other and engage in production sharing as in Southeast Asia. A new international monetary system will develop away from the dollar as a reserve currency. Basing the reserve currency on the dollar does not work because the U.S. will not put world needs ahead of its domestic interests.

The U.S. Economy

Politicians are easily tempted to manipulate or control the international monetary system for short-term political advantage. Drucker criticizes the current administration for pushing up interest rates to encourage foreign investment. In doing so, it exposed the old smokestack industries to competition they could not meet, as well as damaging the competitive position of U.S. farm products. The Japanese are now acting like a previous U.S. administration, pushing exports and becoming overly dependent on the U.S. as a market. In any event, purely national economic policies are no longer effective.

Drucker dismisses the Kondratieff cycle theory as inappropriate for the U.S., although it may have some truth in Europe. At best, the downcurve fits partially, describing the decline of dominant industries, such as the smokestack group, and the shortage of jobs occurring when new industries, such as those in high technology, are slow growing. But U.S. job growth in other areas, and its entrepreneurial approach to business makes this theory incompatible with our reality.

The Future of the U.S. Corporation and the Multinational

Drucker believes the corporate organization is essential to the future of a pluralist society like the U.S. in which the major question is, how do you reconcile a society of organizations and institutions pursuing their own interests to acting for the common good? He worries, however, that the public will not grant corporations the same legitimacy they give government, unions, the courts, etc., to tackle public problems.

Partly, this is corporate management's own fault, for isolating itself, being faceless, anonymous, for paying itself so much, for awarding itself greenmail and indulging in takeovers and acquisitions, and for failing to recognize that the real ownership of their organizations is shifting to their employees, through pension funds and their gradually acquiring a property right in their jobs.

Drucker's view of the corporation's public duty is, first, economic performance. Only after that is assured ought management to seek to activate social responsibility, and that only within their competence. One such "job" will be to recognize and incorporate employee ownership interests. Other tasks are less clear, but Drucker asserts that the agenda for management research in the next 50 years will be to work out in practice what the success of management as a tool for creating and maintaining large organizations means for the society and the public interest.

The surge of mergers, hostile takeovers and acquisitions reveals a fundamental change in the underlying economy, structure and environment of U.S. business.[3] Why have large companies become vulnerable to raiders? Drucker blames inflation for producing distortions in relative value; the structure of some corporations, such as integrated petroleum companies, for no longer being appropriate to the world economy, and management for practicing corporate capitalism that has isolated it from possible friends and constituents. He notes that corporations can beat raiders if they recognize their isolation and organize a constituency. Other factors he notes are the ease with which raiders can get loans without security from banks desperate to find new sources of income as their traditional business erodes. Banks are having to pay more for their money and are being outflanked by the non-banks issuing commercial paper. They are slowly shifting to fees and commissions.

Another profound change is the shift in share ownership from individuals to institutions, especially pension funds, in which the trustees may have no choice but to accept the raider's offer, because of their obligation to bring in the highest return.

The impact of takeover threats forces businesses to operate short term, with managers looking over their shoulders constantly and making dumb financial decisions, dumb at least in the long pull.

One way in which the rush of mergers may be halted could be a default on a raider's part. Failing this, the management of this problem will require structural change in several organizations involved, Drucker believes, including,

- pension funds,
- corporate boards,
- corporate management, and,
- shareholding.

It is noted here and elsewhere in this chapter that Drucker anticipates corporate management will have to abandon its isolation, and seek friends and give mutual support. Management also has a role in the restructuring of pension funds and corporate boards. The introduction of personal management of pension funds through individual retirement accounts may eventually shrink the dominance of the big funds but in the meantime pension funds driven by defined benefits programs are a bomb waiting to explode on the economy. Drucker believes that changing pension plans to defined contributions will give vested employees a greater stake in the future of their company and reduce the company and the trustee's burden.

Management has the additional responsibility of strengthing its board of directors, and realizing that a large enterprise does not exist solely for its shareholders. Drucker anticipates a change in shareholder voting structure that would hinder sales to raiders.[4]

Multinationals

In "The Changing Multinational," which he wrote in 1985, Drucker says the traditional multinational design of a parent company and daughter companies acting as corporate citizens of the countries where they operate, is unworkable.[5] International manufacturing economics requires more centralization because the market is global, and segmented by lifestyle rather than country. He argues for knitting the multinational into a whole system, in which money earned in Germany can be invested in developing business in Brazil. The local management will have less autonomy, but would be expected to know the whole system more thoroughly. Drucker argues for a new crossnational career, multinational management, in which managers can work in any part of the system, understand currency fluctuations as a variable cost and be prepared to shift at least part of production temporarily where costs are lowest.

U.S. Political Directions

Drucker writes off the U.S. government as an organization that cannot attract good people because no one believes in it, or expects it to get anything done. Succeeding administrations preach smaller government and talk of cutting expenses but do nothing. We are inching towards reform but may not do anything effective until a crisis occurs.

He believes we have learned that successful social programs require starting small, contributing the hard work of good people over a long time, and waiting patiently for eventual results. It was 20 years, for example, before Social Security covered all workers. The time frame, the size, the need to experiment and wait for results are all wrong for the political process, Drucker believes.

We do need to experiment with social innovation, but the requirements call for organizations more flexible than government, that can break big, tough problems down into easier tasks and try out alternative approaches. Corporations, as the most flexible non-governmental organizations are the most likely candidates. They should choose problems offering economic opportunities, since they are most likely to be successful when acting in their self-interest.

The future economy will be mixed three ways,

- a private sector, with limited government control, over fraud, safety, and so on,
- a public sector covering defense and justice, and,
- a mixed sector in which government defines, and may fund, the activities, but the private sector carries out the work, in health care, for example.

World Regions and Nations

Europe

Drucker scorns Europe's "rage for high tech," because, he says, the Europeans look at high tech as a magic solution to their employment troubles, without realizing that high technology needs and requires an entrepreneurial infrastructure. Furthermore, high technology produces tomorrow's jobs, not today's. For today's jobs, you need low technology and the Europeans do not want low tech.[6]

Japan

Drucker's long term interest in, and admiration for Japan leads him to make many comparisons of their achievements, especially the Japanese ability to take foreign ideas and apply them effectively to their own goals. He scolds them, however, for their adoption of adversarial trade practices. Unlike complementary or competitive models of trade, neither side will win in the long run. Both lose, the buyer when he buys and the seller, Japan, ten years from now. In adversarial trade the seller sells and does not buy. Eventually, says Drucker, the seller will have given his wares away because the buyer cannot buy and cannot pay for what he has bought. Japan already has the world's largest supply of liquid funds, $640 billion, and is seen increasingly as predatory.[7] Even when Japan takes production to the buyer's country the move still appears predatory.

One possible step is to ask Japan to soak up some of its liquidity by taking a share of problem loans to developing countries. Other more likely developments are protectionism against Japan and recession in the U.S. Drucker warns that Korea and China may also try the adversarial trade path.

Food and Agriculture

Potentially great improvements in agriculture lie ahead. Drucker is optimistic about the use of biotechnology to increase fertility. He also believes much more can be done in basic infrastructure changes in the developing world, such as building concrete bins for grain storage.

Agricultural products in world trade are likely to be cheaper, more plentiful, and more widespread. This has implications for countries in which agricultural products are a major part of the economy, the U.S., for example. Japan, too, does not have to base its industrial policy on the need to earn enough to pay for higher-priced food and raw materials when they are likely to be cheap and in oversupply.

Technology

For Drucker some technologies are hot prospects for innovation, for example;

- telecommunications,
- automation of manufacturing,
- office automation,
- automation of the financial industry,
- medical technologies,
- biogenetics, bioengineering, and biophysics.

He argues, however, that social innovation is as important as technological innovation to the future of the organizations structuring our society. Most corporate enterprises face a period of slow, or no, economic growth in which they will be challenged for social innovations to maintain their health. He suggests considering:

- concentrating on people—since demographics indicates that as the baby boom bulges into management less promotion will be available for them and for younger workers—jobs should begin big and expansive, with plenty of recognition. At the same time, ease out of other jobs or companies, employees who have plateaued.
- improving productivity—which provides the means to reward without promoting,
- look for new growth opportunities but do not expect to diversify into a growth industry.

Information Technology

Drucker looks at information technology as it will affect organizations. The information-based organization will:

- be flat, having fewer levels of management, and consequently fewer relays of information,
- use an information system that absorbs the job of relaying information,
- give the remaining managers more responsible jobs,

- experience management control becoming the ability to get information, and the span of control becoming the span of communications,
- use advanced information technologies but will not necessarily have to do so for the organization to be information-based, (there are historical examples—Drucker cites the British rule by a small, hierarchically flat organization in India),
- grow more soloists and more specialists, resulting in a greater diversity of structure,
- model itself more like a symphony orchestra than like the traditional model, the military,
- manage by objectives,
- need high self-discipline and responsibility,
- share values and mutual respect, and,
- not be likely to be run by financial control.[8]

Telecommunications

As on other issues, Drucker views telecommunications through the lens of his interest in organizations. From his point of view the future of telecommunications is tied to the competitive health of the corporate organizations involved. He observes that in the explosion of telecommunications the telephone has disappeared as a distinct technology. In a sense, Bell Labs is responsible, for producing more advanced technology than the telephone companies can use and receiving no profit from the overabundance.

AT&T was one of the largest and most influential non-governmental organizations in the world and, by in effect lending money to customers to install and use telephones, acted as a development bank for the telecomunications industry. Intelligent monopolies, such as AT&T and IBM, as identified by Schumpeter, live a long time by reducing prices and junking their old equipment. If in the future, without a telephone monopoly, says Drucker, we lose leadership in telecommunications, increase the number of gadgets we have to use, increase our communications costs and find our national security is compromised by fragmentation of the system, we should reconsider the breakup.

Business opportunities exist for pieces of the old telephone system, but Drucker doubts they can take advantage of them. For example, Drucker believes the developing world is a market for advanced telecommunications because it is not heavily invested in older equipment. However he does not believe Western Electric has the marketing ability to compete with international telecommunications companies for this market. Bell Labs could go into business for itself as a worldwide scientific laboratory in telecommunications and electronics, but it is unlikely to do so.

Unions

Drucker considers unions as powerful organizations that have acquired considerable legitimacy and privilege in society by virtue of differentiating the interests of workers from those of management. He notes that they are the one type of organization granted the right to civil disobedience. They have acted as the conscience of society on work issues. They are faced now with the dilemma that the interests of workers and those of management are becoming the same. For example, they must reckon with demographics:

- The share of the total money available for wages and salaries given to older nonworking members of the population is likely to increase from 20 to 33% within the next ten years. Older people are living longer, and fewer young people are coming into the workforce to support payments to the elderly.

Drucker notes that as pension funds now own up to 50% of large businesses in the U.S., the employees are becoming the real owners. For the individual worker, a stake in the company pension fund can become his largest single asset as he ages. As a result employees, or those empowered to act for them, will be brought into pension fund management.

Unless they are willing to be flexible, Drucker believes, unions will not survive. Workers and businesses will bypass them, creating new organizations to do what needs to be done.[9]

Energy

Drucker does not expect rising oil prices. He believes the cost of raw materials and demand will remain low, because our industrial and technological processes are moving from mechanical systems based on physical forces powered by energy to biological systems based on information.

Values and Attitudes

For the most part, young people coming into the workforce today are workaholics. Their future at work will be relatively harsh because we are in the turbulent stages of the transition to knowledge-based work.

The Work Transition

In Drucker's view there are three primary categories of workers, the information worker who uses knowledge to accomplish the task, the mechanical worker whose physical skills are amplified by machinery and energy, and the pre-industrial leftover who has only physical strength as a resource to work with. These categories are unevenly distributed in the world, but only the knowledge worker matters to the future. Countries without the schools and knowledge base will be unable to make the transition into the information-based society. This presents a threat to their future stability, since no society can bear the strain of having 40-50% of its young people unemployed and watching on television how rich countries live.

In the U.S., the transition may not move fast enough to employ all the workers with resources of education and knowledge. Already most new entrants have too much education for mechanical, blue collar work. By 2010 the proportion of the labor force in blue collar work will be the same as that in modern agriculture.[10] For the next 25 years the U.S. will have blue-collar transition problems. The temptation will be to try preserving their jobs, especially as many are older, concentrated in political strength in urban areas and highly unionized. Such attempts are likely to be unsuccessful, as are government retraining programs. Retraining in this transition is a local business opportunity, in Drucker's view.

To employ the knowledge worker, businesses must recognize the capital investment required of the individual, the company and society in schooling, information technology, and continuing education.

For the U.S., its troublesome task will be to bring its own population of pre-industrial workers into knowledge work. These are mostly poor, inner-city blacks whose situation represents failures—in education, in training, and in developing a vision.

Education

Education in the U.S. will improve, Drucker believes, although when or how is not clear. The force depressing educational quality is disappearing and new requirements for quality are increasing in strength. Over time, blue collar factory work has been broken down into relatively unskilled tasks. Drucker believes the high wages paid for this work devalued knowledge and skill and removed the incentives for school performance. As these jobs disappear, and the knowledge-based economy grows, workers are switching to jobs requiring knowledge, skill, and a higher quality of education. Much of this education is now being provided as training on the job by corporations, But Drucker believes today's workers will demand a higher quality of education from schools for their children.

UNDERLYING CAUSES

A fundamental change in our concepts of technology is occurring as activities are organized around information rather than energy. Metaphorically, we are shifting from a mechanical model to a biological model. The fossil fuel industries have been declining for years as a result. Consumption per unit of output will almost certainly continue to decline as more of industry moves to the biological model in which the primary resource is knowledge and information. In this model the process is not organized by physical force but by information, such as the genetic code.

The new capital resource is knowledge, and the skills to use information productively. Drucker notes that knowledge used to be a luxury in society and even skill was not marketable in huge quantities. The medieval guilds cornered available skills and limited the quantity available to preserve their value.

In the future, however, the emerging form of biological organization will create new social needs. Education, for one, will be vital to accomplish the shift to knowledge-based work.

EXHIBIT 10-1

FORCES INFLUENCING THE FUTURIST THINKING OF PETER F. DRUCKER

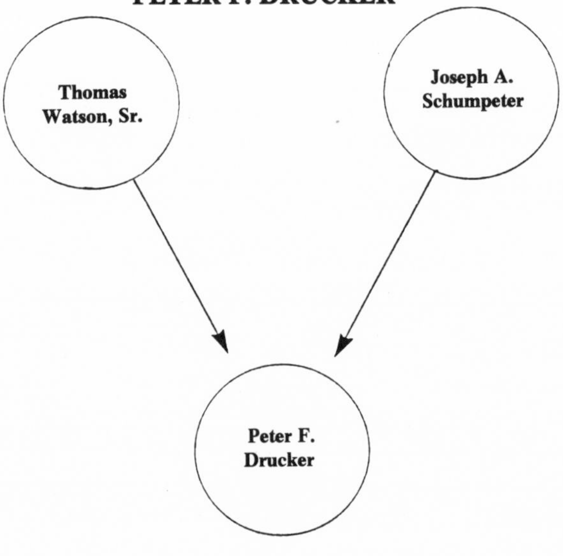

REFERENCES

1. Peter F. Drucker, *The Frontiers of Management*, Dutton, New York, 1986.
2. "The Changed World Economy," *The Frontiers of Management*, 1986, pp. 21-49.
3. Peter F. Drucker, "Corporate Takeovers—What is to be Done?," *The Public Interest*, #82, Winter 1986, and "The Hostile Takeover and its Discontents," *The Frontiers of Management*, 1986, pp. 231-256.
4. Drucker describes these ideas in his articles on hostile takeovers, already cited.
5. "The Changing Multinational," *The Frontiers of Management*, 1985, pp. 61-65.
6. "Europe's High Tech Ambitions," *The Frontiers of Management*, 1984, pp. 76-80.
7. "The Perils of Adversarial Trade," *The Frontiers of Management*, 1986, pp. 98-103.
8. "The Information-Based Organization," *The Frontiers of Management*, 1985, pp. 203-207.
9. "Are Labor Unions Becoming Irrelevant?" (1982) and "Union Flexibility: Why It's Now a Must," (1983), from *The Frontiers of Management*, Dutton, New York, 1986, pp. 208-219.
10. "Social Needs and Business Opportunities," *The Frontiers of Management*, p. 328.

CHAPTER 11

VICTOR C. FERKISS

Victor Ferkiss became known for his work on the politics of developing or lesser developed nations. In the late 1960s, he became interested in the future because of his growing concern about issues related to technology and environmental quality. His Catholicism influences his thinking about the future as it does his political philosophy.

KEY VIEWS ABOUT THE FUTURE

1. By the 21st century we will have one world economy, rich or poor. In that economy, America's choices are increasingly limited by those of other nations and cultures with different views of the world and of the future.
2. Resource scarcity, environmental damage, unconstrained corporate policies, and technology that can alter both human and physical nature and behavior, may doom society not to sudden ecological disaster but to gradual decay and disintegration.
3. Disaster can be avoided only through a cultural revolution and the development of "ecological humanism" as a dominant philosophy.
4. Ecological humanism is a naturalistic, holistic philosophy that would have man live in conscious balance with nature and consensus with other people and societies, based on a shared understanding of community and the public interest.
5. "Technological man," who understands the powers and the risks of technology and is willing to assume responsibility for and control over it, must replace "Bourgeois man," who believes technological imperatives should be constrained only by market forces.
6. It is difficult to prescribe actions to affect the future because of the uncertainty in associating particular means with particular ends. In addition, there is a "religious mystery" at the heart of all human affairs.

BIOGRAPHICAL NOTE

Victor Ferkiss is Professor of Government at Georgetown University in Washington, D.C. where he has taught since 1962. He was educated at the University of California-Berkeley, Yale, and the University of Chicago, receiving his Ph.D. in 1954. He taught in the political science departments of the University of Montana and St. Mary's College (California). Ferkiss served in the U.S. Army in World War II, receiving the Bronze Star, and was a consultant to and trainer for the Peace Corps during the early 1960s. In 1968-69 Ferkiss was a Fulbright Professor at the University of the West Indies, and in 1983 he taught as Eli Lilly Visiting Professor of Science, Theology, and Human Values, at Purdue University.

Four themes dominate Ferkiss's work:

- As a political science academic, he has specialized in the political/economic development of the Third World, especially Africa;
- As a futurist, he has often written about the future of government and the American political process;
- As a political philosopher, he has been concerned with technology, the physical environment, and humanity's ability to avoid global ecological disaster and loss of political freedom;
- As a theologian, he writes about Christianity and the human future on earth.

The fundamental philosophical links between these four themes have become more explicit over time. Ferkiss' work dealing with political development in Africa or in developing nations in general has been largely ignored here. Most attention has been paid to Ferkiss's two major books dealing with technology and human society,[1] several related articles, and another series on religion and the future. Ferkiss's assessment of changes in his worldview over the last two decades is included.[2]

WORLDVIEW

Ferkiss's approach to the world is as a complex fabric combining strands of economic radicalism, Christian conservatism, classical liberalism, and transcendental optimism. Intellectually he insists on optimism but, overall, his message is pessimistic.

His Catholicism gives him both a belief in the fallibility of mankind's ideals and intentions and the limitations on human reason, and an optimism based on the promise of individual and societal redemption. Although Ferkiss rejects the utter pessimism of Jacques Ellul and Heilbroner and calls for creative use of man's technological genius, he is antagonistic towards what he calls "bourgeois man," the "corporate technostructure," and special interest groups and economic classes who seek power at community or society's expense. While not a radical, he is no friend of the corporation nor an admirer of "American managerialism," which is to him the management of technology by the bourgeois man.

He expects society to transform itself, that is, the sum of actions by thousands of individuals will add up to social change of a higher order. This transformation will revise human values and occur through the relatively mundane processes of planning and organizational theory.

SPECIFIC ISSUES

The Economy

The shift of economic activity from production to communication and interaction will tend to emphasize technical expertise in decisionmaking. Fewer people will be needed to keep the machinery of production going, undermining the importance of productive work as an intellectual foundation of industrial civilization. With more wealth and leisure available the pursuit of pleasurable indulgence is likely to increase.

International Economics

Overpopulation is the greatest threat. Technological solutions to the problems of feeding, housing and clothing 7-8 billion people are needed urgently. A complex system of management and communication will be necessary to share our scarce resources and regulate access to clean air and water, nature, and wilderness.

Ferkiss expects that as more individuals and nations become part of international patterns of trade, law and communication, the power over these patterns will move to international organizations. He expects these new international bodies will be expected to curb economic and population growth, control technological innovation and redistribute economic benefits and burdens. Rich or poor, however, by the 21st century the world will have one economy.

At the same time, the post-modern era of technological man is likely to begin and to flourish in the most modern of nations, the U.S.

Environment

Ferkiss was deeply influenced by the environmental and ecological movements of the 1960s and 1970s. While he accepts the thesis that mankind has damaged nature and the carrying capacity of our physical environment through the uncontrolled development of technology, he rejects the idea of a sudden catastrophic collapse as envisioned in *The Limits to Growth*. Such projections, Ferkiss says, all must fail because of the fallacy of aggregation: that is they combine data on a worldwide basis which assumes that "global industrial civilization will march forward in an orderly fashion until it collapses all at once like the fabled one-horse shay."[3] Ferkiss's own view of what may happen is graphic:

> *Long before that time comes, famines, wars, social breakdowns and local catastrophes will combine to bring the machine to a halt, and there will still be human beings living among the ruins like residents of Appalachian hollows, surrounded by rusting hulks of automobiles and abandoned refrigerators.*[4]

This outcome is by no means inevitable. But for now, Ferkiss maintains technology is under the control of "bourgeois man," who has a traditional view of the relationship between man and nature, based on dominance, exploitation, and manipulation.[5]

Technology

Ferkiss believes people can take control of their technology, and avert the rape of nature and falling apart of society. Man is a technical animal and technology is fundamental to his humanity. To take control would require a much more thorough knowledge of technology—a world in which citizens are trained to understand and appreciate the limitations or risks, and the capabilities, of both their machines and themselves.

This is his concept of ecological humanism, which holds:

- that man is part of nature, not apart from it—naturalistic,
- that everything is interconnected, the world is a web—holistic,
- that the world is determined not from outside but from within: we are responsible—immanentist.

In *The Future of Technological Civilization*[6] in 1974, Ferkiss outlines a desirable future based on ecological humanism, which he defines there as the belief that man must live in a conscious ecological relationship with nature and with other men, and that "the ecological perspective on the natural order provides a necessary analogue for the social order."[7] He hopes that the converging activities of individuals throughout the world will transform the values and structures of civilization.

Ferkiss sees technology threatening America's political freedoms. The chief dangers are:

- technological capability to alter man's biological and social nature, or behavior, including "technologies of surveillance and manipulation,"
- technological capability to (or side effects that will) degrade or destroy the physical environment or its carrying capacity.

Two other potential dangers are:

- the end of the possibility of uncontrolled population and economic growth, which sharpens the conflict between competing nations, groups and families,
- the political and moral necessity of diminishing glaring inequalities, which becomes harder as resources become scarcer.

Ferkiss believes the concept of political freedom that has guided America for two centuries is "incomplete, one-sided."[8] That concept, embedded in the Constitution, is based on fear of government. It means only freedom from constraint. We need a more positive concept, freedom for self-realization, which is the ability to choose between alternative futures.

Defense and Disarmament

The threat of nuclear war is held over humanity's head by those in power. Ferkiss identifies other threats implicit in the actions of those in power—population overgrowth, environmental degradation, and resource depletion.

U.S. Political Directions

Ferkiss argues that freedom can be controlled by economic, technical, and cultural forces, and by ignorance or the inability to imagine or see options. Poverty, in particular, can blind people to options. Ferkiss's Christian-economic liberalism emerges when he says: "Social action for common ends is an enlargement, not a diminution, of freedom."[9]

Freedom, for him, must be exercised collectively to be meaningful and self-fulfilling; it must exist in the context of society and the community because man is a social being. It is necessary to reshape the economy to human ends, and to develop a politics based on consensus rather than compromise. This "best case" scenario can only come about if we have daring leadership and if we rediscover a sense of community and public interest, or as Ferkiss says, "civic virtue."[10]

He does not think the best scenario is likely. Three overwhelming forces that will prevent the good from prevailing:

- "corporate technology" or the "technostructure," i.e., the dominance of the political process by self-seeking corporations, in disregard of the public interest;
- resource scarcity in the face of continuing population growth;
- government's promotion of militarism, and its failure to protect civil liberties, or to control the actions of corporations or to moderate economic inequities among its citizens

Ferkiss develops "worst" and "best" scenarios to demonstrate the "outer limits of the possible" over the next two decades.[11] In the worst scenario, the American political system becomes unable to function. There is a disintegration of the intellectual and cultural consensus. We cannot agree on what our problems are, and all issues become fatally dichotomized. Political leadership fails, as Congress becomes the battleground of special interest groups and the President the captive of big business and the press.

This pessimistic scenario appears the most likely to Ferkiss. The description of Congress as increasingly a battleground of petty interests is consistent. In the past, each group in turn was allowed to raid the Treasury (i.e., pork barrel politics) but our economy can no longer afford this. The clashes of interests will become more bitter and less civil, the government will perforce become more repressive. The result will be "neofeudalism" and the decay of our institutions and freedoms.

The "best" scenario will occur if the culture changes radically, and a new consensus on values emerges—specifically the values of thrift, equity, equality, conservation, and harmony with nature. Only in this way can the nation achieve stronger presidential leadership, greater party unity, and "cooperative federalism."

Political Structures

Ferkiss foresees no major structural changes in American government,[12] which has after all remained stable for 200 years. The Republican Party may grow stronger, a trend that has been underway for two decades (with a setback at the time of Watergate). This increased strength may be driven by population movement south and west, by the decline in the influence of organized labor, and by a Republican advantage in financing campaigns since they generally appeal to the more well to do.

The media and the Political Action Committees (PACS) are beginning to have bigger roles than political parties. The media influence had tended to favor the Democratic party, but the trend toward decentralization and demassification (i.e., a decline in the power of the networks in favor of local news gathering) will reverse this trend. The power of PACS and their mass mailings tends to favor the conservative wing of the Republican party.

New Information Societies—Will They Exist?

Ferkiss attacks Daniel Bell's concept of "post-industrial" society.[13] Bell's paradigm, according to Ferkiss, is poorly defined, not backed up by empirical evidence, theoretically misleading, and lamely and uncritically accepted by others.[14]

There is no reason to believe that either new or glamorous technologies or scientific-technological options such as atomic power, computers, or the new biology, have changed the access to, distribution of, or exercise of political power in American society. It is a "theory" or "ideology" rather than a description of trends or a forecast.

To Ferkiss, the concept of post-industrial society is an ideology that "rejects Marxism in favor of capitalist industrialism and predicts and justifies the coming to power of a knowledge elite ruling by rationalistic norms." A truly post-industrial society, Ferkiss says, would be one in which major characteristics of industrial society would be replaced by radically different characteristics. For example, labor would not be a commodity but "an aspect of living," property ownership and power would be widely diffused, scientific and technical knowledge would be widespread, and society decentralized and populist. On the contrary, Ferkiss says, the society Bell foresees is one that has evolved further in the same direction that industrial society has been evolving. It is, according to Ferkiss, more like what Hilaire Belloc called "The Servile State," a society in which the struggle between capitalism and socialism has resulted in a society in which "government dominated the individual in the name of never-to-be-accomplished social goals of equality and harmony, a new society which had no ideology and claimed no name."[15]

The concept of post-industrial society, Ferkiss finds, has little to recommend it logically or empirically, but is popular because it refutes classical Marxism; it defends the status and aspirations of the new class in America of scientists and managers; and it provides an apologia for rationalism and a claim for its future benefits. Post-industrial society manifests the ideology of American managerialism.

Ferkiss' criticism of Bell may come from his fear that belief in the coming of post-industrial society will obscure the necessity for a real transformation: a deliberate change in cultural values and development of new kinds of leadership that can bring about a true harmony between human society and its physical environment.

At present, science and technology develop new products to meet the needs of bourgeois society, based on and interested only in the exchange of commodities. Corporations and the business class make decisions and wield political power. Property-based power has not been replaced by theoretical knowledge and decisions are not being made by planners or any other knowledge-based elite.

Nor, Ferkiss says, will ideology be replaced by rational planning. Myriad interest groups, each with an ideology or a selfish interest, determine political decisions. At best, traditional ideological conflicts reflecting economic differences tend to be replaced by conflicts over lifestyle, for example, the right-to-choose versus right-to-life debate, but this leads to even more bitter ideological battles. Politics are becoming more polarized and more conflicted.

Religion

An historical example of a society transformed was the advent of Christianity, which changed ancient cultures' static view of the future by holding out for the individual the hope of salvation or redemption, and for society, the hope of progress, or collective redemption through social action—"love thy neighbor as thyself."

These transforming principles were made secular by the Enlightenment as individualism and political liberalism. Challenging these tenets today are widespread fears of:

- technology or mechanization,
- environmental destruction and ecological collapse,
- society simply winding down or eroding under pressure, leading to "military-socialism" as Heilbroner foresees.

Christian responses—the social gospel and Christian environmentalism—are somewhat at odds. One implies pro-growth and one anti-growth. The new Fundamentalists are narrowly concerned with personal morality and oppose other Christian responses to the world.

Ferkiss believes society is already decaying, degrading, disintegrating. The new transformation, if it is to come, will be inspired by transcendental forces and occur through mundane processes:

> . . . *(T)hrough the sophisticated approaches of planning and organizational theory we can create means of social coordination which are decentralized, non-hierarchical, and open and which will make possible individual participation and free creativity within an overall pattern of balance.*[16]

Ferkiss insists that, contrary to Heilbroner and Ellul's ideas, technology is not autonomous and deterministic. We design it, we choose it, we can control it. We can accept that we are doomed, or we can resolve to transform ourselves, individually and societally. Personal transformation requires a change in human social psychology, probably based on religious belief; societal transformation requires a cultural revolution, to result in what Ferkiss calls "ecological humanism," a philosophy that rejects the dualism between mind and body, between the natural world and the man-made world, between the individual and the community.

Scientists and technicians of all nations will carry and promote the transformation, driven by their new piety towards the planet. He has recently summarized his view on technology and ethics.[17]

UNDERLYING CAUSES

A Changed Viewpoint

Thinking about 15 years as a futurist, Ferkiss notes that predicting the future is harder than it seemed. He more and more realizes uncertainties in how particular means relate to particular ends.[18] He identifies new developments in his thinking. He now has, for example:

- a feminist perspective,
- a less rationalistic approach, and
- a greater realization of the importance of cultural differences in framing alternative futures.

Contemporary philosophy, he now recognizes, is a "particularly masculine reaction to the total natural environment." Unfortunately, bourgeois man is still firmly in control; we have not yet developed "technological man" but are still dominated by "corporate man."

Technology not only has not been subjected to humanistic/feminist control but is still "an independent variable ruled or constrained only by market forces."

Ferkiss also claims an "increasing consciousness of the ultimate mystery which is at the heart of human existence on both the individual and the social levels."[19] He has also been struck by the reemergence of traditionalism in Third World countries that we had assumed were moving inexorably toward convergence with the western world in thought as well as in technology.

The U.S. may be less autonomous than we assume in shaping its own future; it will be affected by the rest of the world, which has different views of the future, of time, and of the universe.

REFERENCES

1. *Technological Man: The Myth and the Reality*. New York: George Braziller, 1969; paperback, Mentor Books, New York, 1970. *The Future of Technological Civilization*. New York: George Braziller, 1974.
2. "The Future: Not Quite So Easy as it Looked," *World Future Society Bulletin*, XVIII:3, May-June 1984, pp. 10-14.
3. "Christianity, Technology, and the Human Future," *Dialog*, Vol. 13, Fall 1944, p. 261.
4. *The Future of Technological Civilization*, p. 206.
5. *Technological Man: The Myth and the Reality*.
6. *The Future of Technological Civilization*.
7. *The Future of Technological Civilization*, p. 206.
8. "Creating Chosen Futures: The New Meaning of Freedom in America's Third Century," in Norman A. Graebner, ed., *Freedom in America: A 200-Year Perspective*, The Pennsylvania State University Press, 1977.
9. *Freedom in America: A 200-Year Perspective*, p. 254.
10. *Freedom in America: A 200-Year Perspective*, p. 263.
11. "Government in the Year 2000," *National Forum*, LXI:3, Summer 1981, pp. 20-22.
12. "The Future of the U.S. Government: Change and Continuity." *The Futurist*, XVII:1 February 1983, pp. 53-58.
13. "Daniel Bell's Concept of Post-Industrial Society: Theory, Myth, and Ideology," *The Political Science Review*, IX, Fall 1979, pp. 61-102.
14. Political scientists, he says, have in the past damaged their discipline and followed futile or misleading lines of research by accepting uncritically paradigms from other disciplines. He gives as an example the concept of "developing nations," a phrase carried over from economic development as defined by economists, into political science, although nations in this category did not necessarily have significant generalizable political traits and problems.

15. "Daniel Bell's Concept of Post-Industrial Society. . . ," p. 102.
16. "Christianity and the Fear of the Future," *Zygon: Journal of Religion and Science*, 10:3, September 1975, p. 259.
17. "Technology and the Future: Ethical Problems of the Decades Ahead," *Futures Research Quarterly,* Winter 1986, pp. 17-30.
18. "The Future: Not Quite So Easy As It Looked," p. 10.
19. "The Future: Not Quite So Easy As It Looked," p. 10.

CHAPTER 12

BARRY B. HUGHES

Barry Hughes is a futurist and global modeler who has been closely associated with the Mesarovic-Pestel world models. He is also an academic and political scientist. One of his important contributions to the field is his continuing attempt to integrate the widely differing views of other futurists, and thereby impose an intellectual framework on the study of the future. He has not, however, made himself a critic, or a judge, of the futures thinking he draws from.

KEY VIEWS ABOUT THE FUTURE

1. The power of multinational corporations, and of international governmental and non-governmental organizations, is growing. The role of nation states as dominant global actors is diminishing.
2. The possibility of more energy shocks is high, at least for the next 20 years, or until alternatives to OPEC oil are developed. Energy policy, energy prices, or energy related events have potentially great leverage on international economic health.
3. We are undergoing an energy transition from oil to other basic energy sources with major consequences for all social, political and economic systems.
4. The U.S. is less and less a major economic and military power and its decline will cause turbulence and instability, especially in world trade.
5. Forecasters have underestimated the strength of the demographic transition in underdeveloped nations. A faster transition to lower fertility and death rates will mean a slower growth in demand for food, fewer dependents, and less pressure on schools, than has been anticipated for the Third World.

BIOGRAPHICAL NOTE

Barry Hughes is a professor at the Graduate School of International Studies, University of Denver. He taught at Case Western Reserve University, 1970-1980, where he was one of the original group developing the Mesarovic-Pestel global models. He earned his B.S. in mathematics from Stanford, and his Ph.D. in political science from the University of Minnesota. He has been funded by private foundations and the National Science Foundation to develop classroom and microcomputer versions of global models. In the past 10-15 years he has consulted with foreign governments, institutions, and universities, and with U.S. corporations, including being guest scientist and member of the GLOBUS team in Berlin on several occasions. The Organization of Petroleum Exporting Countries, and the Latin American Long Range Planning Project at Simon Bolivar University in Caracas, have employed Hughes as a consultant.

Hughes wrote *The Domestic Context of American Foreign Policy,* published in 1978. This profile is drawn from *World Modeling*, published in 1980; from *World Futures*, 1985, from several articles and from an interview.

WORLDVIEW

As a modeler, Hughes is comfortable with team and group studies of the future, and works with others on developing new generations of world models. He himself points out that the worldview of modelers influences the outcome of models. He has devoted time to understanding and comparing the various world models, and the differing, and competing, worldviews of the modelers, as well as structural variations in the various models.[1] He also notes that all worldviews had better be adaptive because the next 20-30 years are likely to be eventful.

Hughes sorts the major world models and studies of the global future into a two-way matrix reflecting the orientation of the modelers along a line reflecting their general views on relationships between political and social systems and the economy (political economy) and along the other axis, reflecting their broader view of links between politics and the natural biological environment (political ecology).[2] At one end of the axis of political ecology, modernists believe mankind increasingly controls its environment, and technology is the key to a better future. Neotraditionalists, at the other end, believe the environment is sensitive and complex and we should be selective and controlled in our approach to new technologies. They therefore believe a better future comes through making lifestyles more consistent with human values.[3]

Hughes's early modeling work with Mesarovic on the World Integrated Model (WIM) placed him as a neo-traditionalist, with internationalist, slightly radical sympathies. More recently, however, he has moved toward a more modernist perspective on political ecology, and

EXHIBIT 12-1

Paradigm Dimensions in World Models and Future Studies[4]

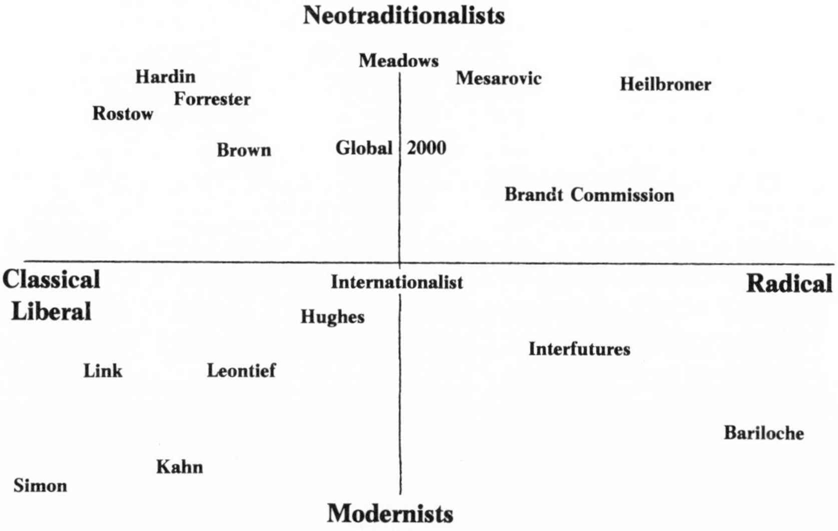

become more liberal in his views on political economy. But as he points out, a third dimension may be evolving, of realists versus idealists; the latter favor individual, voluntary, and sometimes collective and cooperative action based on changes in values. This idealist group, Hughes considers somewhat utopian.[5] He describes Herman Kahn as more of a realist than an idealist.

Hughes looks at the world as a complex system, or set of systems, with hundreds of sub-systems interacting with one another. He believes we need more study of the linkages between systems and between issues.

Forecasts of the future, or potential outcomes which derive from the WIM model, are frequently ascribed in this chapter to Hughes, because he has selected them in his discussion of alternative futures. His views are becoming more optimistic on certain of the WIM forecasts, and these are noted.

SPECIFIC ISSUES

Technology

A strong technological determinism influences much if not most thinking about the future. In his own work, Hughes accepts technological drivers as a base, then builds forecasts of social and political structures on top. Technology drives, but is moved and shaped by intervening variables, such as social and political forces which are themselves shaped by huge forces such as world population growth.

From a modeler's point of view, technology is a wild card because there is no index of technology, or a reliable set of numbers indicating the rate of technological change. Depending on worldview, forecasters either overestimate its potential or ignore it. Hughes favors a combination of extrapolation and expert judgment. He picks three technological areas with potentially fundamental importance to the global system:

- semiconductors and their associated technologies,
- the newer energy technologies, and
- biological technologies, especially recombinant DNA and genetic engineering.[6]

Semiconductor technologies are likely to displace workers across a broad range of employment sectors. In the Third World, these technologies pose both threat and opportunity; threat to the workforce, and great potential savings of capital, energy and resources in commercial and domestic uses.

The newer energy technologies are those which will make possible the transition from reliance on oil to a more diverse energy economy. Hughes notes that these technologies are extremely diverse in type, cost, level and time of development and potential efficiency—and each has its promoters and defenders. Fluidized-bed coal combustion, for example, developed to reduce particle and gas emissions in U.S. coal burning, is now being used extensively by China.

Biological engineering has staggering implications for agriculture, in making plants more productive and more independent of the farmer's care. A permanent increase in the size of livestock is another expected change. Hughes notes also major implications for health care.

Other areas of science and technology with potentially revolutionary importance are plate tectonics, materials science, medicine and space. He even sees potential practical applications developing from the new directions in physics and cosmology.

Energy

We are undergoing an energy transition with major consequences for all social, political and economic systems. The 70% oil and gas share of energy generation will fall to 30-40% of our overall energy budget in the next century.[7] Unlike earlier transitions, this one will require a collective social choice to complete it. The implications of three possible choices may be:

- Nuclear—implies a significant continuing government role, to manage safety, transportation of fuel, waste disposal and siting, as well as supervision of the transmission grid. Monopolies and price controls are also near-certain.
- Solar, or other renewables—implies decentralization, dispersed capital, labor intensity of craft-based skills for installation and maintenance, smaller-scale industries and a reduced government- and corporate-role.
- Coal—implies a new synthetic fuels industry, capital intensive and capital concentrated, with development of new technologies aimed at supporting current patterns of energy and fuel use, in cars, industry, and so on. The government role may be to provide capital for new fuel industries.[8]

Hughes notes that U.S. corporations tend to support a coal-based energy system.

International Economics

Energy policy, energy prices, or energy-related events, such as the oil price shocks of 1973-1974 and 1979-1981, have potentially great leverage on international economic health. Hughes notes that if Iran, as seems likely, wins the Iran/Iraq war, then it will be more dominant in the Persian Gulf and could change world oil prices. World money flows may be severely affected again by energy policy decisions.[9] If incentives for conservation set in place when prices are high are eroded when energy prices fall the future costs will be high when energy prices go up again. Hughes concludes that substantial changes in global energy prices, up or down, are major drivers of all national economies, regardless of current political theories. Policies which build resiliency into a country's energy system may be more protective of economic growth than short-term fiscal policies which respond to the effects of energy shocks.

Unfortunately for corporations, the incentives to build a back-up coal-burning furnace in case of energy price rises are there. Altruistically, the benefits of doing so could be seen as a future social good, limiting economic disruption in the community at a time of energy crisis.

The probability of more energy shocks is high, at least for the next 20 years, or until alternatives to OPEC oil are developed. A typical energy shock cycle will be likely to produce the following effects:

- Energy prices rise. (Spending power drains to oil exporting countries.)
- Workers demand wage increases.
- Inflationary pressure grows.
- Governments apply restrictive monetary controls.
- Growth rates drop in oil importing countries.
- Unemployment increases.
- Third World borrows more money from the First World to pay the higher bills for energy.
- Market recovery mechanisms operate, global economy gradually stabilizes.

Higher energy prices are producing increasing global unemployment, which Hughes believes cannot be blamed solely on changes in the structure of economies, from manufacturing to service, for example, or on the displacement in the workforce caused by the impact of electronics.

Exogenous global shocks, such as sharp rises in energy prices, weaken the traditional tools of domestic policy management. Furthermore, the next exogenous shock, when it occurs, will cost more in terms of inflation, slowed growth and unemployment, than have the others.

Rising global unemployment and governmental deficits are new features of the global economic structure not likely to disappear quickly. Global deficits near 6% of GDP will be difficult to reduce, according to Hughes.[10] The period of U.S. hegemony may be relatively short compared, for example, with that of Great Britain. The U.S. is less and less a major economic and military power and its decline will cause turbulence and instability, especially in world trade.[11]

In the more developed countries the public debt is internally financed, implying internal shifts of money and resources to correct the imbalances. The less developed nations owe money to other countries and repayment means a net reduction in welfare of the entire country. The potential of such a drastic drop in internal worth may explain the flight of private capital from such countries as Argentina and Mexico, which weakens still further their ability to repay their debts.

Hughes is becoming more optimistic about closing the gap in per capita GDP between developed and less developed countries, which was an early concern of world modelers. That ratio, currently about 12.6, has been unchanged for forty years and is not likely to change substantially by 2025, according to the World Integrated Model.[12] For a variety of reasons, Hughes currently believes that although statistics do not support him shifts in global economic and political power over the next 20-30 years will narrow the gap, implying changes in the North-South balance, and a redefinition of haves, and have-nots.

By the 1990s, Western Europe and Japan will be experiencing more oil importing problems than the U.S. Hughes believes that past wasteful practices in energy use will allow the U.S. some slack to tighten its belt when oil prices rise. The U.S. may manage the energy transition more easily than countries which have been conserving for years. A difficult energy transition will slow Japan's growth especially.[13]

Hughes is optimistic about the outlook for the U.S. economy in the short term (1-2 years) and expects that exports will expand following the devaluing of the dollar. The looming image of Federal debt is somewhat offset by the stock market boom which is perceived as creating wealth.

Gorbachev's "glasnost" or openness policy in the USSR is a positive trend for U.S. relations with the Soviets. On the other hand, China's expansion of food production may have negative trade implications for the U.S., at least in the short term.

Food and Agriculture

Population growth and the potential problems of producing food and energy for a world with 8 billion people by 2025 were some of the major concerns driving early global modeling. Hughes now believes forecasters have underestimated the strength of the demographic transition in underdeveloped as well as developed nations. A faster transition to lower fertility and death rates in the less developed nations will mean a slower growth in demand for food, fewer dependents, less pressure on schools, than has been anticipated for the Third World.

The World Integrated Model suggests that South Asia will have the worst food supply problems and the greatest likelihood of mass starvation. The recent dramatic expansion of agriculture and food production in China as a result of the restoration of market incentives, however, excites Hughes. On the down side, the number of the world's malnourished is likely to increase by 10-20% before the end of the century, and in some scenarios by 75%. Hughes believes a 40% increase is most likely, ensuring that an almost constant fraction of the world population will remain malnourished.[14]

One side effect of the transfer of agricultural and food growing technology is a disruption of social patterns based on agriculture, the loss of land tenure, for example. The spread of new production techniques will continue to reduce the world's agricultural laborforce, and encourage movement into cities.

Some newer technologies, such as the development of crops and grains with the ability to fix nitrogen from the air, could reduce world fertilizer needs, as could new irrigation technologies that cut back on water. Hughes also notes the potential of hydroponic agriculture to reduce pressure on land use.

Environment

It is almost certain we will increase the global atmospheric level of carbon dioxide (CO^2) sufficiently by 2025 to experience some effects on the environment. World modeling estimates of the pace of increase vary, and are not sensitive to changes in economic or energy systems. The World Integrated Model shows a 25-30% increase above pre-industrial levels of CO^2 by 2000 and 50-60% increase by 2025.[15]

Among the most troublesome environmental problems will be: the increasing use of chemicals, on the land, especially; land use itself; the overuse of biological systems, such as over-fishing; the introduction of genetically engineered species; and specific toxic waste disposal issues, such as nuclear waste.

Cities

In the long term the various world forecasts of population growth imply we are moving towards a stable state of higher population density and lower fertility. In the near term, the unstable state of rapid population growth will swell Third World cities. By 2000, eight of the ten largest cities will be in Asia or South America, with Mexico City the world's largest urban area with a population of 30 million, based on straight extrapolation.

Values

From Hughes' point of view, most discussions of future values and institutional change are inevitably biased by individual worldviews and preferences. However, there is reason to believe a change in values may be occurring in the U.S., driven by a perception of growing scarcity of resources and damage to the global environment.

Political Directions

The power of multinational corporations, of international governmental and non-governmental organizations, is growing. The role of nation states as dominant global actors is diminishing. As manufacturing and production becomes global and communications technologies create new links, new groupings of power will occur.

Intergovernmental and international nongovernmental organizations are growing in numbers and complexity. Their creation is frequently driven by function, by the need to administer and control new technology, to manage resource problems, and to influence the management of social and environmental issues. Greenpeace and Amnesty International are examples of the latter type. Hughes notes that the creation of global organizations to handle issues of common security is new in this century.

Multinationals are growing fast in size and numerically. More will appear, from Europe, Japan and the developing countries. Although the extent of their future political power is not clear, Hughes points out that the five international grain trading houses (Cargill, Continental, Bunge, Louis Dreyfus, and Andre), the food processing companies and the agricultural product suppliers play important roles in the global food system.

At the same time as newly powerful groups and sub-groups are forming, there is also a resurgence in power-seeking along national and ethnic cultural lines. This may be a major issue for the Soviet Union. Such a resurgence may be reflecting a drive towards greater diversity and decentralization that is worldwide. Economic and technological forces may be pushing this trend along, towards smaller units of manufacturing more widely dispersed, away from the domination of the large and the centralized—and away from domination by the U.S. manufacturing and economic paradigm.

The Future of the Corporation and the Multinational (MNC)

Multinationals are potentially important actors on the global scene, but not necessarily more important than developing non-governmental and international organizations that cut into the sovereignty of nations. Production technology is a force driving MNCs to multinational operation and their industrial base is broadening as their numbers grow. The industrialization which appears to be spread by MNCs to less developed countries can be explained by product lifecycle theory.

However MNCs are subject to the economic policies of nation states and, should these turn towards protectionism, the growth of MNCs will halt. In the U.S., pressure for trade protection is likely to ease. The maintenance of low tariff barriers and the absence of financial barriers are critical to the future of MNCs—Hughes is optimistic about both. Attempts to stop the movement of capital across borders will continue, but will not hold. Hughes expects to see the opening up of equity markets and the availability of capital from countries with a surplus. Banks will follow, and sometimes even lead the way for, MNCs.

Corporations ought to be looking at the long term horizon, 20-30 years, and many are doing so, believes Hughes. He dismisses labor unions. They are falling behind, reluctant to look at or plan for the future.

Defense and Disarmament

Beyond a concern for the proliferation of nuclear weapons, and a belief that there is a high probability of their use in regional wars over the next 20-30 years, Hughes has little to say about defense matters. Star Wars is the most important example of a technologically driven development which will make structural and political change (for example, disarmament) more difficult.

UNDERLYING CAUSES

What anyone believes about the underlying causes of any effect depends on worldview and assumptions about future behavior, according to Hughes. Long wave economic cycles, for example, can be cited to show that the economy will always recover, and on the other hand to show that the economy is bumping against limits, which it may recover from this time, but not the next. To Hughes, the linkages between issues, and between systems and subsets of systems, are what is important. He implies that the more we understand linkages and their effects, the greater our ability will be to forecast realistic world futures. Energy, as a "master resource," is a primary driver of other global systems and its cost and availability is key to world development.

EXHIBIT 12-2

FORCES INFLUENCING THE FUTURIST THINKING OF

BARRY HUGHES

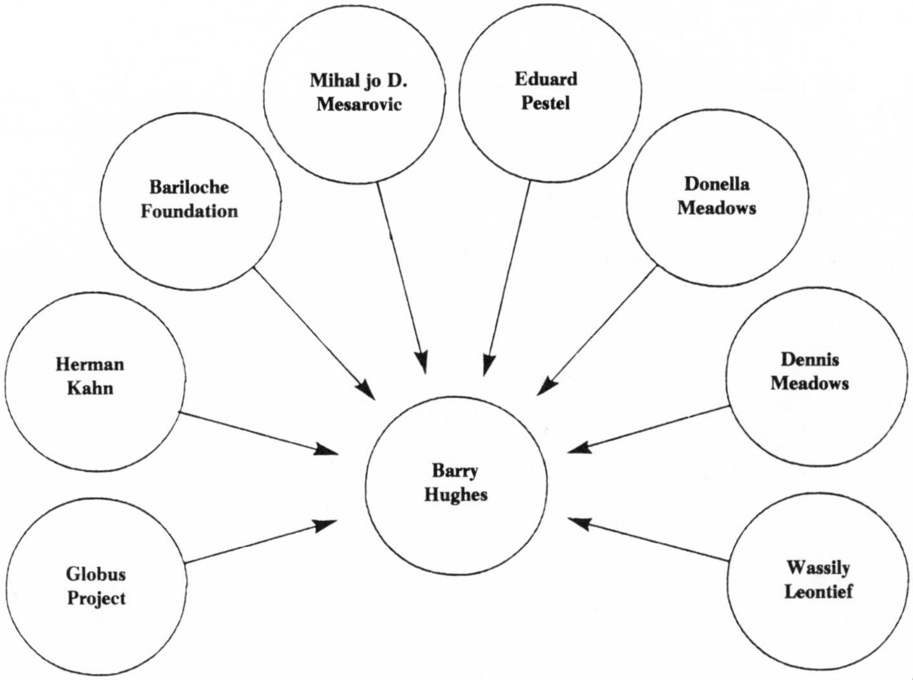

REFERENCES

1. Barry B. Hughes, "World Models: The Bases of Difference," *International Studies Quarterly,* 29, 1985, pp. 77-101.
2. See Barry B. Hughes, *World Futures*, John Hopkins University Press, 1985, for a detailed discussion of the various worldviews.
3. *World Futures,* Table 3.1, p. 34.
4. *World Futures*, Table 3.3, p. 48.
5. *World Futures,* p. 50.
6. *World Futures*, p. 158.
7. Interview with Hughes, February 13, 1987.
8. *World Futures*, pp. 112-113.
9. Barry B. Hughes, "The First Two Oil Shocks: Policy Response and Effectiveness," *Policy Studies Review*, May 1986, 5:4, p. 722.

10. These trends are graphed in Hughes, "The First Two Oil Shocks: Policy Response and Effectiveness," *Policy Studies Review*, May 1986.
11. Interview with Hughes, February 13, 1987.
12. Barry B. Hughes, "World Models: The Bases of Difference," *International Studies Quarterly*, p. 95.
13. Barry B. Hughes, *World Modeling*, Heath, 1980, p. 201.
14. *World Modeling*, p. 199.
15. *World Modeling*, p. 201.

Additional Readings:

Barry B. Hughes "Domestic Economic Processes," in Stuart A. Bremer, (ed), *The GLOBUS Model: Computer Simulation of Worldwide Political and Economic Developments,* Boulder, Colorado, Westview, 1987.

Barry B. Hughes, *Disarmament and Development: A Design for the Future?,* coauthored with Stuart A. Bremer, Englewood Cliffs, NJ, Prentice Hall, forthcoming 1989.

CHAPTER 13

ALEXANDER KING

As president of the Club of Rome and an international civil servant of wide experience, King brings a global approach to the future. Rather than seeing himself as a futurist, for King the study of the future is only one of many perspectives to an interdisciplinary understanding and management of the global system. In this chapter there are few prescriptions of what to do about global problems. King and the Club of Rome are committed to fostering a more profound understanding of world problems among leaders and decisionmakers of all political and ideological stripes.

KEY VIEWS ABOUT THE FUTURE

1. We are in a 30-50 year transition or evolution to a global society of greater numbers, changed values, new political and administrative structures, new institutions and new technological bases.
2. Technology molds society; usually the more prosperous societies benefit the most. This will be true, at least in the short term, of microelectronics.
3. A number of emerging global environmental problems are likely to require technological solutions on a planetary scale—atmospheric and climatic changes, for example, and water pollution.
4. Transnational corporations are the most effective mechanism for technological transfer, despite the suspicion in which they are held by Third World countries.
5. Populations of rich countries could be clustered in luxurious shelters with the masses of poor ranging over the rest of the world.
6. Demography, unemployment, and rising expectations are driving a slow opening of the USSR's society and institutions.
7. The smooth running of cities and countries depends on the efficient functioning of technical devices, yet they are vulnerable to disruption and their malfunctioning could quickly bring many activities to a standstill.
8. The structure of national governments is anachronistic, with overly short electoral cycles and slow problem solving mechanisms adequate only for the problems of simpler societies.

BIOGRAPHICAL NOTE

Alexander King is president and co-founder of the Club of Rome. Since 1974, he has also been chairman of the International Federation of Institutes of Advanced Study (IFIAS), a group which promotes and carries out multidisciplinary research on global problems. From 1961-1974, he was director general for scientific affairs and education of the Organization for Economic Cooperation and Development (OECD). He had a distinguished scientific career at Imperial College, London, and was head of the British Scientific Mission in Washington in World War II. He has had a long-term interest in multidisciplinary studies and while he was chief scientist of the British government's Department of Scientific and Industrial Research in the 1950s, he completed a number of such studies, including one on the social, political, technical and economic consequences of automation. He also promoted research in the social sciences at universities. Now 80, Dr. King lives in Paris.

He is the author of *The State of the Planet*, a report prepared by the IFIAS, and published by Pergamon in 1980, and introduces and writes a chapter in *Microelectronics and Society—for Better or for Worse:A Report to the Club of Rome*, Pergamon, 1982, as well as a number of other publications and articles dealing with global trends and the effects of technology on the global future.

WORLDVIEW

In a recent article for *Interdisciplinary Science Reviews,*[1] Dr. King describes the main function of the Club of Rome as being to foster among decisionmakers and the public a more profound understanding of world problems and a greater awareness of the long term benefits of change. This characterizes it as an educational, rather than an activist, organization with no political power, but considerable international influence. The Club is a group of 100 individuals from 47 countries which publishes reports to its members—the most notable and most widely distributed was its first, *The Limits to Growth* which sold more than 7 million copies—and promotes conferences, education and training. A reappraisal of *The Limits to Growth* is to be published, titled *The Limits to Growth Revisited.*

The major concerns of the Club of Rome to the end of the century are:

- war and violence as a symptom of a deeper malaise in society,
- the consequences of a doubling of world population,

- the management of a global society in the face of complexity and rapid change,
- the generation of sufficient human wisdom to act constructively on a global scale, and
- the impacts of science and technology.

To some extent, the views expressed by the Club are those of Alexander King. King himself has been influenced by the Club's first president and co-founder, the late Aurelio Peccei.

King's is a worldview, a planetary outlook. He draws on multidisciplinary perspectives, including thinking about the future. For the most part his views are pessimistic because he believes the world's problems are outpacing our attempts and ability to deal with them. All of the major trends affecting the next few decades are characterized by:

- the rapidity of change,
- complexity, and
- uncertainty.

The uncertain nature of trends and uncertainties about their future strength and direction requires more careful and continuing monitoring of emerging developments. *The Limits to Growth*, for example, was not a projection or a prediction but an illustration, showing that we need to understand what extrapolation of the trends implies if we are to defeat their disastrous effects.

One of King's most powerful images pictures a future world in which a few countries shelter 20% of the population, the rich elite, favored by birth, using the tools of science and technology to benefit themselves and surrounded by the remaining ocean of 80% of the people, young, hungry, poor and shut out.

The Club of Rome, however, is optimistic about the potential of nations and institutions to manage the global future.

King believes technology molds society, but usually the more prosperous societies benefit the most. New information technologies, however, promise to be beneficial and widespread in their economic effects over the long term. In the near term, information technologies will replace work and workers across all sectors of the economy; the transition to a new level of social development in an information society may be rough, with increased social unrest and social and institutional change.[2] The great bureaucracies which have arisen on an expanding policy of governmental provision of services will be early candidates for automation and since the public generally dislikes them for their coldness, will be early replaced by smaller, partially automated, and more flexible units.[3]

A Global Society

We are in a 30-50 year transition to the evolution of a global society of greater numbers, changed values, new political and administrative structures, new institutions and with a new technological base. The major consequences of this transition will be:

- large changes in the distribution of international trade and industry—and King only hints at what these might be—and,
- big shifts in power.

To manage the transition and to build a global society, certain shifts are necessary in human behavior and values:

- changes in lifestyle,
- changes in consumption patterns of developed countries,
- economic and political shifts to move the world in the direction of more harmonious overall development.

King does not say how these shifts are to be made, except by educating decisionmakers in the developed nations of the need for change.

SPECIFIC ISSUES

Science and Technology—Microelectronics

Of all new technologies driving the global transition referred to earlier, microelectronics is the most revolutionary. Because of its potential to increase productivity through automation across broad sectors of the economy, large numbers of the global workforce will be displaced. King expects a long period of endemic unemployment followed by a richer society, with a higher quality of life as the increased productivity pays off and people find other occupations than work as we know it today.

King notes that in more affluent societies, consumers are spending more on travel, private education and health care, private transportation, and on high technology products which provide services. An example is the increasing purchase of recorded entertainment, music, movies, and television.

The microelectronics industry will be intensely competitive amongst highly industrialized nations.

The U.S.

- Advantages

  —Federal government support of integrated circuit development, for the space program and for defense, especially for very high speed integrated circuits (VHICs).
  —the leader in use of integrated circuits.

Japan

- Advantages

  —long term industrial and government policy to promote a strong domestic computer industry.
  —protection of that industry from foreign competition.
  —new microelectronics industries are units within large enterprises, have better access to capital than Silicon Valley start-ups.
  —is introducing microelectronics into as wide a range of industries as possible.

Europe—late arrival in the field, and lagging

- Advantages

  —Government investment in the creation of firms to develop the next generation of memory chips and in the convincing of industrialists to use them.

King concludes Japan will be the pacesetter because of its long term industrial policy and its genius for reaching decisions through consensus.[4]

Environment

King notes that a number of emerging global environmental problems are likely to require technological solutions on a planetary scale.[5] Much of what threatens the environment is reversible by technical solutions, at a cost, but no more than that of the current global budget for advertising. In the long term, however, population growth pressures the environment, leading to potentially irreversible changes, deterioration, and greater difficulty in adjusting to larger populations. King is full of disquiet about global climate. Among his concerns are,

- the changes in atmospheric ozone,
- increasing atmospheric carbon dioxide,
- acid rain.

Human actions, such as forest clearing, are exacerbating the greenhouse effect. In any event, according to the consensus among climatologists, we are faced with a period of climatic uncertainty, perhaps a new Ice Age, and possible extremes of heat and cold, drought and flood. These problems are essentially global and cannot be solved by the isolated actions of individual countries. Improved international mechanisms are called for. It is politically unrealistic to expect that countries will take direct action to slow down or prohibit, for example, the burning of fossil fuels to prevent the disruption which the greenhouse effect is likely to cause to climatic and agricultural patterns; but, much could be done by wise prevision to buffer the effects.

Energy

The global energy demand is rising with the new scale of human activities—an increase of people, autos, cities and governments and an increase in the size and scale of most human artifacts, buildings, factories, numbers of domestic appliances, and so on. Costs are likely to rise. Even a small increase in population will mean much greater use of energy and materials. King suggests the use of microelectronics in industry and systems control will be important in reducing energy demand since these techniques are less energy-hungry.

We will inevitably need renewable energy systems, energy policies, and diverse energy sources. King doubts nuclear or coal based energy systems can meet the need because of their potential high risk and high environmental costs. It will take at least 40 years to establish any new energy system. More could be done with nuclear energy, but it is unclear if we will. Photovoltaics is an attractive alternative. Fusion is a long term strategy with a number of problems in development and potential side effects.

In the 1970s, King favored a quick push to develop renewable energy technologies, especially solar.[6] Renewable energies are a part of the bioresource that in his book *Bioresources for Development,* King describes as a continuously fed storehouse, resilient, versatile, renewable, self-balancing, bulky, limited by natural cycles, interconnected and essential to human survival. Use of non-renewable resources and uncontrolled economic growth threatens the bioresource and the natural environment. Development of bioresources, on the other hand, offers promises of food and energy for less developed countries in Asia, Latin America and Africa.

Food and Agriculture

In the mid-term, enough food can be produced, but the uncertainties require global monitoring. The real problems are economic, political and logistical. We are entering a period of surplus and famine, with increasing fear that food will be withheld as a weapon. In the long term the population may overwhelm the global food supply. Purposeful management of locally available bioresources may supply more food and energy for some areas.

Examples of useful approaches are:

- waste recycling programs;
- biogas as used in China and parts of South East Asia;
- inland pond fish cultivation;
- algae as an intermediate step in food production as seen mostly in rural and peasant economies;
- the application of systems science to problems of total or integrated bioresource management;
- the promise of contemporary biological research, in enzyme technology, genetics, and use of solar energy.

THE GLOBAL ECONOMY

The Corporation

Transnational corporations are the most effective mechanism for technological transfer, despite the suspicion in which they are held by Third World countries.[7] However the technologies transferred tend to be more appropriate to the competence and needs of developed countries and do not readily become rooted unless there is sufficient technological infrastructure. King notes that achievement of a threshold of technical competence is a nation's entry card to the globe's common pool of technical knowledge and innovation.

Although corporations have an important role in promoting the spread of technology, King considers them among those institutions poorly adapted to cope with contemporary problems because they tend to seek only short term solutions. Nevertheless, some multinationals, Shell, Exxon, Unilever and Fiat, for example, are oriented to the future, but others are slow to take a long range approach. Like governments and other bureaucracies, they do not recognize the web of interdependencies in which they exist.

He notes that most industrialists and representatives of large corporations in the highly industrialized countries believe that with automation, all domestic goods and services can be produced with only 10-15% of the workforce. In the end, the Luddites may be right—machines will put most people out of work, including those in the pool of cheap labor in the industrializing countries.

The Workforce

In the long run, Malthus may prove right here also. Doubling of the world population will treble the workforce. The provision of jobs will be a major world problem, and serious social difficulties could result. We will be faced with the prospect of having to change work attitudes, the length of hours, and working life. In the near term information technologies will replace work and workers across all sectors of the economy, and the transition to a new level of social development in an information society may be rough, with increased social unrest and social and institutional change.[8] On the other hand, with sufficient foresight on the part of governments supported by an informed public, the new technologies could usher in a new type of society, more democratic and more equitable, which would provide leisure and self-fulfillment to the individual and a general improvement of the human condition.

The International Economy

Economic interdependence among nations will increase, as will their sharing of problems and their mutual impact. The current rate of economic growth cannot be maintained. King notes that some countries will take a moral position on growth. He cites Norway, which rejected the economic growth that would have followed the unrestricted sale of its North Sea oil.

> *(In) a period of slower growth and greater constraints, the present highly industrialized countries will be competing with one another for a share in a more sophisticated but possibly more restricted market.*[9]

Smaller countries are more at the mercy of external forces and their power of action is greatly restricted. Some small countries, such as

Denmark and Japan, have no resources except their populations and this drives a continuing reassessment of their policies toward other nations.

Unless the gap between the rich and the poor nations is bridged to some extent, and some of the present frustration and hostility of poor toward the rich is removed, strong tension inevitably will develop. Populations of rich countries in the future could be clustered in luxurious shelters with the masses of poor ranging over the rest of the world.

The Soviet Union

The USSR will be an Asian nation in 20-30 years, based on the projected differential fertility of its Asian and European Caucasian population. Based on a recent interview and correspondence with Gorbachev, King takes a more hopeful view of the USSR's potential for institutional change.[10] The Russian leader acknowledges the need to restructure Soviet society and is more open to and interested in change, according to King. Besides demographics, the drivers of change in Russian society include:

- unemployment, a problem masked for years as widespread underemployment,
- a younger generation with greater expectations for freedom and the opportunity to travel.

In King's judgement, the Soviet Union is opening up carefully, making an effort to lighten their bureaucratic burden, and may offer new opportunities for trade ventures. Dissidents are still distrusted, but in the USSR, as in other countries, ideology is eroding.

Global Demographics

By the end of the century the proportion of people in developed countries—North America, Western Europe, Eastern Europe, and Japan—will make up less than 20% of world population. At its present growth rate, for example, Nigeria will have 600 million people by the end of the next century. King points out that huge numbers of people are only one of the problems created by population growth. We must also face pressures on the environment created by more human activity and the increasing affluence of a large part of the population. Little work is being done on the consequences for food, agriculture, natural resources, politics, migration, border conflict and violence.

Migration and cross-border movement of large numbers of people will be a worldwide issue, including the Mexico-U.S. border.

Africa represents a complex, nearly intractable problem for other nations which, nevertheless, will have to be concerned. The continent is a part of the world system, important for its resources, for its people and the events which may begin there. It may be the source of new epidemic diseases as it has been the source of AIDS.

Cities

The forecast that 30 million people will live in Mexico City by the early 2000s is unthinkable and probably will not occur because among other factors there is not enough water. However, a very large number of cities with millions of inhabitants will rise all over the globe, especially in the underdeveloped world.

More and more the smooth running of cities and countries depends on the efficient functioning of technical devices, yet these are vulnerable to disruption and their malfunctioning could quickly bring activities to a standstill. King doubts cities this size are manageable at all, at least as we understand city management today.

Industrial Development

Rising costs of energy will drive refining of oil and processing of ores closer to their sources of production. Much of this transition is likely to be aided by the transnationals in their own economic interests.

Growth rates in the volume of exports of manufactured goods, especially textiles, garments and shoes from Hong Kong, Singapore, South Korea and Taiwan, have slowed and are likely to be decreased further by the impact of microelectronics in U.S. and European industries. The U.S. textile industry will spend about $2 billion a year in the 1980s on automation, reducing its workforce by about 300,000.[11]

Transportation

The capital, effort, resources and materials are not available to double world infrastructure in 30-40 years to meet the needs of huge cities and increased world population.

Government and Political Directions

The structure of national governments is anachronistic, slow, with overly short electoral cycles and problem solving mechanisms adequate to the problems of simpler societies. The confrontational nature of most public life, the expanding bureaucracy and the increasing complexity of issues make most government decisionmakers unsuitable for handling world scale problems. This is also an argument for the growth of non-governmental organizations such as the Club of Rome, which can be ideologically neutral, cheaper to run, represent grassroots constituencies, and promote bootstrapping strategies, some of which are being used effectively in less developed countries, such as in Africa. The Club of Rome sponsors a foundation for International Training in Toronto which now has about 80 projects, at about a quarter the cost of similar government programs.

Defense and Disarmament

World disarmament is crucial to achieving world balance in the use of resources. Half of the world's scientists are engaged in militarily related research, which is a waste of human resources.

The threat of war is the most dangerous and pressing of all issues facing humanity. World harmony will be exceedingly difficult to achieve, however, unless human values change.

Values

King believes man's biology works against his survival in the modern world. Although aggression, greed, fear, lust, and other similar attributes may have served a purpose in ensuring survival in a more primitive world, these characteristics are obsolete. What is needed is a projection of the individual's egoism to embrace survival of a larger society.

There is a widespread impression that the values of society are in transition, and a belief that decaying public morality represents a weakening of the will of people and societies to respect in practice what they sense as true.

The internal adoption of new attitudes and values will not be accomplished quickly enough to solve urgent global problems. King suggests potential external approaches:

- Establish a worldwatch—a world monitoring system that continually reports status and progress to all citizens.
- Build a new international order to reduce economic disparities between nations.
- Find means of persuading all of us to postpone our own gratification to build a livable world for our grandchildren. Education is one

means of doing this, although a slow one. The religious movements are weak and not likely to be effective.

- Match the material successes of the human race with an equal growth in wisdom. Science may contribute to this task.

Education

The strengthening of social sciences is King's imperative item, given his values change agenda. Overall, a more transdisciplinary approach is needed, especially in universities. The power of education, and the potential of the educational system for bringing about social change, is overlooked and underused in his view.

Universities, with a great record for leadership and innovation, are now among the least interested and interesting institutions in their potential for change.

Most of the Third World countries are unlikely to catch up with the microelectronics society unless they can reach the critical threshold of scientific competence to use and manufacture the technology. King notes that the new information technology will give the Third World access to the world's knowledge, limited only by the ability to select what is useful out of the enormous mass.

Among third world countries, India may already have reached the competence threshold and Mexico and Brazil are approaching it.

Crime and Violence

World society is on the brink of ungovernability. We can expect rising violence and instability with the growth in population. Contemporary societies are fragile—extremely vulnerable to planned or unplanned disruption. Malfunctioning of their infrastructure could paralyze a city or even a nation.

Religion

Churches have disappointed and let us down with their lack of orientation to the future and interest in world problems, King believes. The World Council of Churches is active in a small way, and there is interest among Buddhists in world issues. Islam is past-oriented, totally.

UNDERLYING CAUSES

The accumulated knowledge generated by scientific research, its methods and its applications through technology could be more effectively used towards harmonious world development but has generally favored the rich.

Our global problems continue to grow; inflation, unemployment, the arms race which siphons off global resources, national indebtedness, and a continuation of environmental deterioration, because we have neither the will nor the worldwide management structures to solve them. Aid programs are insufficient or inefficient or the concepts of development are inadequate.

King proposes, as an interim step, a regional approach, creating regional and sub-regional alliances and economic groupings to utilize complementarity. He advocates regional defense mechanisms and guarantees of equality for smaller ethnic or culturally coherent sub-groups within regional groupings. Mechanisms exist within the UN for consultation and negotiation between various regional groupings for considering joint action regarding global problems.

Global and regional planning must stress resilience not rigidity. Some global problems are contagious, like inflation and doubts about the stability of economic systems.

EXHIBIT 13-1

FORCES INFLUENCING THE FUTURIST THINKING OF

ALEXANDER KING

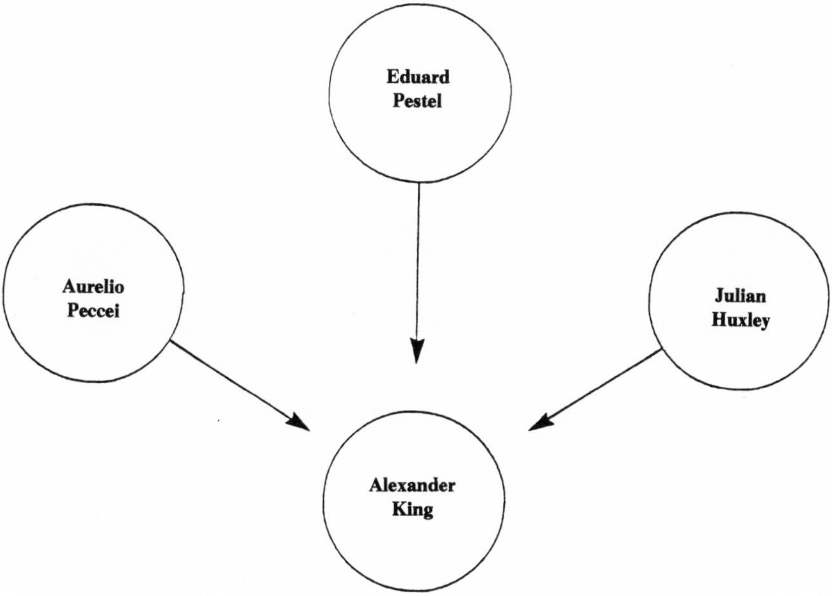

REFERENCES

1. Alexander King, "The Club of Rome: Reaffirmation of a Mission," *Interdisciplinary Science Reviews,* 11:1, March 1986, p. 13.
2. Personal interview, January 20, 1987.
3. Alexander King, "Introduction: A New Industrial Revolution or Just Another Technology?" in Gunter Friedrichs and Adam Schaff, eds., *Microelectronics and Society, For Better or For Worse,* A Report to the Club of Rome, Pergamon, 1986, pp. 1-37.
4. This is from King's discussion of the evolution of the microelectronics industry in *Microelectronics and Society,* pp. 314-318.
5. Alexander King, "The Club of Rome: Reaffirmation of a Mission," *Interdisciplinary Science Reviews,* p. 13.
6. Alexander King, "The Global Perspective," *Nebraska Journal of Economics and Business,* 18:3, Summer 1979, pp. 5-18.
7. *Microelectronics and Society,* p. 319.
8. Personal interview, January 20, 1987.
9. King, "Microelectronics and World Interdependence," in *Microelectronics and Society,* p. 313.
10. Personal interview, January 20, 1987.
11. King, "Microelectronics and World Interdependence," in *Microelectronics and Society, p. 325.*

CHAPTER 14

RICHARD D. LAMM

Governor Lamm is the only U.S. political figure of his generation who has made a systematic and substantial attempt to explore the future. His enormous popularity as governor derives from his performance and his willingness to lay his views on the line. This chapter presents his perspective on the future. In his look toward the political and policy issues of tomorrow, he sees ahead a more controlled, restricted, and regulated environment for the U.S.

KEY VIEWS ABOUT THE FUTURE

1. Public institutions, elected and appointed officials, and individual citizens are unwilling to make the hard choices becoming increasingly necessary.
2. A severe economic crisis looms ahead for the U.S., and economic and political conditions in the rest of the world are deteriorating.
3. The U.S. political system will be more radical, that is, extreme in its measures, in its attempts to control fiscal and social crisis, and turn its back on world disasters by reducing aid and closing its borders.
4. Extremist social movements will arise in response to crisis, promoting social change.
5. The U.S. government will avoid making hard choices on the deficit, on pension obligations, on health care, on immigration, and on defense, until forced to do otherwise by disruption and disorder.
6. An optimistic view of the future based on technological development is false. Technologies are only important insofar as they alleviate or exacerbate social issues.
7. We can expect problems with crime and terrorism, faltering education, law and lawyers, and alarming international and global developments.

BIOGRAPHICAL NOTE

Governor Lamm completed his third and last term as Governor of Colorado in January 1987. He was elected to his first term in 1975 after serving eight years in the Colorado House of Representatives. In early 1987, he taught for six months at Dartmouth as a Montgomery Fellow. He is now an attorney with the firm of O'Connor and Hannan, in Denver.

He was born in 1935, has a Bachelor's degree in business administration from the University of Wisconsin, became a certified public accountant in 1960, and received a law degree from the University of California in 1961. He taught law at the University of Denver from 1969-74. He taught a course, "Hard Choices", at the University of Colorado-Denver Graduate School of Public Affairs. Lamm is head of the Center for Public Policies and Contemporary Issues at the University of Denver.

He is the author of five books: *The Angry West*, with Michael McCarthy in 1982; *Pioneers and Politicians*, with Duane A. Smith, 1984; *Megatraumas: America in the Year 2000*, 1985; *The Immigration Time Bomb: The Fragmenting of America,* with Gary Imhoff, 1985; and the novel *1988*, with Arnold Grossman, 1985. He won the *Christian Science Monitor's* "Peace 2010" essay competition in 1985.

This chapter is based primarily on Lamm's *Megatraumas*, modified by other writings, and further developed in an interview.

WORLDVIEW

> *In the end, more than they wanted freedom, they wanted security. They wanted a comfortable life, and they lost it all—security, comfort, and freedom. When the Athenians finally wanted not to give to society, but for society to give to them; when the freedom they wished for most was the freedom from responsibility, then Athens ceased to be free.*
>
> *Edward Gibbon*[1]

As a futurist and politician, Governor Lamm has a reputation as a doomsayer; he is sometimes referred to as "Governor Gloom." He extrapolates negatively; that is, he chooses to describe only the down side of future trends, building a case for his main point: that the U.S. and the world are heading towards a crisis which current political systems, institutions, and values are not competent to handle. As with many negative extrapolists, the Governor's objective is to drive home the extreme dangers that we face with the hope if not the expectation that this awareness of impending disaster will jar us into a new mental set and guide our behavior in new directions.

The future faces us with hard choices, most of which we are not now equipped to make. He is most concerned with the inability of our political systems to adapt to the future, and is pessimistic about the willingness of people and institutions to be proactive unless forced by an economic and constitutional crisis which will collapse many of the structures of power. The present system he criticizes as being incremental in decisionmaking, locked to the past, and presuming a stable future.[2]

The Governor as Author

Except for *Megatraumas*, Lamm's books have been written in collaboration with a co-author of developed political, ideological and policy views on the chosen subject. *The Immigration Time Bomb*, for example, relies on the immigration policy expertise of Gary Imhoff, who researches policy for the Federation for American Immigration Reform. In each of the books, Governor Lamm develops his theme of hard choices ahead, based on the implications of the policy case made by his co-author. *Megatraumas,* therefore, is a distillation of the Governor's own views on the future without the interposition of another author's policy agenda. It is a book rich in trend data.

In *Megatraumas*, Governor Lamm acknowledges Garrett Hardin, Harrison Brown, Peter G. Peterson, and Lester Brown, of Worldwatch, all of whom have a pessimistic view of the future and of individual and societal capabilities. He acknowledges John Naisbitt, perhaps somewhat ironically, given the latter's positive uplift approach, in *Megatrends* and in *Restructuring the Corporation*. (See the influence diagram at the end of this chapter.)

Our vision of the future is conditioned by our expectations of scientific progress and technological solutions which leads, in Governor Lamm's view, to a false optimism.

> *Our basic, long-term problems are not being solved—they are being covered over. The future, in fact, is much bigger, darker and more problematical than anything our bright new technology can dominate.*[3]

The Coming Crises

He believes the 1980s are a threshold of enormous changes, as was 1914, because great pressures are building with the potential for straining and ripping society's fabric. We are, for example, spending too much of the nation's resources on defense, health care, homes, luxury goods and deferred obligations, and too little on the education of scientists and engineers, on R&D, and on manufacturing, necessary for future economic viability. Our biggest problem is our uncompetitive society, industrially and institutionally.

The coming crises may be weathered only by the use of martial law and a program of national austerity, followed by survival that is dependent on individual self-discipline, thrift, and sacrifice.

America is heading towards a crisis because its leaders:

- Assume continuing prosperity.
- Ignore needed reform in systems such as health care.
- Are not willing to control immigration into the U.S. (the new immigration legislation is only a half-step and its success is dependent on its handling of such issues as amnesty and the reunification of families).
- Allow elections to become bidding contests.
- Borrow assets from the future, in terms of waste, environmental deterioration, and expanding debt.
- Are failing to secure a natural resources base.
- Are allowing the educational system to deteriorate.
- Are not telling the truth to the people.[4]

The Governor assumes that many of the political and policy choices he believes necessary cannot be made without major changes in societal attitudes and values. Therefore support will be generated by radical social movements that arise spontaneously to do the job of changing public opinion and behavior. However, he notes that the appearance of a charismatic and strong leader able to guide the nation through a series of hard choices will be due entirely to luck.

An Optimistic Note

Pressed to look at the up side, the Governor cites four positive points for the future of the U.S.

1. Women entering the workforce. The success of such social movements as the women's movement and the environmental movement are apparent; however the underlying reasons why are not clear to him.
2. The creativity that arises out of the freedom available in our system. A similar creativity may be found in Hungary, compared with the USSR, or in South Korea rather than North Korea.
3. Immigration may be a positive influence on the nation, although he continues to see Mexican immigrants as a burden because they lack the commitment of other immigrant groups to education, hard work and upward mobility.

4. The large reservoir of natural resources possessed by the U.S. (even though these are shrinking).

Positive acts to head off disaster would include educating U.S. workers to an understanding of the world situation, saving more, revitalizing U.S. education, acting to stay healthy, practising restraint, balancing the budget and putting new life into the domestic economy. All these we should work to achieve before 2010.

The Role of Corporations

Lamm ignores any significant role for corporations, labor unions, and religious or philanthropic groups, in causing or preventing our imminent traumas. He focuses on structural problems, and lays the responsibility on political leadership. Corporations (and unions) can be influential by organizing and cooperating on mutual goals, such as a reduction in health care and educational costs. However, corporations like governments will be galvanized only by crisis, in his view.

There is a strong moralistic tone as a countertheme in his writing and speechmaking which assigns blame more personally. This ambiguity is important because a search for moral rather than structural solutions to problems would steer the nation on a different course. For example, his assertion that the U.S. lacks a national purpose and a manifest destiny implies a lost moral direction.

The Futurist as Governor

Futures thinking has informed Lamm's private time, rather than his official functions, perhaps because he sees a futurist as a lonely prophet rather than an organizational insider. His own list of accomplishments in Colorado are those of a modern governor interested in "good" government rather than those of a futurist bringing a futures perspective to the state.[5] Nevertheless futures thinking has been introduced through a Colorado Year 2000 project, and through the formation of a planning group responsible for the state's five year plan.

SPECIFIC ISSUES

Technology

In Governor Lamm's approach to the future, technologies are dealt with only as they alleviate, exacerbate, or respond to social issues. In this, he is out of step with many other futurists, who see technology as a driving force. He sees no scientific or technological developments counteracting our fundamental political, organizational and institutional problems. And he admits he does not understand the role of science and technology as well as he would like.

Crime and Computers

In his scenario, the 1990s are America's most violent decade, caused largely by a public wish for freedom from responsibility for society's ills. Computers are aiding law enforcement and also providing new opportunities for educated criminals. The increasing use of 'the electronic policeman' helps police catch criminals and, since the enactment of a national identification bill, a computer keeps watch on citizens who must all carry identification cards.

On the other hand, computer crimes, most carried out by well-educated criminals, are a fast growing statistic.

Education and Computers

As the educational system declines, computers and related technologies will replace teachers. However the rate of college dropping out will increase.

Health and Computers

The computer's capacity for monitoring and control could be made an instrument of government policy and provide the solution to one of society's most troublesome problems—the increasing cost of health care. A national clearinghouse would be established to track and monitor doctors, hospital beds, and medical equipment.

Employment and Computers

Governor Lamm assumes computers will spur the move to a two-class society by eliminating middle level and medium-skill jobs.

Future Information Societies

The rise of the electronic communications network, linking individuals regardless of location and time, hammers another nail in the coffin of the traditional city, which he expects to continue to decay in the U.S. because the business and trade proximities it supplies are no longer as necessary as they used to be.

Defense and Disarmament

The U.S. overspends on defense without decreasing its vulnerability to a resource war and is undercutting its own economy by transferring wealth into the defense sector.

Governor Lamm forecasts a positive public reaction to future attempts to reduce the defense budget, believing the military system is overstaffed and inefficiently run. Avoiding a nuclear war between now and 2010 is a practical and achievable goal.

Energy

According to the Governor, the OPEC embargo of 1973 ought to have taught us to expect another energy crisis following on the political instability of the Middle East, which is a "political Mt. Saint Helens." His scenario includes continuing conflict among Arab states but with no particular event responsible for the crisis.

Two political outcomes are likely, energy rationing and mandatory conservation.[6]

The Economy

Most of *Megatraumas* views the world from the hindsight of the Year 2000 after the election of the first woman president of the U.S. From this vantage point, the causes of deterioration in the U.S. economy are described as follows:

- Overall, the villain is a trade deficit which was $130 billion in 1984, and accumulating. Restrictions on grain sales to the USSR was a factor in making the U.S. the world's largest debtor nation.

Other factors:

- an overvalued dollar,
- cutthroat foreign competition, based on cheap labor and worldwide unemployment.
- foreign countries' trade restrictions and tariffs—lack of a free market for U.S. goods.
- inadequate investment in new plant and equipment; for example, in the 1970s and 1980s, a critical turning point, Japan was investing 10% of GNP to the U.S.'s 3% of GNP.
- stagnation of productivity.
- an acquired and deserved reputation for shoddy goods.

- fewer new ideas, declining innovation—illustrated by the falloff in new patents.
- U.S. government and businesses, no longer hard Yankee traders, allowing themselves to be cheated and imposed upon by foreign traders.
- poor investment of educational resources—too many lawyers and accountants.
- the end of cheap oil and energy.[7]

A social Darwinism accompanies the deterioration in the U.S. economic position, characterized by the loss of a portion of the middle class and the growth of a two-class society. Highly skilled workers in the new technologies benefit, unskilled workers in the service industries are paid less, and have insecure jobs. As a result, more people will be poor.

Enormous pension obligations and a larger proportion of the elderly in U.S. society may create intergenerational conflict by 2000. If the political structure waits until then to correct inequities in the retirement system and to reduce the burden on the Federal budget, it may be hampered in doing so by the growing political clout of the elderly.

International Economics

The power to control—and thus deny—the flow of critical metals and minerals is likely to be a crucial factor in future global economics.

Japan comes out well in almost all the Governor's policy comparisons, in defense spending, in its investment in plant and equipment, in its priorities for education and in the success of its protectionist trade policies. Japan's organizational genius in serial assembly serves it well, and to sift and adopt Japan's manufacturing approaches would serve the U.S. well, especially since the Japanese approach to U.S. industry has been like that of the poolhall hustler pretending to be innocent of the game long enough to learn the opponent's style and beat him.

Health

One of the Governor's whipping boys is health care, which he describes as a runaway out of control system, an economic cancer catering to a society obsessed with the need to deny death. Thirty percent of all Medicare, for example, is spent on the last months of a patient's life.

He expects a new social movement to establish an individual's right to die at a moment of his or her own choosing and without interference from the medical care system.

Education

The quality of public education is likely to continue a long term decline, contributed to by a drop in college enrollments as students discover a degree is no longer worth the cost and does not, except for the few, produce a well paid job. Colleges are likely to lower standards to encourage enrollment and to suffer from a surfeit of elderly professors as their tenured faculty ages and they lack funds to replace them with younger teachers.

Information technologies are flung into the breach but do not fill the gap.

National apathy about the importance of education to the nation's economic health drives this trend, according to the Governor. He believes self-interest guides most individual choices of study. This results in a glut of lawyers and physicians, as well as an increase in litigiousness and increasingly costly health care. As a wealth-creating institution, our educational system performs indifferently.

Environment

The U.S. has poisoned itself with its own wastes. The national bill for cleanup of toxic waste and groundwater contamination is coming due, presenting a major environmental and public health problem by the year 2000.

Food and Agriculture

The U.S. faces a crisis in its loss of topsoil, as well as serious shortages of water and the effects of climate change occurring as a result of the greenhouse effect.

World Regions and Nations

Overpopulation in many countries is leading to many future evils in Governor Lamm's view, not least an increase in terrorism and limited war. Terrorism may be motivated by politics of the left and right and also by a desire to be noticed in an increasingly anonymous global society.

Poor nations will continue to demand food from the U.S. Only the developed and developing nations are keeping Africa from megafamine. Our willingness to incur these obligations is driven by our religious values, the Governor believes, but he anticipates the U.S. will be less able to maintain support as world hunger increases. To make saying 'no' to requests for international aid plausible, he describes a paradigm shift in Christian religious thinking, a move to reality theology.'

This new theology fosters triage ethics and reinterprets the Gospel to present God's world as harsher and more punishing of disturbances of its ecological balance.[8]

Underdeveloped countries whose development is stalled, have dim prospects. Some bad news:

- Egypt—experiences serious shortages of agricultural land.
- Argentina—lives with endemic revolution.
- The USSR—becomes an aging society, with its ethnic balance tipping power toward its Oriental cultures.

U.S. Political Directions

Immigration is an explosive issue for the U.S. for the next 15-20 years, because, as he says, "a sea of hungry young people surrounds us." Tough policy options on immigration are among the hard choices he anticipates for the U.S. Congress.

In his scenario of life in the U.S. after the crises of the 1990s, he pictures that by 2000 immigration into the U.S. will be limited to immediate relatives, and scores of camps will be established to contain a tide of illegal immigration caused by population pressure in Central and South America.

Among the future consequences of uncontrolled immigration are the following:

- Hispanic generated immigration riots—in Los Angeles in 1997, for example,
- separatist and secession movements in the Southwest—the new nation of Aztlan,
- increasing unemployment,
- declining border control,
- an increase in terrorism,
- energy and resource shortages, and
- disruption of the social order.[9]

U.S. society's ability to assimilate new entrants is being reduced by uncontrolled immigration and policies for treating migrants that will create more ghettos.

UNDERLYING CAUSES

Who is to Blame?

Overpopulation and misuse of resources are driving the world's problems.

In the U.S. Governor Lamm accuses his own generation of political leaders of reacting to the horrors of the Depression and of World War II by mortgaging the economic future of the nation to create security, luxury, and a militaristic peace for those who survived the two events. In time, and he forecasts 1990-2000 as the time, the bills will come due, creating economic and constitutional crises provoking harsh measures—thus presumably creating another scarring 'event' for future generations to react to.

This view implies a roller coaster vision of the future as governments and individuals rebound from crises to prosperity and back.

Lamm is hardly an isolationist, but his strong emphasis on being realistic ("reality theology" and "reality politics") argues very strongly that the nation must think of itself first, set its own affairs in order, and recognize that its first priority is its own long term viability. In some sense, in a world of impending disaster, we must stand strong and not attempt to do everything for everyone.

With no positive image of the future, the best the Governor can hope for the U.S. is a long-term decline and a gentle slide into an economic and social condition like that of England today.

EXHIBIT 14-1

FORCES INFLUENCING THE FUTURIST THINKING OF GOVERNOR RICHARD LAMM

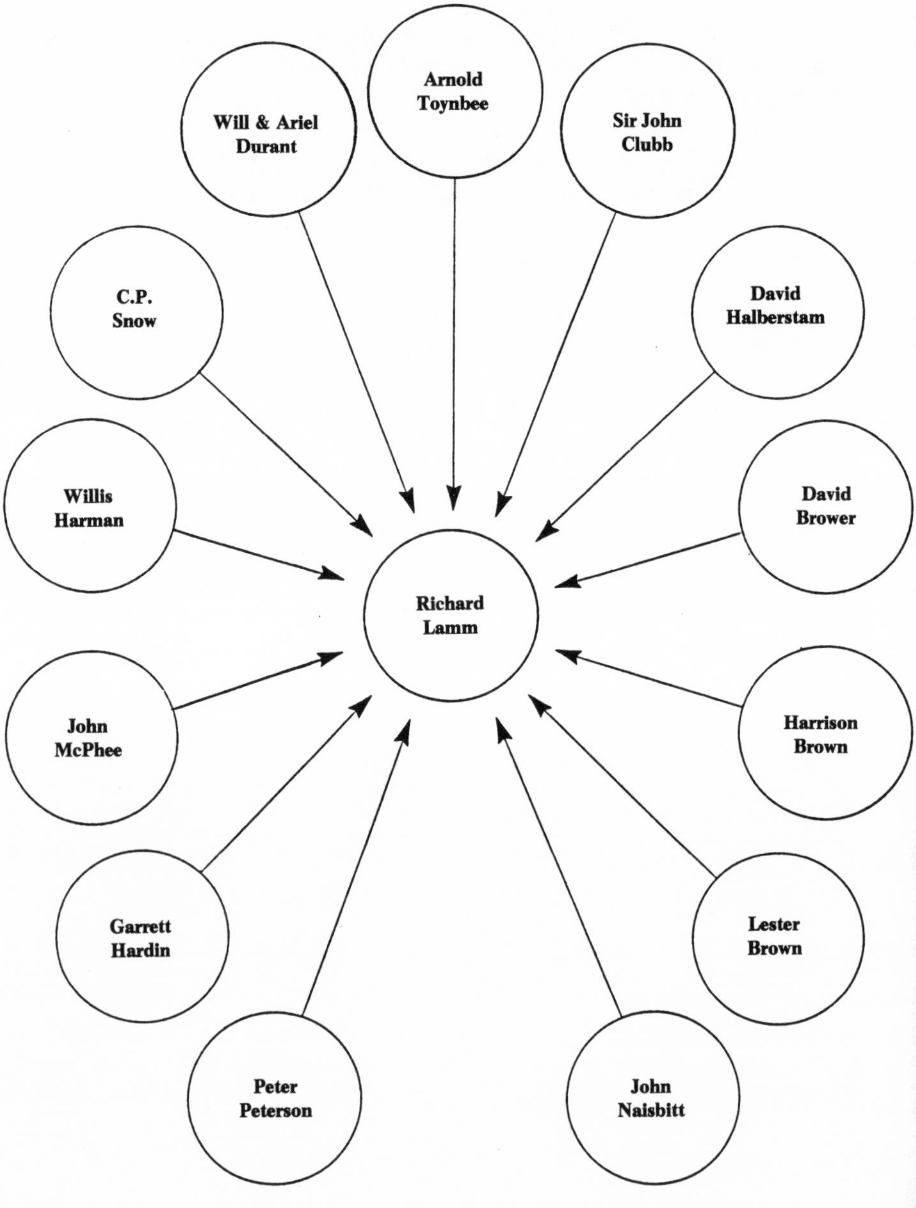

REFERENCES

1. This quote from Gibbon is printed on a card Govenor Lamm hands out and sums up his thinking about the problems of America.
2. Lamm, Governor Richard D., *Megatraumas: American at the Year 2000*, Houghton Mifflin, Boston, 1985, p. 1.
3. Lamm, *Megatraumas*, p. 2.
4. Lamm, *Megatraumas*, p. 21.
5. The Governor's accomplishments in Colorado include:
   a. Health care—progress on health maintenance organizations (HMOs).
   b. Population is up, but welfare rolls are down.
   c. Non-supporting fathers are being pursued.
   d. Greater automation of the state government.
   e. A better focus on business in higher education.
   f. Colorado is eighth highest in job creation, sixth in manufacturing job creation.
   g. The cost of government has gone down every year.
   h. A five year plan for the state has been introduced.
   i. Senior government bureaucrats are reviewed annually.
6. *Megatraumas*, p. 158.
7. *Megatraumas*, p. 25.
8. *Megatraumas*, p. 143.
9. Lamm, *Megatraumas,* Chapter on immigration, pp. 66-81, and Lamm, Governor Richard D., and Gary Imhoff, *The Immigration Time Bomb: The Fragmenting of America*, Dutton, New York, 1985.

CHAPTER 15

MICHAEL MARIEN

Michael Marien is the outstanding bibliographer of the futures field. His on-going reconnoiter provides the wealth of material found in *Future Survey*, **and** *Future Survey Annual.* **In consequence, he has become one of the foremost critics of futures thinking and of its practitioners.**

KEY VIEWS ABOUT THE FUTURE

1. Events, ideas, and technologies shape the future.
2. The intellectual task of seeing and integrating the many pieces of knowledge we have of our complex physical, environmental, governmental, and social systems is our outstanding world problem. Most observers are far too complacent in their worldviews.
3. A new age of ignorance is upon us as the gap between what we know and what we need to know widens. We need new skills, and new worldviews.
4. A global economic collapse could be more devastating than the explosion of one, or perhaps several, nuclear weapons and is more likely, at least in the short term. An economic collapse can be prepared for by raising international consciousness; but such a prospect could increase the likelihood of its occurrence.
5. New information technologies will have less effect on schools than many anticipate because these institutions have more purposes than learning. Although the idea of individual access to the world's storehouse of intellectual wealth is appealing, educational offerings will continue to compete against a proliferating array of enticing entertainments in and out of school.
6. Multiple transformations are reshaping society, in technologies, in demography, in energy, but a shift to so-called "new age" values is not likely to be one of the transformations in the short term. There is no evidence of a widespread change in values.

BIOGRAPHICAL NOTE

Michael Marien lives in LaFayette, New York, where he works at home reading, reviewing, and abstracting for *Future Survey,* a monthly abstract journal of books and articles on trends, forecasts and proposals for the future. It is published by the World Future Society. He founded the journal in January 1979, and he also edits the *Future Survey Annual,* derived from the monthly. In the annual, Marien's subscribers can read his picks of the year's publications and his annual chart of important hopes and fears for the future.

Marien earned a BS at Cornell in 1959, an MBA in organizational theory at Berkeley in 1964 and a Ph.D. in interdisciplinary social science from Syracuse in 1970. He has monitored the writings of futurists, system theorists, as well as reformers and visionaries for almost 20 years. He is co-editor of *What I Have Learned: Thinking About the Future Then and Now*, Greenwood Press, 1987.

This chapter is based on an interview with Marien, and a review of his writing. Much of what he communicates about the future is evident in the huge volume of reviews and abstracts he compiles for *Future Survey.* Marien estimates that the *Survey* is read by corporate managers and planners (25%), academics and academic administrators (25%), consultants (15%), public sector officials and planners (10%), and the remainder a diverse group of professionals. He would like more planners to read the *Survey*, and for it to reach more concerned citizens. From about 12,000 pieces of non-fiction literature on the future Marien has abstracted 8,500 cites in *Future Survey.*

Those thinkers who have influenced him most are the sociologist, William Ogburn, Herman Kahn, Bertram Gross, de Jouvenel, John Gardner, Yehezkel Dror, and during the 1970s, Ivan Illich and Theodore Roszak. To put this in perspective, however, the greatest positive and negative influence has been from everyone he has read, to a greater degree than any individual. "I learned from everyone." Marien cites as negative influences, Daniel Bell, Buckminster Fuller, and John Naisbitt, describing their work as pretentious and overrated.

WORLDVIEW

Michael Marien brings order and shape to the hundreds of ideas he encounters each year by abstracting the material for *Future Survey.* For his own, and his subscribers' enlightenment, he categorizes and lists key ideas and approaches to the future. He holds intellectual work to high standards and therefore considers it morally imperative to be critical, hostile, and even satirical in approaches to the future he considers unintelligent.

One might think that contemporary standards of rational thought would insist that all facets of every problem be identified, and that all proposed solutions should be carefully weighed, debated, refined, and—where possible—combined. Such a scholarly ideal is virtually the antithesis of the parochial chaos of contemporary thought.[1]

Marien identifies three broad categories of driving forces, events, ideas and technologies. In his view, weaknesses in much thinking about the future are a narrow frame of reference and one-sided arguments. A recurrent minor weakness is the failure to allow for the force of major events that shape human affairs. Good ideas implemented by those in power can reduce the likelihood of bad events, can make society resilient, help people lead better lives. We are short of these large, guiding notions because our intellectual infrastructure is made up of separate and isolated disciplines. We lack the ability and motivation to cross boundaries, collect the good ideas, and integrate them into coherent images. Sometimes a crisis created by an event, such as the Vietnam war, can encourage boundary-crossing.

Competent futurists, according to Marien, should counter intellectual fragmentation with broad, integrative work.[2] Observing the North American variety of the species, Marien developed a tentative taxonomy based on whether they were in the mainstream of futures thinking or at the margin. In the mainstream he groups the synoptic generalists, the quantitative forecasters, the normative generalists, the pop futurists, the multi-identity futurists, and the specialized futurists. On the margin are the futurized specialist who thinks about the future of his specialty, the closet, or hidden, unadmitted futurist who thinks about the future but does not ally himself with "the field," the future futurist, (or student futurist) and the forgotten futurist, whose work may have become classic but is neglected because he or she has died.[3]

Marien believes our intellectual task to understand, integrate, and use the many pieces of knowledge we have of our complex physical, environmental, governmental and social systems is the greatest task of world management.[4] We stumble because we cannot organize and focus our energies sufficiently to do the task, and because of ideological and egotistical indulgence.

SPECIFIC ISSUES

Key Potential Events that May Shape the Future

- A nuclear weapon explodes, not necessarily in war, perhaps as an accident or terrorist act. Marien sets this as a 50-50 probability by 2000, but one which could positively alter the course of human affairs. A nuclear event would of course be tragic but could have a beneficial outcome in the long-run if, by killing people and upsetting ideas, it led to the end of, or significant reduction of, the arms race, thus redirecting available wealth away from military production. This could only be possible if a nuclear explosion remained a limited event and was not followed by a larger war.

- A global economic collapse could be more devastating than a nuclear explosion and is more likely. An economic collapse can be prepared for by raising international consciousness of its possibility; but such a debate could increase the likelihood of its occurrence.

Key On-going Events that are Shaping the Future

- World population growth and worldwide pollution are large events created by millions of incremental small events whose sum is negative.
- The spread of AIDS.

Societal Transformations

Marien believes multiple transformations, not well-understood by anyone, are reshaping society, in technologies, in events and ideas, but a shift to so-called "new age" values is not one of these transformations in the near future, at least. He accuses so-called "transformationalists" of equating intentions with results, and sees no evidence of a widespread change in values.[5]

The Information Society[6]

Our capacity to communicate will be multiplied by the new technologies but we will not necessarily communicate better. Automation, while displacing a large part of the female office workforce may tend to move the office into the home. But the trend is overrated by people fantasizing a technological fix for commuter traffic jams. He notes the following other impacts of information technology:

- commerce—an increase in teleshopping may lead to better information exchanges between buyers and sellers.
- health—more access for the individual to medical knowledge, more self-monitoring, more implanted monitors, and more use of computer-based psychotherapy.
- entertainment—a glut of options, better quality technically, not necessarily artistically.

- education—the information society will have less effect on schools than many anticipate because these institutions have more purposes than learning; day care, for example. Although the idea of individual access to the world's storehouse of intellectual wealth is appealing, educational offerings will contrive to compete against more enticing entertainments.
- knowledge—the information society demands a new standard of literacy and competence. On the other hand, a new age of ignorance is growing as the gap between what we know and what we need to know widens. We need new skills and new worldviews. The knowledge gap should be a question of national security, receiving national attention and be the stimulus of an ongoing national forum for discussion and debate.
- politics—the technology has promising possibilities for democratic access that will not necessarily be realized if society moves more towards collecting information on and monitoring its citizens electronically. Narrowcasting specific messages to target certain voters is a more likely development.
- mass communication—mass broadcasting gave us shared experiences. The new concentration on diversity, different audiences and narrowcasting fragments information into specialized interests, a trend likely to produce a rich diversity of experience and a splintered chaos of conflicting perspectives.
- families—better communications technologies will be available if family members want to make more contact with each other, but at the same time, the variety of specialized entertainments available at home may strain family bonds.
- quality of life—not necessarily better, for most of us. Workloads will be poorly distributed. Professionals will work longer hours and others may not have enough work to do. We will be obliged to talk more to machines. A computer may become a best friend and teacher.

Movement into the information society could be halted by catastrophe, such as an electromagnetic pulse from an above-ground nuclear explosion. Or it may be sidelined somewhat by revolutionary impacts of other developing technologies, in bioengineering, for example.

Technologies

Marien clusters information technologies, biotechnologies and materials technology as a revolutionary group. Energy technologies trail at present because the social and economic impetus moving new energy ideas is at low tide. Military technologies, especially those of the Star Wars initiative, have revolutionary potential, but an uncertain political future.

The mood swings of a nation like the U.S., shifting from a shallow pessimism in the 1970s to an even more shallow optimism in the early 1980s, can affect emerging revolutions in many technologies, such as computers and telecommunications, biotechnology, nuclear weaponry and energy. In optimistic times, the nation encourages new technologies. In a pessimistic mood, as it was a decade ago, the U.S. becomes more concerned about technology that is appropriate and safe rather than high. Several forces or events could bring back that pessimism:

- a technologically created catastrophe, or an American Chernobyl or Bhopal—demonstrating that it can happen here.

Under a new political regime:

- a re-evaluation of human needs resulting in a somewhat lower technology approach, and possibly, a lowered prestige for natural scientists,
- a re-evaluation of national and corporate profit opportunities in high technology, questioning our need for a high-tech race, and
- a new policy of satisfying human needs in order to promote national security; higher prestige for social scientists.

Education

Marien names three important actors in education who are underplaying their roles; universities, public libraries, and corporations. Universities are missing their opportunity to promote a worldview with an integrative school of future studies and world studies on every campus. Public libraries are neglecting their responsibility for increasing civic awareness of major issues. Corporations must educate themselves and their communities about the dynamic environment in which they operate especially the deteriorating public "commons" that we all must share, the physical infrastructure, for example.

Institutions

Current institutions of higher learning are ineffectual, Marien complains, because they generate hundreds of solutions or partial solutions to public problems and cannot invent, or lack incentive to invent, a mechanism for bringing people together to integrate the ideas and decide on priorities.

Marien has recorded 75 ideas on reforming the economy and 60 methods for managing the arms race.[7] This profusion comes, he believes, in the first instance, from the fragmentation, triviality, and hubris encouraged at institutions of higher learning. The institutions of the intellectual infrastructure need renewal if they are to provide a forum for serious consideration of world issues. The World Future Society potentially offers such a forum, although not achieving national or international status and attention. Since the *Global 2000* report to the President in 1980, outstanding U.S. government-sponsored thinking on world issues has lapsed. Marien suggests debate should especially be focused on an examination of technological threats and promises for world stability, peace, and wellbeing.[8]

U.S. Political Directions

Policies of anticipation and preparation can equip us for disasters such as hurricanes, or other unexpected events that might disrupt society. Marien believes, however, that even as we improve our preparation we may, ironically, be falling behind. In education, for example, as we improve the system arithmetically, the need for improvement increases geometrically. We think that we know more about the economy today than we ever did, yet the problems and potential for disaster seem to be worsening. Marien, a Democrat, is unsympathetic to current policies, especially in foreign affairs.

He advocates focusing on the national value of human resources and the importance of avoiding waste, especially through foreign follies, such as funding the Contras. His concept would direct the U.S. to full employment, to some form of universal health insurance with cost penalties for those who endanger their health, to services to reduce teenage pregnancy, to voluntary civilian national service for young people, to a consensus on dealing with drug abuse, to reform of the criminal justice system, decent housing for the poor, and a greater emphasis of science and technology towards social mechanisms and human solutions to problems, especially the growing threat of AIDS.

Marien characterizes two ideas of a post-industrial society as opposed. One, that of Daniel Bell and Herman Kahn, describes a service or an information society of high technology, global interdependence, wealth and leisure. The other, described by E.F. Schumacher, Theodore Roszak and Willis Harman, among others, views the emerging society as decentralized, ecologically-oriented and employing appropriate or human-scale technology. This, according to Marien, is a potential re-emergence of the Hamilton-Jefferson debate and represents the poles of an axis at right angles to the traditional right-wing, left-wing axis of political thought.[9] Along this alternative axis futurists divide into two groups, those engaged in forecasting measurable trends, the acceptance of conventional measures and structures of society and being "reasonable" and "objective," and those "normative generalists" who focus on idealistic visions of revolutionary transition.

Environment

Marien believes we need a new economic accounting for the environmental and human costs of ecological degradation. Such an accounting ought to bring more money to pay for environmental clean-up. Sooner or later we will have to pay, one way or another.

Energy

Decisions on research and development in energy are based on less than full cost of the specific source. A more truthful accounting would be likely to further discourage use of nuclear power, and encourage other options, some of which are dormant at present. We have many options.[10]

Defense and Disarmament

Marien favors reducing by 20-50% U.S. spending on weapons. In order to justify beating swords into ploughshares, however, (1) world tensions must be reduced, (2) a broader definition of national security is needed, and (3) military procurement must be reformed. As one of many bridge-building efforts, a joint U.S.-Soviet mission to Mars may be the idea that would keep the scientists and engineers employed and be a highly visible peaceful and cooperative enterprise.[11]

Values

Marien identifies multiple transformations, in technologies and in demographics for example, but rejects the transformationalists' view that a shift to "new age" thinking and lifestyles is occurring or will occur spontaneously. Spontaneous swings and shifts in general and public attitudes do happen for reasons not well understood. It has been suggested that public consciousness spirals to new levels at certain intervals. A more likely possibility—to Marien—is a combination of event-triggered attitude change and policies which institutionalize that change. Marien believes we have shifted away from the 1970s expectation/hope of transformation to an appropriate technology culture, and this move to the "high-tech" 1980s has some connection to our becoming more comfortable with computers and their potential impacts and possibilities.[12] But we may be shifting again to some greater sense of "we-ness" and concern for public interest, as is suggested by Schlesinger's theory of 30 year political cycles.

A catastrophic event, however, such as an economic collapse or a limited nuclear war, could cause public attitudes and values to shift to low-tech "sustainable" approaches, while also encouraging evangelism and survivalism.

UNDERLYING CAUSES

Ideas and images motivate a society and drive its policy and actions. If the intellectual infrastructure of the well-educated and the institutions of higher education continue to foster triviality and fragmentation and fail to integrate ideas then, Marien believes, our governing capability declines. Futurists and decisionmakers alike have an interest in maintaining the flow of constructive ideas and bringing them together to address public issues.

EXHIBIT 15-1

FORCES INFLUENCING THE FUTURIST THINKING OF MICHAEL MARIEN

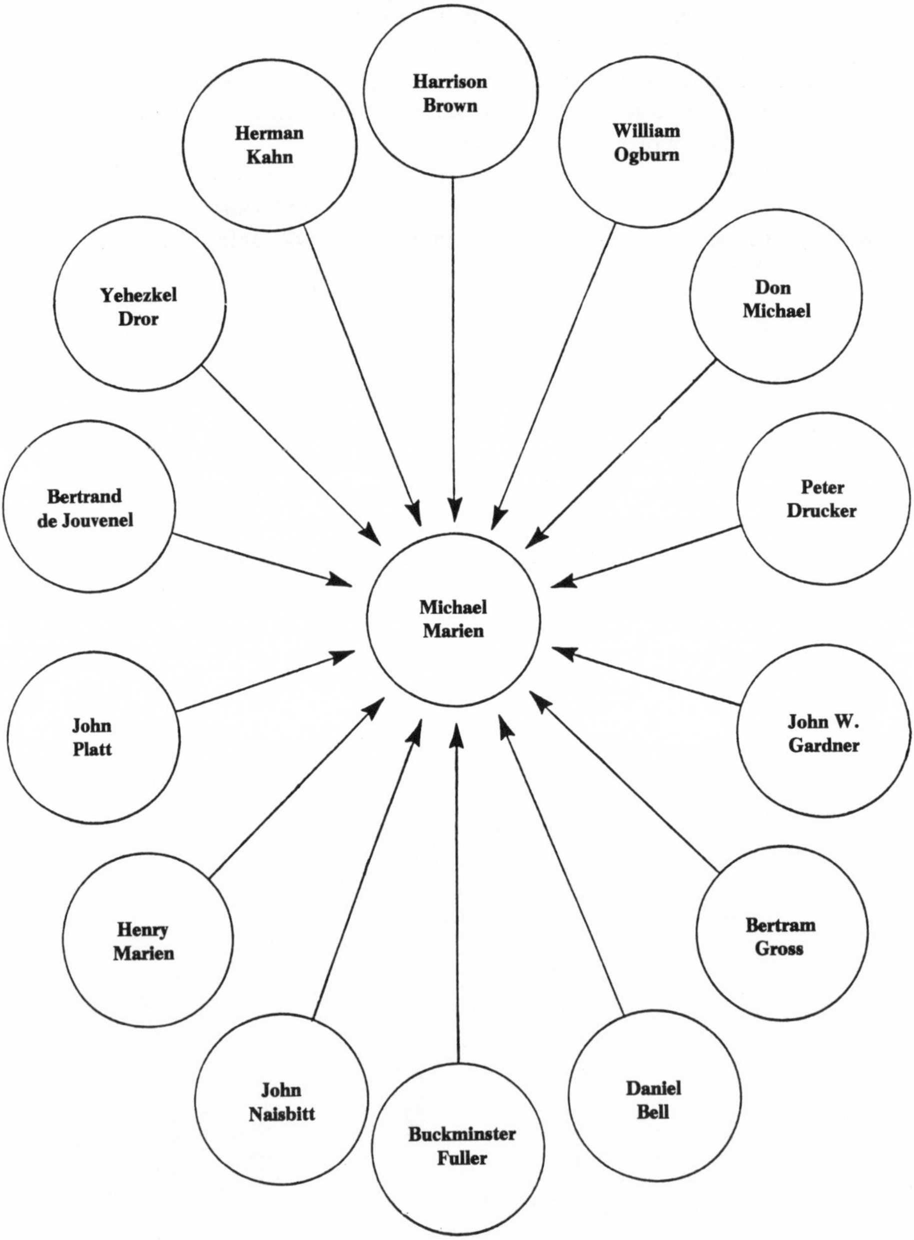

REFERENCES

1. *Future Survey Annual 1985*, World Future Society, Bethesda, MD, p. vi.
2. "Toward a New Futures Research: Insights from Twelve Types of Futurists," *Futures Research Quarterly*, 1:1, Spring 1985, pp. 13-35.
3. *Futures Research Quarterly*, Spring 1985.
4. "The Two Post-Industrialisms and Higher Education," *World Future Society Bulletin*, XVI:3, May/June 1982, p. 18.
5. From an interchange in the *Journal of Humanistic Psychology*, Fall and Winter, 1983, between Marien and Marilyn Ferguson, author of *The Aquarian Conspiracy.* Marien's first article in the journal, "The Transformation as Sandbox Syndrome," *JHP*, 23:1 Winter, 1983, began the exchange.
6. "Some Questions for the Information Society," *The Information Society*, 3:2, 1984, pp. 181-197.
7. *Future Survey Annual 1984*, pp. 185-189.
8. "How Can Sleepers Waken—and Stay Awake? Some Hopes for the Australian Commission for the Future," *Prometheus*, 3:2, December 1985, p. 251.
9. *World Future Society Bulletin*, May/June 1982, p. 19.
10. *Future Survey Annual*, "55 Ways to End the Energy Crunch," 1980-1981, p. viii.
11. Also see Appendix 1, *Future Survey Annual 1984*, pp. 185-186, for many potentially good ideas.
12. "Hope, Fear, and Technology: Changing Prospects in the 1980s," *Vital Speeches of the Day*, 51:5, December 15, 1984, pp. 137-142.

Additional Readings:

Michael Marien, "125 Impacts of New Information Technologies," Appendix 1, *Future Survey Annual 1986*, pp. 185-186. [*Marien notes:* The most important of these impacts are discussed in "Assessing Information Technology in Time and Space: You Ain't Seen Nothing Yet," to be published in Tom Forester (ed), *Information Technology and Society*, (MIT Press, 1989)].

Michael Marien, "What is the Nature of our Embryonic Enterprise? An Open Letter to Wendell Bell," *Futures Research Quarterly*, 3:4, Winter 1987-1988. [*Marien*—in which the extent of fragmentation is described, as well as reasons why futures studies is not (yet) a field.]

CHAPTER 16

DENNIS L. MEADOWS

Dennis Meadows is a global modeler, simulation gaming expert, engineer and practitioner of a lifestyle of voluntary simplicity. He is co-author of *The Limits to Growth,* a report for the Club of Rome, one of the most widely-distributed, disputed, and controversial books on the future ever published.

KEY VIEWS ABOUT THE FUTURE

1. It is difficult for most people to accept the future in terms of plausible alternatives, rather than hoping for a return of an attractive past which is an alternative no longer available.
2. Technology cannot long outstrip its cultural support. Society must evolve to provide an infrastructure for the new techniques before their use can be sustained.
3. The strategic implications for nations of decisions made by large corporate entities, linked globally in real time by telecommunications, are serious.
4. Our perception, looking back from 2050, will be that to have been born just after World War II in the U.S. was to have been born into a good time, and that life since then has been increasingly less pleasant for the average American.
5. The big question is: how can we organize society to provide a good life for all without requiring continual growth in production and in the use of energy?
6. If the warning (in *The Limits to Growth*) is ignored we will lose any opportunity to adapt gracefully to important physical limits. We will become the unprepared victims of political and social events, such as oil shocks, that are the socio-economic symptoms of approaching the physical limits of growth.

BIOGRAPHICAL NOTE

Dennis Meadows is professor of engineering at Dartmouth College, New Hampshire. One of his central interests is the theory and application of computer simulation models for analysis of complex socioeconomic systems. He is also involved in the design and use of microcomputer-based management training games. Currently he is director of The Balaton Group, a consortium of institutes in 22 countries that focus on policies to provide high resource productivity on a sustained basis. He is engaged in a study of the political and economic implications of natural resource depletion, with a special focus on fossil fuels and forest resources. He has a B.A. from Carleton College, where he graduated magna cum laude, and a Ph.D. in management from MIT, in 1969.

Meadows directed the MIT research team, with Donella Meadows, Jorgen Randers, and William W. Behrens III, that produced a report for the Club of Rome's Project on the Predicament of Mankind, *The Limits to Growth,* in 1972.[1] The report, as a book, sold 7 million copies worldwide and has been translated into at least 35 languages.[2]

Meadows spent a year in 1983-84 as director of integrative and special studies at the International Institute for Applied Systems Analysis (IIASA), Laxenburg, Austria. He is associate editor for *Simulation and Games, Technological Forecasting and Social Change,* and *System Dynamics Review.* He is U.S. project leader for the Soviet-American Bilateral Agreement in Environmental Education and president of the International System Dynamics Society, as well as a member of the North American and International Simulation and Gaming Associations.

Meadows himself lives in voluntary simplicity, as a vegetarian, in a communal house, raising vegetables and animals, yet using advanced technologies, such as in information processing for microcomputer modeling and research.

With Donella Meadows and others, he is also the editor of several books including, *Toward Global Equilibrium*, 1973, *Dynamics of Growth in a Finite World,* 1974, *Alternatives to Growth - I*, 1977. This chapter is based on a review of these and other publications and an interview with Meadows. Since *The Limits to Growth*, he says he prefers to work on new methods for constructing and implementing computer simulation models. Recently, this has involved him in introducing microcomputer-based games to a range of students from high school to government officials. He is executive director of the International Network of Resource Information Centers (INRIC). For this group, Meadows has run courses on modeling of regional and environmental problems for government officials in more than 20 countries, mostly in Western and Eastern Europe.

Meadows was attracted to system dynamics at MIT and it proved to be a technique well adapted to a study of the future. After he met members of the Club of Rome, he extended his work on the forecasting of commodity prices to global issues. This led to his work on global modeling and *The Limits to Growth.*

WORLDVIEW

Dennis Meadows gained the reputation of a doomsayer with the publication of *The Limits to Growth*, but since then he has moved away from broad analysis of world problems to concentrate on specific problems or issues and the societal and political moves needed for their resolution.

He describes himself as a dissenter from the generally held view that we have the potential for perpetual growth and improvement in personal welfare. For him the big question for the future ought to be, how can we organize society to provide a good life for all without demanding continual growth in production and the use of energy?[3]

It is difficult for most people to accept that an attractive steady-state society is a plausible alternative. People tend to compare any future possibilities with an era or a time in the past they liked; they implicitly want to return to the 1950s and 1960s, for example.[4] That was an attractive time for the U.S., when prices were low and energy was cheap. Such an industrial golden age will never come again.

New indices of progress are needed. The ones we have principally measure economic growth; they do not indicate, for example, the resilience of our economy and society to unexpected shocks. Consequently, few corporate managers understand that the days of unlimited growth are over, and no corporation has developed a long term plan that embraces the notion of limits to growth.

Nevertheless, mechanisms are developing to constrain corporations, just as similar mechanisms have developed in industrialized nations to slow population growth. Meadows sees corporations as continuing an ineffective struggle against these mechanisms which increasingly will limit their growth. For example, every time a public interest group forces a corporation to pay for environmental cleanup, capital is diverted from expansion.

Based on the impact of the worldwide dissemination of *The Limits to Growth*, The Club of Rome believes the report is influencing attitudes. Challenges and counter-challenges greeted the report's conclusions, but although skepticism continues, the notion of limits to growth has become more widely known. Meadows hoped the report would stimulate debate and change opinions about economic growth as a desirable goal. He intended to influence the worldview of the student who might some day be chief executive officer of a multinational corporation. For those who worked on the project, the work offered an opportunity to study long term world trends, and a certain notoriety for their ideas.

Using a world systems model based on work by Professor Jay Forrester at MIT, *The Limits to Growth* examined interactions among five factors influencing growth: population, agricultural production, natural resources, industrial production, and pollution. The report concluded that unless growth in industrial production, pollution and population were drastically reduced, there would be, sometime in the 21st century, a crisis in which it would no longer be possible to maintain prevailing standards of living around the world. That this is a worst case scenario not likely to happen as predicted escaped many readers of the report. Since the report's publication, Meadows and the other authors have interpreted, explained, expanded on, and defended their conclusions. In 1980, Meadows commented that he saw *The Limits to Growth* as an awful warning of the consequences of poor, or no, long term planning for a no-growth society. If the warning is ignored, he said, we would lose the opportunity to adapt gracefully. We will become the unprepared victims of political and social events, such as oil shocks, that are the inevitable socioeconomic symptoms of approaching the physical limits of growth.[5]

The *The Limits to Growth* model excludes extensive consideration of the effects on growth of price or of new and emerging technology, and the possibility for a transformation in human values. Meadows believes price is an effective constraint on resource use, although it can be outweighed by other factors. It was left out of the model because its inclusion would not have altered the basic conclusions.

Meadows also concludes that human values drive the direction of innovation. Based on past experience, a gradual shift in opinions and attitudes towards limiting growth is more likely than any sudden transformation.

SPECIFIC ISSUES

The U.S. Economy

Meadows subscribes to the Kondratieff wave theory. A cluster of phenomena associated with a steep downcurve of the Kondratieff cycle will strongly influence the U.S. and the world economy. About 15 years from today, the U.S. will be starting back on the best part of the Kondratieff upcurve after a period of inevitable turbulence.

In the past a war, occurring after the downcurve, has enabled nations to junk obsolescent industrial capacity and begin again, as well as rearranging capital and debt structures. Without the option of a war, the U.S. must discover a way to dump excess and obsolete capacity and get rid of its debt. Meadows believes the debt cannot be paid and must be written off or devalued drastically through inflation. The process of writing off unpayable debts in the Third World has already begun by U.S. banks.

Defense and Disarmament

The U.S. has built a military infrastructure around national security and military aspirations that it cannot support for long, especially as a debtor nation. The U.S. cannot afford to sustain such large flows of capital into the weapons economy, so that over the next 15 years, the political structure of the world and the internal political structure of the U.S. will change, with the U.S. no longer being the biggest kid on the block.

A trend towards disarmament will be pushed by the Soviets. Their priority will be to cut back the world weapons economy in an effort to avoid their own bankruptcy. The U.S. economy may be hard hit by a cutback in the world arms business.

More than half of the scientific and technological manpower in the U.S. is devoted to the military economy, with serious adverse consequences for competitiveness in non-military fields.

Another issue is the effect on the freedom and openness of science when a large number of scientists are obligated to a central and highly politicized military authority.

International Economics

Meadows believes the toughest global problems will include those related to allocating diminishing resources. Technological advance can extend the period required for adapting to relative scarcity, and it can permit some shifts in usage patterns, but drastic social and economic changes will in any event be required. Among the processes that will require social and political responses are:

- the shift by industry towards drastically increased use of recycling technologies,
- the accommodation of society to ever more expensive oil and to political dependence on the low cost petroleum producers,
- the resolution of demands by the poor for a share of the wealth produced principally by the richer nations,

- the reversal of past trends towards chemically-intensive agriculture to move towards technologies that deliberately regenerate the productivity of the ecosystem,
- the evolution of economic systems to reward conservation more than production and to emphasize the maintenance of current stocks rather than the generation of new flows,
- the development of new data systems and political criteria that stress an economy's robustness rather than its growth and equity, rather than average income,
- the coordination of international action to avoid irreversible damage to the global commons—ozone depletion, ocean pollution, fish banks depletion, deforestation of the tropics, erosion of soils, and carbon dioxide accumulation.

To Meadows, the likelihood of more discontinuities, either in physical, social or political world systems grows higher as we push against the boundaries of these systems. Worsening of the world debt crisis, for example, could cause a global financial shock, the details of which are unclear.

World Regions

There are two Africas, Moslem Africa and Black Africa. Black Africa is facing the most serious problems, including AIDS. The future of the two Africas will depend in part on the extent to which the countries importing African resources, Europe and the USSR, become involved in the continent's affairs.

Many nations, those in Africa are examples, are merely political artifacts. These are likely to break up and reform along religious, tribal, or ethnic lines. In Africa this may produce further chaos. In the Soviet Union, any opening up of the system's rigidities may have implications for its cohesion and the possibility of new alignments.

U.S. Political Directions

Meadows, while modest about his understanding of the political priorities pursued by the U.S., believes that between massive growth in the U.S. foreign and domestic debt on one hand and the growing proliferation of nuclear weapons on the other, U.S. policies are leading towards ever narrower options.

His ideal political direction is towards political and economic mechanisms that will promote a sustainable society. Using Herman

Daly's concept of a steady-state economy as one with a constant stock of physical wealth and people maintained in a fluctuating balance, Meadows argues that such a society need not be primitive either culturally or technologically. It does, however, imply use of renewable energy sources or the diminished use of nonrenewables. People in this society would come naturally to prefer activities low in their use of energy and materials.

The route to this society involves short-term sacrifice, the use of fail-safe technologies to guard against human error and disruptive accident, and a long, slow process of rebalancing societal systems.

The Future of U.S. and Multinational Corporations

Distinctions between corporations and national government entities will continue to blur. General Dynamics is now, for example, no longer an organization separate from the U.S. government's military establishment. Meadows bases this argument on the increasing size of some corporations. Because they are so big, their actions begin to have national economic and strategic implications.

One factor increasing their impact is the development of telecommunications links around the world. These links permit giant entities to be coordinated globally in real time. A purchase in Hoboken can be instantly reflected in inventory in Singapore. Besides political effects, the emerging links will pose new sets of industrial and management control issues. One such issue, for example, will be the political impact of management in New York or Amsterdam laying off employees in Hong Kong or Brisbane. Meadows points out that the U.S. attempted to manage Viet Nam war from Washington in this way and that did not work. Minor breakdowns in global business links may annoy, but catastrophic failure could disrupt the global financial system.

Environment

Even though the public may long for the lost golden age of U.S. industrial expansion, their concern for the environment has built a movement that cannot be readily turned back by appeals for growth, Meadows believes. A new public understanding of the interaction between economic growth, environmental effects and the wellbeing of the individual underlies the movement's strength.

Nagging environmental problems will come to be explosive issues in the next 15-25 years as a consequence of long term overuse of resources. For example, some of these are:

- the economic and ecological consequences of the loss of forests, especially the tropical forests,
- the damage from acid rain pollution in forests, bodies of water, and structures,
- the depletion of ozone,
- the accumulation of toxic wastes,
- the pollution of most ground waters, and
- the erosion of prime soils.

Any one of these problems, if a disastrous event occurs, such as an episode of water pollution that causes deaths in a large city, can exert great leverage on the public's attitude to the environment. The public's attitude in the U.S. includes assumptions about technological solutions which it prefers over changes in individual behavior or organizational practices. Technology can improve choices on the disposal of toxics, for example, but the least expensive and best long term choice on waste disposal is to produce less waste, and this requires lifestyle changes.

Health

AIDS will run its course over the next 25 years, and it is likely to influence the world profoundly, as well as the U.S. and U.S. business. As an epidemic, AIDS has not killed, and is not likely to kill as many people as some other epidemics but as a disease, it has certain new characteristics:

- The presence of a very large number of relatively young people who will know for several years that they are going to die introduces a new feature into society, with influence on societal ethics, civil disobedience, and so on.
- Health care services will be overloaded.
- People will have to learn how to live and work for years in the midst of friends and co-workers who are contagious victims slow to show signs of the disease.
- The effects on the Third World will be devastating because it cannot absorb the changes nor afford the care available in the First World. It will also lose a significant fraction of its trained personnel.

The effects on Africa, especially, will be extreme. In certain places in black Africa, a third or more of the males between 20 and 40 will die before the end of the century.

AIDS is a discontinuity in the long term trend towards improved public health in advanced nations, and a disastrous setback for parts of the developing world. Like other discontinuities, it rends the social fabric and induces changes faster than society can adapt. If we maintain our present, Western values, philosophies of treatment, and habits then AIDS may bankrupt the health care system. Meadows believes the U.S. should expect its citizens to take personal responsibility for their health and to shift health care towards prevention rather than treatment.

Education

Meadows is skeptical of the influence of information technology on education, because people have hailed the arrival of the computer-educated society for 30 years. He believes the technology can be and is available, but the educational content will be simplified and trivialized. More education is already being done by businesses than by colleges. This, however, is frequently narrowly focused on commercial interests.

Cities

As a consequence of decline in real wealth, home ownership patterns in the U.S. are likely to become more European, with more renters, as fewer people anticipate ever owning a home.

Values

Our values will eventually include a perception that if we were to look back from 2050, to have been born in World War II in the U.S. was to have been born into a good time, a good life, and that life since then has been less pleasant. Some examples of what will cause that shift in perception:

- influenced by AIDS, a change in our sexual mores,
- increasing evidence of environmental damage will alter our attitude to the environment,
- based on diminishing real wealth, we will have less expectation of ever becoming prosperous, and
- social, political, and economic attitudes are likely to become more conservative.

Energy

By the mid-1990s, as cheaper oil stocks are depleted, the world will experience new oil shocks at least as serious as earlier ones. Meadows believes Japan is preparing for the next shock while the U.S. does little.

Future energy use forecasts are often flavored with hopeful assumptions about new energy technologies over the horizon that will permit an easy transition from rising oil prices to an abundance of cheap power. In most cases on closer examination, these technologies turn out to be neither cheap nor abundant. Meadows' message is—there is no cheap energy, nor will there ever be.

Technology

Artifacts of a society that derive from technical laws can change more quickly than moral or social structures that are interconnected with those structures. Technology cannot outstrip its cultural support. It is true that technology and science can give more data and provide tools to outflank the control systems of society as may occur in biotechnology. However society must evolve to build an infrastructure for the new techniques before they can be used widely and sustainably. Star Wars, for example, will not happen; not only is the technology not there, the cultural and societal support is missing.

Important developments in technology likely to have revolutionary effects on the U.S. and world business are:

- The continuing development of microelectronics over the next 15 years.
- Other computer related technologies such as voice input to microprocessors—in about 15 years we should be able to input voice data in a robust fashion, in other words, be able to ask a computer a question over the telephone.
- Superconductors—in 15-20 years will create a technological upheaval.
- Expert systems will have revolutionary effects 20 years ahead.
- Biotechnology.

UNDERLYING CAUSES

A change in public attitudes, such as attitudes towards large families and fertility that occurred in industrialized countries, may bring about profound societal change without anyone being able to say when, or why, the attitude change occurred. However the time period is almost always long. An event, or a changing set of conditions, that begins a process of change gradually gathers momentum until it has its full impact 10-15 years later.

EXHIBIT 16-1

FORCES INFLUENCING THE FUTURIST THINKING OF DENNIS MEADOWS

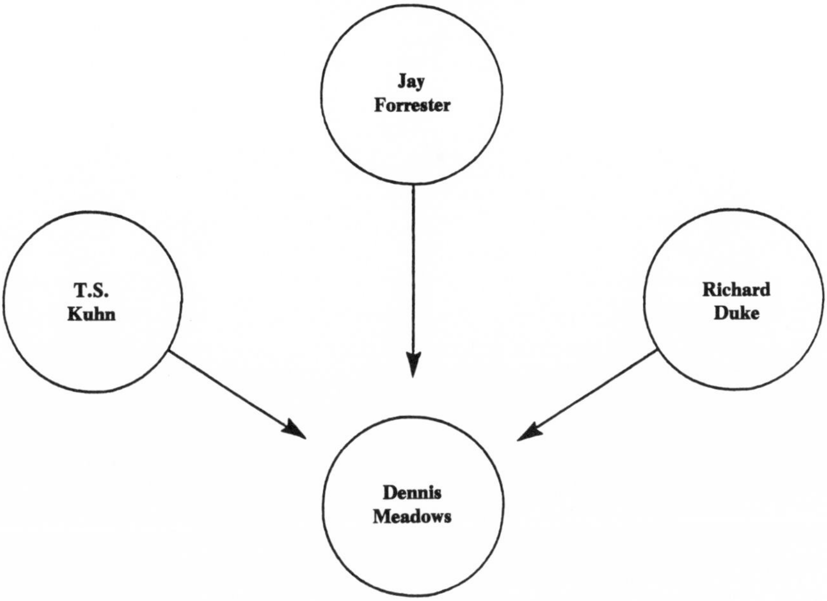

REFERENCES

1. Donella H. Meadows, Dennis L. Meadows, Jorgen Randers, and William W. Behrens III, *The Limits to Growth*, A report for The Club of Rome'a Project on the Predicament of Mankind, Universe Books, New York, 1972.
2. Figures from Alexander King, President of the Club of Rome, 1987.
3. "The U.S.—A Sustainable Society?" in *Making It Happen: A Positive Guide to the Future*, U.S. Association for the Club of Rome, 1982.
4. Dennis Meadows, "Are There Limits to Growth?" *The Wharton Magazine*, 4:2, Winter 1980, p. 16.
5. "Are There Limits to Growth?", 1980.

CHAPTER 17

JAMES A. OGILVY

Jay Ogilvy is a futurist with a formal background in philosophy and a professional focus on the study of human values.

KEY VIEWS ABOUT THE FUTURE

1. The U.S. is favorably placed for a move into a diversified information economy. The cultural homogeneity and order of Japan and Germany have been tremendous positive factors in industrial production, but are less of an advantage now when flexible approaches and diverse solutions are called for.
2. People buy experience, not merely information. The market for experiences, unlike that for most consumer goods, is likely to be inexhaustible, as well as intangible.
3. Government is shifting away from bureaucracy towards more horizontal structures with overlapping relationships. These heterarchies are more appropriate than hierarchies to an information society.
4. In the long term, economic institutions, notably the large corporation, are taking over governance functions from political institutions, much as nation-states took over from the church.
5. Information technologies are moving through a transition, "the age of incompatibility." When that is over their capabilities will expand enormously beyond what we now imagine.
6. The future of agriculture is in smaller farms worked with intelligent use of information. Most R&D in agriculture has been directed at increasing yields. Because of the newly important global issue of sustainability of the land and its products, this is likely to shift.
7. The 1990s may be wild and crazy as the baby boom generation goes through mid-life crisis. The baby boom demonstrated a commitment to change in the societal upheavals of the 1960s and early 1970s. As they reach their mid-forties the reassessment of their life goals and values will shake up the corporations, institutions and societal groups in which they are executives, legislators, administrators, and participants.

BIOGRAPHICAL NOTE

In 1987, Jay Ogilvy became director of the Revisioning Philosophy Program at Esalen Institute, Big Sur, California. Between 1983 and 1986, he was director of research at SRI International's Values and Lifestyles Program (VALS).

Ogilvy has degrees in philosophy from Williams (BA) and Yale (Ph.D). In 1979 his book *Many Dimensional Man: Decentralizing Self, Society and the Sacred*, was published by Oxford University Press. He is a co-author with Paul Hawken and Peter Schwartz of *Seven Tomorrows: Toward a Voluntary History*, Bantam, 1981. In *Seven Tomorrows*, the authors wrote scenarios of the U.S. future in the 1980s and 1990s. The book makes some of the collective work of the futures research group at SRI available to a wider audience. A number of people besides the authors had a hand in developing the ideas on which the scenarios are based, including especially Willis Harman and the late Arnold Mitchell.

This chapter is based on an interview with Ogilvy and a review of his work.

WORLDVIEW

Two of the most important trends shaping the future are the growing global economy and development of the information technology that is making possible business on a global scale.

Ogilvy has been consistent in advocating pluralism, tolerance, diversity, and compromise in society to manage increasing complexity.

Seven Tomorrows asserts that we will need a greater collective intelligence to manage increasing complexity, but assumes that the development of an advanced communications network, by improving our collective memory and ability to retrieve information, will augment our ability to reach a higher level of consciousness and give us as a society a new and highly developed nervous system.

Although he is an optimist about society's capacity to build and maintain diversity, Ogilvy is not a transformationalist. A sudden shift in values and attitudes is unlikely, in his view.

He also notes a trend towards decentralization—a move away from homogeneity, away from the melting pot, towards the regional, the ethnically or culturally different, from the federal to the state, from the big to the smaller group. Fed by distrust of big business, big government, and big education, this trend to decentralization could result in resistance to national initiatives.

On the other hand, corporations, especially multinationals, could act as a force for economic order and stability and may inherit responsibility for providing services from an increasingly ineffective public sector.

SPECIFIC ISSUES

The Information Society

Ogilvy notes that people are not buying bytes when they buy information, they are buying an experience. The market for experiences, unlike that for most consumer goods, is inexhaustible, as well as intangible. Information technology is being used to improve and expand the quality of experience, in everything from the special effects of movies to the design of better shovels. The well-informed shovel, as well as the well-informed Star Wars movie epic will educate consumers to the information society without their being more than marginally aware of the revolution happening around them.

Ogilvy believes societies develop their economies and their social structures on solid and concrete products and values. Over time, these become less solid and more intangible, ephemeral and abstract. The U.S. economy was based on land and agriculture, then industrial products, and now, more recently, on information. The energy supply was coal, moved to oil and gas, and now includes sunlight and wind. The financial industry was based on gold, then paper, and now, increasingly on credit. Individual values have moved from the solidity of the Ten Commandments, to cultural relativism to a nihilism in which nothing is firm or fixed. At the same time, a long term shift towards automating all physical work and expanding mental work is occurring.

The U.S. Economy

The U.S. is favorably placed for the move into a diversified information economy. The cultural homogeneity and order of Japan and Germany has been a tremendous positive factor in industrial production, but is less of an advantage, and may even be a disadvantage, in a diversified information economy. In this new economy the basic function of business is no longer in efficient standardization, but in flexible approaches and diverse solutions. Compared with other societies, the diversity of U.S. society makes Ogilvy optimistic about the U.S. economy through the next ten years.

Ogilvy sees the U.S. on an economic tightrope maintaining its fiscal balance above the abyss of national debt. At one end of the balance pole is innovation in small and medium sized companies and at the other, the economic potential of the new information economy.

It is to the advantage of the U.S. to have its large baby boom generation moving into its most productive years, with a smaller generation following, thus lowering the future demand for new jobs.

U.S. Political Directions

Two issues for governance driven by the move to an information economy are:

- A shift away from the bureaucratic structure of government towards more complex horizontal structures Ogilvy calls heterarchic,
- The globalization of economies, societies and cultures.[1]

Industrial corporations and governments required extensive standardization to mass produce goods and to provide mass education and services. Standardization was best achieved by a bureaucratic structure. However in information societies, innovation and differentiation are more appropriate to meet diversified markets and differing public needs. Ogilvy suggests government will follow the private sector in abandoning the bureaucracy in favor of a heterarchy in which others must be taken into account. For state governors, for example, important others may be heads of state and business leaders from other nations because information about foreign trade no longer passes solely through Washington channels. In a heterarchical structure leaders may lose some autonomy, but may gain power through developing strong alliances.

In an exercise for public managers, published in *The Bureaucrat*,[2] Ogilvy developed three scenarios of government for the next 15 years. In one, bureaucracy expands to 19.5% of the workforce, tending to strangle domestic innovation and international competition. In the second, suspicion of bigness leads to the reduction of large organizations, especially those of government. Most government functions are privatized, others are pushed to the states. Tax gathering and defense are accomplished with a minimum of bureaucracy and the help of technology and a policy of minimalism. One result of less attention to defense is that peace breaks out.

Heterarchy is introduced as the third scenario. In this future, distinctions between public and private sectors begin to blur. The government goes into business with profitmaking services, non-governmental organizations manage international trade and commonly held resources, such as the oceans. Planning is decentralized and responsive to market conditions with a longer time horizon. From Ogilvy's point of view the third scenario is the most flexible, able to avoid the stifling effects of bureaucracy and the potential anarchy of minimalism.

The Future of Corporations

In the long term, economic institutions, notably the large corporation, are taking over governance functions, such as education, health, and welfare, from political institutions, much as nation states took over from the church. The church did not disappear, but the nation state ruled. Now it may be the time for the economic institution to manage the people.

In this context, the multinational corporations are especially interesting because they are not tied to political boundaries. In a globalizing economy, those institutions independent of national interests will be more significant shapers of the future than those institutions, such as governments, whose existence and power is dependent on maintaining their national boundaries. Multinational corporations are big and spread widely enough to deal with the big problems. Ogilvy notes the study of acid rain in Europe as an example of an issue which cannot be tackled effectively by any single country.

The economic institutions have not yet woken to the shift from the public to the private sector, and have not admitted to any responsibility for the transfer, or its outcome. This is not a complete shift but a fuzzing of the line between public and private sectors. Corporations are taking care of many services formerly in the public sector: health, education, and welfare are examples. In education, for instance, the Carnegie Commission discovered corporations are spending $40 to $60 billion on training and education, which is about equal to the U.S. budget for higher education.

Technology

Biotechnology will be a big technology but probably not commercially significant until the end of the 1990s.

Information technologies are moving through an awkward stage of what Ogilvy calls, "the age of incompatibility." When that is over their capabilities will expand enormously beyond what we now imagine. The development of these technologies will lead to new theories of the economics of information that are not based on our current industrial model.

Faster transport technologies are probable. Flights to Toyko in an hour and a half will speed the developing global economy.

Education

Cycles which appear to have been disastrous to the educational structure may be the natural swings of a functioning system, although Ogilvy is doubtful of the outcome because he sees the U.S. system in deep trouble.

Three issues for the future of education are:

- The moving on of the baby boom, which implies a declining demand for schooling in some areas and no numerical growth overall.
- An increasing diversity and decentralization in the kinds of education offered, which may increase the range of quality and limit access to the highest quality of education.
- New educational needs of the information society.

Television, radio and mass media have picked up the burden of promoting cultural homogeneity. Children now learn more about the "American experience" from television and radio than from school. He also suggests that computers will render pedantry, with its close attention to detail, redundant—there will be no reason for people to compete with computers in being accurate—therefore an education in creativity and how to learn from error will be more important.

The consciousness movement, in which are included such programs as est training, is becoming another alternative to traditional education for its ability to fill needs for experiential and spiritual education.[3]

Health

People will continue to be better informed on health and wellbeing, but excess enthusiasm for fads and fitness may wane. Ogilvy notes a trend towards softness that may be characteristic of a more moderate approach underlying a long term trend towards personal responsibility for health and fitness. Business will continue to support the long term trend. However softness is appearing in everything from industrial products to fabric. The aging baby boom may be going softer in their lifestyles. Their expectations for hard fitness and rigorous exercise may be moderating. According to Ogilvy one should look, for example, at such indicators as butter consumption which has recently increased in the U.S.

Agriculture

Agribusiness is on a collision course with reality. The agricultural system is headed for catastrophe. Instead of pummeling nature into what we want it to do with chemicals and pesticides and herbicides, finding out how nature works and helping her along would be more intelligent, in his view. The future of agriculture is not in family gardens, or giant farms, but in smaller farms worked with intelligent use of information. Most R&D in agriculture has been directed at increasing yields. This is likely to shift because the newly important global issue will be sustainability of the land and its products.

Defense and Disarmament

Ogilvy is optimistic about our ability to avoid full-scale nuclear war, pessimistic about controlling the use of nuclear weapons by smaller nations. Religion, and the societal and institutional baggage carried by the concept of religion, is an important and uncertain factor in nuclear arms control. Neither science nor society has succeeded in separating religious belief from war.

The international stability that could be created by multinationals pursuing their global business interests is a reason for corporations to be interested in solving the problem of war, according to Ogilvy. They are capable of encouraging solutions to the economic transition from war-based to peace-based economies.

Religion

Participation in certain kinds of religious and spiritual experience will increase. These include pentacostal, fundamentalist, meditative and other forms that require active participation in a heightening of consciousness. Mainstream Protestant sects, such as the United Methodists and Episcopalians, may continue to decline.

More people have strong religious beliefs than is generally assumed, however. In recent surveys by SRI about 62.5% of the people asked said they believed the world was created in six days. About 35% said they were born-again Christians. A move towards religious experience may not imply less interest in worldly affairs. The Connecticut Mutual Life Insurance company sponsored a survey in 1980 that found the highest correlation between a social conscience and any other attribute was that between religious conviction and political activism.[4]

For some, a new attraction to religion, or to spiritual experience, may be in reaction to the inevitability of societal change and to the challenge of a steadily increasing flow of information on everything from nuclear arms to health and sex.

Values

The 1990s may be wild and crazy as the baby boom generation goes through mid-life crisis. The baby boom demonstrated a commitment to change in the societal upheavals of the 1960s and early 1970s. As they reach their mid forties the reassessment of their life goals and values will shake up the corporations, institutions and societal groups in which they are executives, legislators, administrators, and participants.

In the 1970s, the big issue for the front half of the baby boom was employment and unemployment, as everyone tried to find their places at work at the same time. In the 1980s, the front half of the bulge generation are working, achieving, paying a mortgage, getting children through school. In the 1990s the front half reaches its forties and begins to confront limits on what can be achieved. Social change has been a characteristic of the baby boom, partly because its enormous size creates pressure on social structures but also because many of its members became used to, tolerant of, and committed to change as a way of life. Therefore in the 1990s, he says, we should expect some unconventional, varied, and expressive behavior inside, and outside, organizations.

Millennial fever

A generational crisis in the U.S., may be accompanied by a worldwide outbreak of millennial fever in the late 1990s. This could take the form of new cults and sects.

New centrality of the family

Ogilvy expects the family and the home to become more central to the lives of many people. Shaping the return home is the restructuring of work away from the physical and away from the fixed workplace, fixed hours model. What will also occur is new attention to child-raising and a lowering of career aspirations by women, and by some men.

UNDERLYING CAUSES:

Attitudes and values change slowly. Human nature changes most slowly, over millennia. A sudden or even a fast transformation to a new set is not likely for the majority of people, although it is possible for smaller groups to shift their thinking and values. Many approaches, notably religious, have aimed at shifting human nature, none have been completely successful. Marxism, for example, as an attempt to assert the conscious mind over myth, market and fantasy, is unsuccessful because it underestimates the power of non-rationality.

An underlying premise of the *Seven Tomorrows* is that subjective perceptions about facts are more important to thinking about the future than the objective facts themselves because these perceptions govern the way people choose to act, and thus determine the kind of future they will have regardless of factual information. Thus a perception of resource shortage may influence energy policies even when actual resource levels are high.

EXHIBIT 17-1

FORCES INFLUENCING THE FUTURIST THINKING OF

JAMES OGILVY

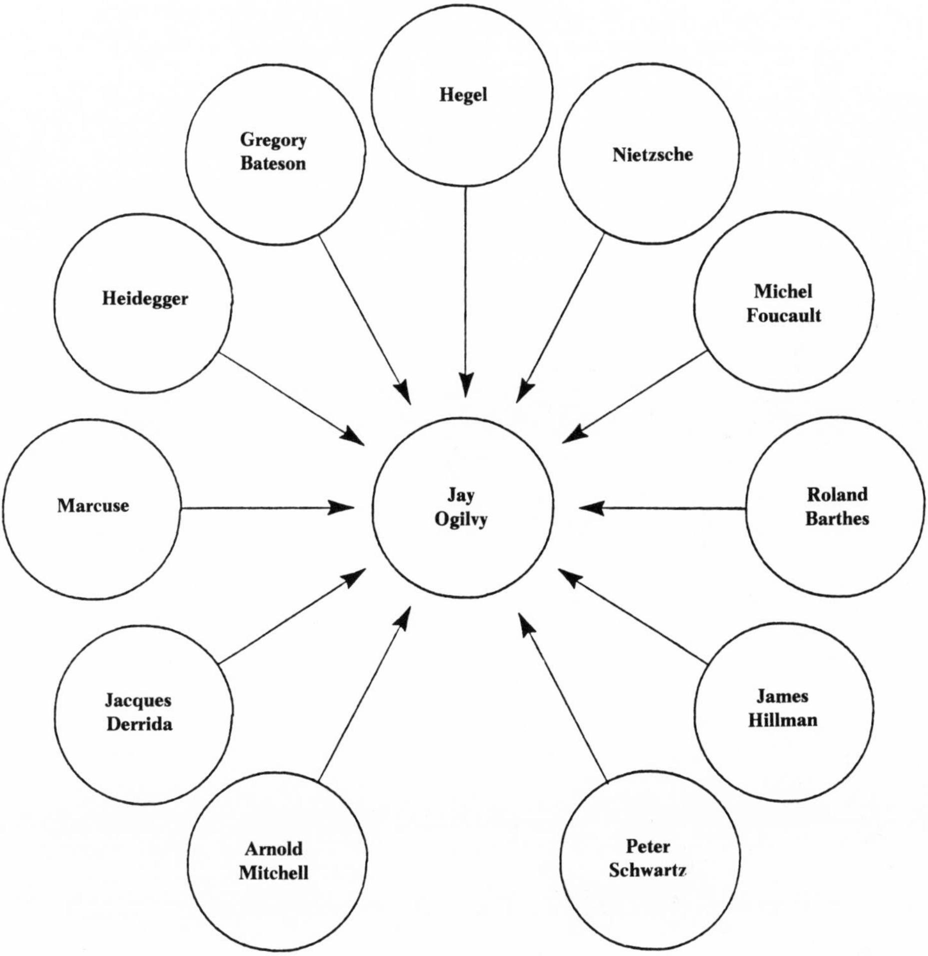

REFERENCES

1. "Governance in the Information Age," The Council of State Governments, no date.
2. "Scenarios for the Future of Governance," from Elsa A. Porter, ed., "From 1972 toward 2000," a special forum on the future of governance for the 15th anniversary issue of *The Bureaucrat*, 15:4, Winter 1986-1987, pp. 13-16.
3. "Education, Evolution and the Future," *Journal of Thought*, 16:3, Fall 1981, pp. 47-59.
4. "Symposium on Religion and Politics", *Telos*, 1983-84, 58, Winter, pp. 141-143.

CHAPTER 18

GERARD K. O'NEILL

Gerard O'Neill, a distinguished physicist and advocate for space development and space colonization, is notable for his long time horizon—a century or more; his strong technological optimism; and his deep and rigorous belief in human efficacy—that is, our ability to solve problems and make a better future. In his book, *2081, a Hopeful View of the Human Future,* **he uses scenarios effectively, writing engaging short stories of life a century from now. In these scenarios, however, and elsewhere in his work, O'Neill emphasizes technology over social, institutional, political, and psychological factors in shaping the future and defining our choices.**

KEY VIEWS ABOUT THE FUTURE

1. Technology can solve most human problems, because most of them are related in some way to resource limitations that can be overcome through technology.
2. Mankind can and should escape the severe resource limitations of earth by establishing highly-industrialized self-maintaining colonies in space.
3. Like earth's oceans, space is a vast reservoir and a resource, full of free energy and basic materials.
4. We can and should begin now to establish colonies, using today's technology and taking full advantage of solar energy and lunar materials.
5. The source of all change is technology. "Irreversible change is confined. . . to a single area: technology and its consequences."[1]
6. Change is desirable because a static society becomes rigid.
7. The society advocated implicitly by the authors of *Limits to Growth* involves unacceptable "constraints that would bind not only those of us alive now, but our descendants to the end of time."[2]

BIOGRAPHICAL NOTE

O'Neill, who served in the Navy from 1944-1946, joined the faculty of Princeton University on receiving his doctorate in physics from Cornell in

1954, and has been there throughout his career. He specialized in elementary particle physics and nuclear physics, and since 1969, in space development. Now an emeritus professor, O'Neill founded and is president of the Space Studies Institute (SSI) at Princeton. He is an instrument-rated pilot, a Fellow of the American Physics Society and the American Institute of Aeronautics and Astronautics, and in 1977, a recipient of the Glover Medal and the Phi Beta Kappa Science Book Award, for his book, *The High Frontier.*

In 1969, soon after the first moon landing, O'Neill posed freshman physics students the question: "Given that mankind will eventually colonize space, is a planetary surface the right place for an expanding technological civilization?" He and his students came to some surprising conclusions and interesting hypotheses.[3] Over the next three or four years, O'Neill continued his own calculations, and in 1974 published an article on space colonization in *Physics Today*,[4] which attracted wide attention. In 1975 NASA funded the first of three intensive summer studies in space colonization at Ames Research Center. In 1977, *The High Frontier* was published, and O'Neill established SSI to fund or carry out research on subjects related to space colonization. Its goal is "to enable humans to move into the high frontier."[5] In 1985, O'Neill was appointed by President Reagan to the National Commission on Space.

Of his life goals, O'Neill says:

> *To me the ideals of human freedom, of individual choice, and of concern for others have always been of the greatest importance. Much of my favorite reading is of authors who wrote in the early part of this century, when right and wrong seemed more clearcut than they do today, and when individual achievement was more highly regarded. I find my greatest personal satisfaction in a warm and intense family life and in those achievements, modest though they may be, which I know to be my own. I hope that at the end of my life I can look back on work honestly done and on fair dealings with others.*[6]

WORLDVIEW

O'Neill is a technological optimist. Technology in general, and space exploitation in particular, can solve those problems of human society which arise from the dilemma of finite resources and unlimited population growth.

> *The human race stands now on the threshold of a new frontier whose richness is a thousand times greater than that of the new western world of 500 years ago.*[7]

Individual freedom is more important than wealth or a stable society to O'Neill, and this freedom is more likely to be won within a technologically-achieving society. A society that damps down all risk, fearfully husbands resources against future need, preserves stability at all costs, is one which will become rigid, denying freedom and unable to progress. O'Neill believes societal change spurred by the free-flowing developments of science and technology is rapid and irreversible. In his view of the future, scientists and engineers are given their heads—and the capital—to perform prodigious and beneficial feats of scientific and technical development. Nagging social problems are reduced or disappear as humanity moves up the road of technological progress. He suggests in *The High Frontier*, that, more than democracy, which in any case does not seem especially exportable, the U.S. can contribute best to increasing the world's wealth by using its great technological competence and potential to lead the way into space.[8]

Technological progress in five areas is likely to determine what the world will be like in the next 100 years:

- Space colonization
- Computers
- Automation
- Energy
- Communications

Until about 1980, nearly all of O'Neill's non-technical writing dealt with space colonization, notably in *The High Frontier*. His 1980 book, *2081: a Hopeful View of the Human Future*, was a broader look at the potential of technology for transforming day-to-day life on earth as well as in space.

Having worked out the technologies for building enclosed habitats in space which will support a population in ideal climate and atmospheric conditions and describing them in *The High Frontier*, he then applies these concepts to problems arising on earth. Many future technologies for supporting planetary life will look like space designs. Thus he suggests rehabilitating old cities by roofing them over and producing a perfect climate inside; controlling pests and pollution in agriculture by enclosing crops in closed-cycle greenhouses; carving out habitats underground for factory production, and vacuum tunnels for high-speed magnetic transport. Furthermore, development of space-useful technologies, such as artificial biospheres and closed cycle life support systems on earth, will teach us about building and maintaining them in space.

In *The High Frontier*, in later writings and in the publications of SSI, a coherent scientific and technological view emerges of the future of space colonization. O'Neill believes science can provide an ideal physical environment for humans in space. The social organization of this ideal environment will be up to the inhabitants to design. O'Neill is laissez-faire on political and social structures, believing that many factors besides deliberate choice shape and broaden the outlook of societies, easily accessible international air travel being a good example. These space communities are not likely to be Utopias, in O'Neill's view.[9] Utopian movements have emphasized escape from outside interference enforced by tight discipline within the community, as well as the selection or rejection of certain technologies. Space communities will escape further than any other human community has been able to, but the opening of new ideas and the possibilities of new social structures suggested by their unique environment and the technologies available to them will encourage diversity and experimentation.

O'Neill believes that we have "a responsibility beyond mere curiosity to learn as much about the future as we can, because we must choose those actions that will ensure not only the survival of humanity but an improvement in its condition."[10]

SPECIFIC ISSUES

Space Colonization

O'Neill insisted in 1976 that a first space colony could be in place before 1990, using conventional materials and technology, including a modified space shuttle and chemical space tug, and using "ordinary civil engineering practice." By 1984, according to O'Neill, "the engineering has been worked out in considerable detail."

The importance of space colonization is that it will change the future from one driven by the economics of scarcity to one of the economics of abundance. In space, we could live at a much smaller scale of human density. He acknowledges in *The High Frontier*, that man went to the moon on a burst of national confidence in technology that was an effective propellant for the U.S. space program. In the longer term, however, space will be colonized as a new frontier, as an opportunity for the bravest, boldest, and most adventuresome to move beyond an overcrowded world. He says almost nothing about risk, but implies that although the space colonies will be comfortable environments once built, the building of them will be a rough and tough adventure.

O'Neill reasons that with abundant resources and unlimited space, people could establish small communities and the relationships between individuals and between communities could be cooperative rather than competitive. Thus there may be less hostility between people. The great benefit to the earth will be abundant energy microwaved back from solar-powered generators in space.

His central ideas about space colonies are:[11]

- A new ecological range exists for human life, the orbital space between the earth and the moon, in which large colonies can be self-maintaining, drawing on solar energy which is always available.
- Such colonies can be constructed in the immediate future, on a short time scale, without any tools more advanced than the rocket boosters and other technologies now available. More advanced technologies would be supported (for the program) only if their benefits were clear and unequivocal.
- An investment of about $6-8 billion, comparable to that for the Alaska Pipeline, would be enough to establish a partially automated industry in space capable of producing 100,000 tons of products annually, with a value of more than $10 billion.[12]
- Nearly all the construction materials can be taken from the surface of of the moon, avoiding the costs of transporting them into space from the earth.
- The materials would be launched from the lunar surface by an electric catapult called a mass driver, three of which have been built as models in Space Studies Institute projects. The first model, with 33 gravities, needed five miles to accelerate to 2.4K per sec. Mass Driver III, with 1,800 gravities, can reach that speed in 500 feet.[13]
- The materials would be processed with solar energy. The new colonies would build and maintain power generators in synchronous orbit around the earth to supply the earth with electricity by low-density microwave beams.

Computers and Miniaturization

O'Neill notes that there are two ways to make computers intelligent: by "brute force" (i.e., greater power and speed), and by research into the associative and creative processes of the human brain.

Computers can be several hundred times the speed of today's, if they are small. The limitations on miniaturization imposed by the need for a human interface will be avoided by speech recognition and speech generation.

Before the end of the century it will be possible to store all the information in a good-sized library in a device the size of a business card.

Automation and Robotics

No fundamental breakthroughs are required, but progress has been impeded by the cost of programming and the difficulty of pattern recognition, and by mechanical factors (e.g., friction, wear, dirt, leaks) and the difficulties of finding and repairing failures. We are just beginning to solve the problems of vision (pattern recognition) and are making progress in developing sliding contacts to reduce wear and tear.

The precision of movement now possible within a millimeter or so, will be increased by measuring distance acoustically and by other means.

We now have machines that build other machines. Eventually we will have machines that replace themselves. These self-replicating machines are important to O'Neill's program of space colonization because they can be sent to remote places (the moon, or the asteroid belt, for example,) to replicate themselves under local conditions, using local materials and local energy and avoiding the enormous cost of lifting all materials out of earth's gravity well.

Energy

O'Neill anticipates our current energy sources becoming scarce and expensive and thus a barrier to progress in all areas. He sorts among various technological options for solutions:

- Conservation and efficiency are essential first steps but in the long run a higher standard of living will demand increased use of energy. In the U.S., our lifestyles, and our freedom of choice are supported by high rates of energy use. The U.S. cannot easily tolerate more than 10-20% reduction in energy use and resources are not currently available for the rest of the world to use energy at the same rate.[14]
- Energy options are driven by efficiency, pollution, land use, heat load, costs, ease of use and of conversion, and versatility of applications. Environmental impact will be more important as population and energy use increase. The effects of increasing atmospheric carbon dioxide will be one such problem, and a big one.

- For transmission, the possibilities are either electricity, or chemical forms that can be stored or shipped: synthetic ammonia, hydrogen, or synthetic hydrocarbons.
- Liquid fuel for transport and transportation, i.e., for vehicles of all kinds, will continue to be necessary.
- Old forms of energy will persist; nuclear energy will be used less because of the risk of radioactivity; renewable energy is not adequate because it demands far too much dedicated ground space per unit of energy. OTEC (ocean thermal) and SPS (solar-powered satellite) are promising because they require no major breakthroughs, are environmentally benign, and could supply sufficient energy.
- Fusion power requires new, difficult, more advanced technology, and will have radioactive waste to dispose of.

Telecommunications

There are limitations on all modes of communications; for example, satellite transmission will run into fundamental limitations of the bandwidth and tradeoffs in size of transmission and receiving equipment and costs. Ultimately satellite communications will be more expensive for high population density areas than fiber optic landlines but will continue to be used for transmitters on the move, those carried by persons as well as on ships, planes, and automobiles.

Cities

O'Neill writes of one roof for all, suggesting cities will renovate and cover their most desirable sections with movable three-part roofs made of metal frame, reflecting aluminum, a layer of glass and a layer of mesh screen. The typical covered city will be a mile square, house 10,000, maintain an ideal climate, with semi-tropical trees and plants, and be surrounded by parks and gardens. These habitats and the enclosure of agriculture he describes will be prototypes of, or developed at the same time as, space habitats and agricultural systems.

Food and Agriculture

O'Nelll expects development in and greater use of enclosed, closed-cycle spaces for growing food. The "greenhouse revolution" he anticipates will enable us to produce food more efficiently, with less land use and greater control over pollution, pests, and impurities. Land saved by the extensive use of greenhouses could beneficially be reforested.

Transportation

By 2081 we may have "floater" trains, supported by magnetic fields operating in vacuum tubes, possibly coast to coast. The proper place for trains is underground, according to O'Neill. Automated tunneling will reduce labor costs, reduce risks, save the economic and social costs of a surface right of way, and greatly reduce the demand for energy.

Jet planes are not economical for trips of less than 400 miles. Our problem is to engineer planes that fly efficiently and safely at both high and low speeds; one answer may be a pivoting oblique wing plane.

Automobiles will have on-board computers and highway automatic guidance markers.

Future Information Societies

In a computer and communications society, O'Neill expects the uninteresting chores, the commute to work, the trip to the store, cleaning house, paying bills, and so on, will be taken over by electronic communications and robot services. People will have higher incomes and more choice in their activities. If they choose to go to work because it is interesting or exciting, they may do so, but they are likely to work fewer and more flexible hours. Clerical and other mundane work tasks can be done at home on the computer. Grocery shopping will be done by computers, shopping for luxuries, in person. Textbooks will be on thumbnail-sized wafers, magnified for reading onto flexible sheets, artbooks and magazines will be beautifully printed on fine paper, for aesthetic delight.

Crime

Not all is delight. By 2081 almost everyone on earth will wear an identification anklet which will serve two purposes, as a universal credit card, and a locator device for a central computer tracking all persons. In such a controlled society, where money is rarely used, crime will decrease, according to O'Neill, although he anticipates a rise in crimes of terrorism.

Health Care

O'Neill forecasts the adoption of a national health insurance program in the U.S. well before 2081, implying this will be driven partly by a need to reduce the cost of malpractice insurance. He also expects greater use of computer diagnosis and the development of completely automated operating rooms.

International Economics

The world population will be 10 billion by 2081, and at that time population pressures will begin to be eased by an emigration into space of more than the natural annual rate of growth. By 2131, world population will be down to about 9 billion.

The world will be poorer and hungrier, except for those nations in rapid technological evolution. The annual income for a family of four in the U.S. will be about $200,000 in 1980 dollars by 2081.

The Soviet Union in 2081 will be much as it is now, except that the average citizen will be slightly better off, and own a car. Given his belief in the importance of individual freedom, O'Neill is, not surprisingly, pessimistic about the Soviet Union's ability to take part in technological change.

Africa is likely to be the worst-case continent, primarily because of the continuing prevalence of dictatorships and tribal disputes. Some nations within Africa will prosper by delivering universal education by satellite.

Defense and Disarmament

The 21st century world will still be heavily armed, fragmented into nation states, subject to nuclear terrorism and outbreaks of conventional wars. The development of computer monitoring may provide greater control over the world's population, but not peace. Some developing technologies may improve international communications, pocket-sized electronic translators, for example. O'Neill assumes the development of a new language for international communication, Common Basic, which contains words of all languages.

Other Technologies of Importance

O'Neill sorts several other technological possibilities into the likely, the unlikely and the downright impossible. We may well see by 2081:

- Superstrong materials with molecules arranged in tiny ordered crystals, especially useful for flywheels and space elevators.
- Sex selection and genetic modification to increase health and intelligence.

- Preserving an individual's tissue from childhood, and cloning it when the person needs new organs.
- Artificial body organs made of teflon.

We are less likely to see:

- Regeneration of nerve fibers, because nerve cells cannot regenerate.
- Significant extension of human lifespan; we cannot now see the way to it. Both cancer and aging, however, may be symptoms of a breakdown of the DNA-repair mechanisms in somatic cells.
- An increase in reported psi phenomena; these have not been proven, but have not been disproven.

Some things can be dismissed, because they violate the laws of causality, or have inherent impossibilities:

- Faster-than-light travel,
- Time travel,
- Anti-gravity.

There are twin mysteries only to be speculated about, although we might be on the way to answering them one way or the other by 2081:

- The "meaning of consciousness," i.e., is there a transcendent self independent of the body?
- The uniqueness of life, i.e., are there extraterrestrial conscious beings? O'Neill reasons that either we are alone in the universe, or we have been observed from the beginning by sentient beings, who must also be friendly or benign.

UNDERLYING CAUSES

Advanced technology benefits the individual, economically, in improved choices and quality of life. A conserving, conservative, stable, low risk, socially-oriented society is unacceptable to O'Neill because he believes it stifles innovation and burdens one generation with the unsolved problems of an earlier one, leaving future generations with unacceptable constraints.

O'Neill speculates that our society, characterized as it is by a hunger for new knowledge and a search for scientific answers to the mysteries of the physical world is part of a brief period in the history of the world—a scientific age—that may last only about 1000 years. By the end of the scientific millenium, humans may have answered most of their questions and be turning away from science and towards intellectual, artistic and social interests.[15]

Change and advance in human society occurs in periods of turbulence and confusion. O'Neill suggests our exploration into space marks a big jump forward, one likely to be accompanied by unpredictability, and uncertainty for many years until we gradually achieve the goal of living in space.

EXHIBIT 18-1

FORCES INFLUENCING THE FUTURIST THINKING OF

GERARD K. O'NEILL

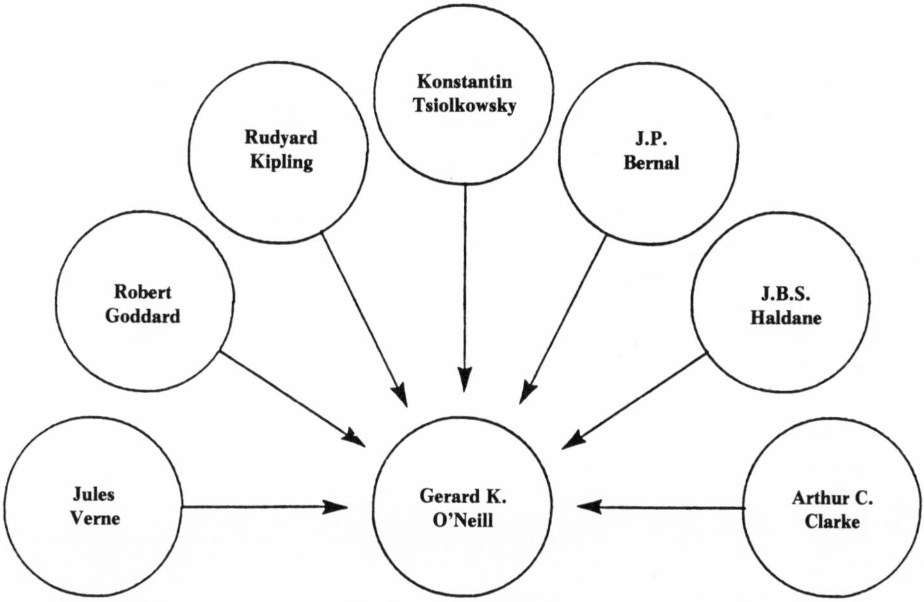

REFERENCES

1. *2081: A Hopeful View of the Human Future.* Simon and Schuster, New York, 1980, p. 19.
2. *2081: A Hopeful View of the Human Future.*
3. (O'Neill with Ginie Reynolds), "Habitats in Space," *The Science Teacher,* Vol. 44, No. 6, September 1977, p. 23.

4. "The Colonization of Space," *Physics Today*, Vol. 27, No. 9, September 1974.
5. "The High Life in Space," *Omni*, Vol. 7, No. 1, October 1984, p. 73.
6. This is a quote from the entry in *Who's Who* for O'Neill.
7. "Space Colonies: The High Frontier," *The Futurist*, February 1976, p. 26.
8. *The High Frontier*, William Morrow, New York, 1977, p. 36.
9. *The High Frontier*, p. 200.
10. *2081: A Hopeful View of the Human Future*. Simon and Schuster, New York, 1980.
11. "Space Colonies: The High Frontier," *The Futurist*, February 1976.
12. William T. Bryant and Gerard K. O'Neill, "Breakout into Space," in Frank Feather (ed.), *Through the 80's*. World Future Society, 1980, p. 121.
13. Space Studies Institute *Update*, Special Report on High Frontier Research, 1986, Princeton, pp. 2-3.
14. *The High Frontier*, p. 26.
15. *The High Frontier*, p. 170.

CHAPTER 19

JOHN R. PIERCE

John Pierce is a distinguished American electrical engineer. While Emeritus Professor of Engineering at the California Institute of Technology, he is also associated with the Center for Computer Research in Music and Acoustics at Stanford. He enjoyed a long and distinguished career at Bell Laboratories. Pierce is an expert looking at the future of his specialty. He is not a futurist, by his own evaluation. Therefore, the most weight is given here to his views on the future of his special area, telecommunications and computers.

KEY VIEWS ABOUT THE FUTURE

1. Totally digitalized information technology is emerging to process speech, sound, text, data, graphic and pictorial information commonly, and with equal ease.
2. The major effects of this integration will be in these areas: the convergence of all modes of information handling and the development of new communities of interest.
3. Computers and electronics will be part of everything; we are entering an era of mechatronics.
4. Fiber optics will be a dominant technology, complemented by communications satellites.
5. The integrity of information is a larger and more pervasive issue than privacy.
6. Competition and monopoly solve many problems, not all. To achieve maximum growth in the technology, we need standardization, and to achieve standardization, we need cooperation.
7. The extensive use of telematics may lead in a closely knit society to infringements of privacy; unemployment may result from automation; malfunction of information systems may endanger our property and life; some cultural patterns may become extinct; and existing regulation may hamper the convergence of modes.
8. The use of computers may mean a lower level ability and less training will be sufficient for many jobs.

BIOGRAPHICAL NOTE

John Pierce, born in 1910 and trained as an electrical engineer, was at Bell Laboratories from 1936 to 1971. He was a professor of engineering at Cal Tech from 1971 to 1980 and, although emeritus, he is active in Stanford's Department of Music and Acoustics working on the computer and music. He received a National Medal of Science from the President in 1963.

In 1984, Pierce co-authored with Hiroshi Inose, Professor of electronic engineering at the University of Tokyo, *Information Technology and Civilization*, (Freeman). The book was commissioned by the Club of Rome and ran into heavy sledding when presented to the Club of Rome at a 1982 conference in Tokyo. The principal criticisms were that the book was too technology-oriented and light in emphasis on social, political and economic impacts of new information and communications technologies. The book was also criticized for its scant treatment of the opportunities presented to, and the impacts of, information and communications technology on third world countries. The Club agreed that the book was technically excellent and as a report to, rather than of, the Club of Rome, met its objectives.

Some useful comparisons can be made with Pierce's earlier book, *Signals: The Telephone and Beyond*. Written in 1981, it is pessimistic about the future of communications in the U.S. as likely to be shaped by regulation and legislation aimed at social goals, rather than reflecting the potential of telematics technology. He deplored the breakup of the Bell system with its disastrous implications for Bell Laboratories and saw this as thoughtless action in the name of competition at any cost. In the later book Pierce comes to a more complex position recognizing multiple roles among competition, cooperation, government, the private sector, regulation, and other factors. This chapter is based on these two books and an interview with Pierce in which we also discussed his more general views on the future.

THE WORLD OF TELECOMMUNICATIONS AND COMPUTERS

Today's information technologies can be distinguished from information technology in the past in three regards:

- The convergence of all modes,
- The development of communities of interest,
- Inevitable, but as yet unclear, impacts on culture.

The convergence of modes and the associated speed, reduction of cost, and increased power of information technology can encourage communities of interest that span many countries. Fast and economical air travel has worked together with the convergence of modes in fostering such transnational communities of interest. Such communities of interest are an inevitable outcome of the convergence of modes and the increasing effectiveness of the transmission, processing, storage, and retrieval of information. They are valuable both as a means of advancing human knowledge and as a means of illuminating it, perhaps overcoming cultural biases. [1]

Pierce emphasizes the impacts of new information technologies on life. He sees a broad range of effects on everything from integration of social activities to industrial efficiency, from effects on medical care and personal security to the enrichment of the traditional arts and culture. But he tends to stand back from forecasting many of the specifics because of a fundamental belief, "No matter how powerful, information technologies are merely tools." Hence their development is determined by their social context.

He does imply, however, that advanced telematics, including computers and communications technologies, will begin to substitute for many other activities and resources. Some of these substitutions are highly significant and prophetic of structural changes in society.

- Communications will substitute for commuting, allowing more people to live in areas they find attractive but which are not necessarily close to a work site.
- Computers are likely to substitute for job skills and erode the need for job training.
- Artists and musicians are complementing and substituting knowledge of electronics technology for traditional craft skills.
- Satellite-aided navigation will augment, and perhaps substitute for, maps and charts.
- Although moving slowly, information technologies are substituting for individual craftsmen in the home construction industry, producing the mobile, and the manufactured, home.

Computers and electronics are the big breakthrough areas, and will continue to be for at least the next decade. Everything will be instrumented, have its electronic components; this is the concept, mechatronics. The power of computation is going up, the costs are going down.

For optimum growth in the technology, we need standardization. Successful standardization must standardize on things as they exist and have been shown to work well, not on paper studies or even on incomplete experiments.[2] Universal electronic mail associated with the telephone would require greater standardization, for example. Other countries, such as Japan and those in Europe, may reach this goal before the U.S., because they are willing to cooperate and to build consensus to a much greater extent than the U.S. has been capable of doing. Pierce believes the U.S.'s use of monopoly and competition to achieve economic goals is successful, but there are certain problems, such as standardization, which develop complexities capable of swamping individual judgment and requiring cooperation and a degree of consensus. The lack of standardization will continue to limit growth in systems such as electronic mail, which needs to be extremely widespread, and probably international, to be successful.

Cooperation is a desperately needed tool of social and technological management.

> *Both monopoly (for government services, at least) and competition have their strong adherents, but cooperation is regarded with suspicion by almost everyone. It is rendered difficult or impossible by both regulations and anti-trust law. Yet, we see no way in which the full potentialities of information technology can be realized without a great deal of cooperation among information providers, communication companies and equipment manufacturers, between the public and private sectors.*[3]

Pierce's view is that cooperation, undertaken to improve productivity and technological development, may spill over to improve other areas of society, such as relations between labor and management. He cites examples of countries and corporations which have cooperated successfully to meet social and technical goals. Japan, in its handling of air pollution in Tokyo, is contrasted with the unsteady and shaky progress on pollution in California. Hewlett Packard has successfully organized units manageable in size, and encouraged them to set goals that are clear, achievable, and well understood by all.

SPECIFIC ISSUES

Fiber Optics

Fiber optics is highly promising, but Pierce doubts the U.S. can achieve full growth in the technology over the next 10 to 20 years because greater cooperation is required. Coaxial, of course, is a technology of the past. Satellite communication Pierce sees as ideal for planes and ships, but ranked behind fiber optics for ground communication.

Artificial Intelligence

Pierce believes clever machines will be of great use, but we are on the wrong track if we build them to imitate ourselves.

> *The capabilities of human beings and machines differ profoundly. Machines can act much more rapidly than people and can take many rules into account infallibly, while people can easily sort relevant data out of complex inputs or memories. Recognition in spoken language is one example of human capabilities, another is the ability to drive through traffic.*[4]

> *It seems inevitable that clever machines will be of great help to human beings and will benefit their civilization. However, we believe that artificial intelligence in the sense of imitating human capabilities is the wrong approach. The fruitful course is to make machines do for people those tasks in which they easily outstrip people in capability, and for people to do those things—including using and directing machines—for which they are best suited.*[5]

Software

The human-machine interface will continue to be important, Pierce believes. Its relative ease will be a factor in the readiness of people to substitute computers for other activities, such as travel to work.

> *The proper use of machines and "simple," "friendly" interfaces between human beings and machines are important in the present and will be increasingly important in the future.*[6]

> *In fact, software costs now exceed those of hardware, and the ratio of software costs to hardware costs is increasing.*[7]

Privacy and Information Integrity

Most people are concerned with the effect of information technologies on their privacy, but for Pierce, the integrity of the information itself is also a problem. He believes we are addicted to a "garbage-in gospel-out" belief about computers.

This issue (of privacy) is too narrow. A better concern is the integrity of information. Information is of value only if it informs us correctly; it can be dangerous if it does not. Thus, the source of information should be identified, and the way that data are gathered and processed should be made known. Further, the meaning of summaries of numbers derived from data should be understood.[8]

We ought to be concerned about when confidential information is gathered, how it is put into the system, that it is destroyed when no longer needed, and guarded while it is held.

The emerging issues of privacy and information integrity are likely to be subtle and frequently technical. Pierce believes, however, that although the news media may not take a technical approach, it serves to clue us that there may be an issue into which we should dig deeper.

The Role of Government

One would expect Pierce to advocate that the government be a major player in achieving standardization and indeed he does, but he is reluctant to say government should enforce cooperation, or regulate industries to achieve technological growth. He would rather have a model of cooperation, encouragement and support played out by the government to demonstrate its clear objectives in certain areas:

- closer coordination of basic research,
- standardization,
- support of education and culture.

Government should work for closer coordination of basic research in universities, in government institutions, and in industrial laboratories. The competitive and cooperative aspects of information services should be carefully balanced so as to utilize limited resources of money and human energy efficiently. Standardization by governments or industrial associations should be encouraged in order to ensure the maximum compatibility of equipment consistent with future progress of information technology. Information suppliers and vendors should be organized to promote the flow of information while ensuring its integrity. And all of the above activities should be carried out in concert with the rest of the world.[9]

Pierce believes regulation should occur only under two conditions, when people are directly affected and when it is essential to interconnect systems.

Satellites

The two major satellite issues appear to Pierce to be weight, and competition from fiber optics.

> *At present, the greatest technology uncertainty concerning communications satellites is how future satellites, which are getting larger and heavier, will be launched. Past civilian satellites have been launched with such vehicles as Delta, Atlas Centaur, or Ariane. The U.S. plans to rely on the manned space shuttle to launch future satellites.* 10

> *We may expect very rapid growth in satellite communications in the future, but we may expect a very rapid growth in other modes of communications as well. Lightwave transmission via highly transparent optical fibers promises to have a revolutionary effect on all communications, whether over long, intermediate, or short distances.* 11

Computer Applications

The trend Pierce describes as "mechatronics" is the integration of computers into almost everything. The pervasive use of computer components, and the enhanced power and sophistication they give to the tools they are integrated with are likely to have unforeseen, and perhaps even dangerous effects.

> *As we look at various areas of computer application, a significant trend sometimes referred to as mechatronics is generally found. Computers and mechanical systems are being rapidly integrated in office machines, machine tools, vehicles, cameras, and many other devices.* 12

> *As a result of the extensive use of these tools, privacy may be infringed in a closely knit society, unemployment may result from automation, malfunction of information systems may endanger our property and life, some cultural patterns may become extinct, and existing regulatory measures may hamper the convergence of modes.* 13

One significant effect may be that computers may replace skill and training needs for a number of jobs, which can be done by lower skilled and lesser trained workers.

Computer power is going up, costs are going down.

Digital systems with more than a hundred thousand components are now operating almost trouble-free, with a total estimated downtime of only a few hours over twenty years. More than ten thousand components may now be mounted on a chip of some thirty square millimeters and consume very little material and electric energy. Chips with hundreds of thousands of components will be common in the near future.[14]

At present, the computer based on the 32-bit microprocessor costs several tens of thousands of dollars, but within a few years such powerful microprocessors may cost only a few thousand dollars, about a hundredth of the cost of a present large central processor with similar capability.[15]

The protection of computer products may be managed with technical solutions, or by making the software in large quantities and so cheap theft is not worth the effort.

One encouraging factor is the increasing use of firmware. Firmware is a specific program built into a microprocessor or an attached read-only memory (ROM). Although a microprocessor is a general-purpose computer, when firmware is built in it performs a specific function. If the function is identified as novel, the firmware may be patentable. Firmware also makes it difficult for pirates to copy the program.[16]

Videotex

Pierce makes the point that videotex and teletext will have substantial effects on individuals but that they definitely need standardization.

A user may wish to use one interface unit to receive both teletext and videotex. An information provider may wish to sell information through the videotex services to several countries. To do so standards must be agreed on for display format and transmission, national as well as international.[17]

Future Information Societies

Information based societies will emphasize high technology products because these consume less energy and raw materials and have higher value added. These products will substitute for lower technology products.

> *Information technology will play a major role in reaching these ends. Information technology, including process control computers and industrial robotics, reduces the consumption of energy and raw materials, enhances the productivity and performance of conventional industrial products, and relieves workers from unnecessary monotonous labor.*[18]

A typical example would be a computerized road traffic control system that efficiently improves the infrastructure, detecting and measuring the amount of traffic in a complex system and centralizing that information in a central computer.

> *Air traffic control systems are another example. A radar system detects a number of aircraft en route or around an airport and, with the help of transponders on board and computers on the ground, displays on its cathode-ray tube the image of each aircraft along with a tag that indicates the aircraft's speed, altitude, and flight number.*[19]

The Arts in an Information Society

Pierce sees technology as always having had a decisive influence on the arts.

> *From what we can see, the most likely impact of such technology is that of a tool in the hands of the artist. The computer can allow the architect (or other designer) to explore extensively appearance, structural soundness, and cost. Computer graphics can be used to create still or moving images of objects that exist only in the memory of the computer—and the mind of the artist. In principle, numerically controlled machine tools can be used to fashion individual sculpture and ornament. Computers can be used to produce, manipulate, and reproduce musical scores. Digital technology can be used to record and preserve music with unprecedented quality and permanence. Computers can be used to create wonderful musical sounds that never were—sounds that may change the very nature and organization of music. And computers might be used to organize all of these into a new interactive art.*[20]

The New Information Workers

Artists, unlike other workers whose skills may be less in demand when computers enter their workplace, are acquiring new skills and jobs in information technologies. Pierce sees the artist as a potential model for the new information worker, whose primary interest and vocation may be in an area other than what he does for a living, yet what he does for a living is neither menial nor drudgery.

The potential for greater cooperation between management and unions and between management and workers exists in part, at least, because information societies put severe limits on what can be done without cooperation. Workers who communicate to work, for example, cannot be supervised visually, nor can they be easily organized, yet they still require labor advocates and management direction. Pierce notes that the U.S. will probably have an easier time learning cooperation than will older societies such as the United Kingdom and Europe where class divisions have become institutionalized.

Cities

Information technology will worsen the situation for cities, believes Pierce, because they are outmoded structures. Corporations tend to move away and leave behind those for whom no jobs will fit.

Science and Technology

Science and technology are creative and revolutionary factors in our world, and will continue to be. And we need better ways to support science and technology. By and large, science and technology are thriving.

The space age will not develop the way many thought it would, i.e., in exploration of the universe in the time period we are considering. It will develop in terms of communication satellites, spy satellites, navigation satellites, and weather satellites. In most of the next 20 years, all cars, trucks and ships will be tied to some satellite navigation system, all of which will work at less than a mile. Specialized ones will detect and spot well under a mile.

Space manufacturing is simply crazy. It was put forward as a way to justify man in space. The irony is if you could do anything worthwhile in space it would be better done by automation and robots. Man is designed for terrestrial space and is very poor and clumsy in outer space, whereas robots have difficulty in terrestrial space, but automation is ideal for outer space.

Among the areas of science that promise positive benefits are:

- genetic engineering

  —From molecular biology and genetic engineering, although he claimed no expertise or sharp, clear knowledge, he anticipates major benefits. Government got off on the wrong track by paying attention to those who were concerned about the human genetics issue. He sees the real opportunities lying in doing the things that chemistry can't do; the science to provide medical cures and care.

- energy

  —The technologies are full of promise for practical application, in contrast to high energy physics, which is pricing itself through the roof and promises to deliver few practical results, aside from understanding of the universe. Nuclear energy is not getting the kind of attention where big payoffs could lie ahead of us.

Some Long-Term Developments

- Necessities are becoming more expensive, and luxuries are getting cheaper. Air travel and home electronics are getting cheaper, while housing is getting more expensive.
- Many novel things have altered our lives, such as the telephone, the automobile, the pill, and space communication. But Pierce remains concerned, as a non-futurist, that we cannot predict these things reliably.

Education

Pierce believes we should not attempt to educate children for the future, yet he himself implies changes are occurring in education as a result of the implementation of information technologies. Technologies are also creating multiple opportunities for education out of school. Air travel, for example, is a cheap luxury which takes little time at low cost, which has brought large numbers of people the opportunity to travel all around the world for brief periods.

UNDERLYING CAUSES

The transition to an information society, and the weakening of our traditional approaches to business and government, are currently engaging corporations, unions and government in petty squabbles which are likely to be solved only in crises. Within what is a confusing picture, some examples of right-thinking organizations and individuals stand out: AT&T's commitment to universal telephone service; Bell Laboratories dedication to long-term objectives in electrical communications technology; Hewlett-Packard's clarity of goals, and manageable size of its units; and the broad perspective of the Chairman of the Board of Nippon Electric, Koji Kobayashi, in choosing only to do what would benefit the organization.

Complexity tends to overwhelm our judgement and our ability to make our trusty social tool of competition work effectively in managing our society. Pierce strongly encourages more cooperation and celebrates the Japanese ability to cooperate and deal with their problems. We need to promote actively the use of human judgement, to reverse practices which inhibit it, and to use our new and newly emerging information technology tools to manage and order the complexity.

REFERENCES

1. Hiroshi Inose and John R. Pierce, *Information Technology and Civilization,* W. H. Freeman & Co., New York, 1984, p. xi.
2. Personal conversation with Pierce.
3. *Information Technology and Civilization,* p. xvii.
4. Ibid., p. xiii.
5. Ibid., p. xiv.
6. Ibid., p. xiv.
7. Ibid., p. xvi.
8. Ibid., p. xv.
9. Ibid., p. 172.
10. Ibid., p. 40.
11. Ibid., p. 40.
12. Ibid., p. 63.
13. Ibid., p. 103.
14. Ibid., p. 54.
15. Ibid., p. 58.
16. Ibid., p. 64.
17. Ibid., p. 91.
18. Ibid., p. 111.
19. Ibid., p. 115.
20. Ibid., p. 168.

CHAPTER 20

PETER SCHWARTZ

Peter Schwartz has specialized in the future environment for business, especially from the point of view of corporations operating in many countries and differing business climates.

KEY VIEWS ABOUT THE FUTURE

1. The fundamental challenge for the multinational corporation is internal and external complexity.
2. We are experiencing a significant phenomenon of integration which is shaping the rules for life in the 21st century. This integrative force is the global spread of information technology.
3. Technology, economic and market forces are the primary drivers of change, with values and social and political structures tending to maintain the status quo.
4. The world's financial flow is a system so large it overwhelms any single nation's attempts to regulate it. The new financial interrelationships tend to render domestic economies unmanageable.
5. One of the largest users of the emerging global computer and telecommunications complex will be the financial industry. The entertainment industry, as a user, also will expand to enormous size worldwide with needs that will determine technological development.
6. U.S. oil demand could fall more than 50% by 2000. Innovative energy policy action may be needed to maintain higher prices artificially—at or above $20 a barrel—in order to continue pressure to reduce demand. Plausible outcomes for the U.S. of maintaining the price of oil will be highly efficient cars and no net imports of oil.
7. The bright economic promise of some African countries in the 1960s has disappeared and most of central Africa is on the edge of breakdown. The world has already demonstrated little interest in or concern for the stability and economic health of Africa, and is likely to offer minimal help in the event of disaster.

BIOGRAPHICAL NOTE

Peter Schwartz recently returned to the U.S. after five years in strategic planning with the Royal Dutch/Shell Group in London. There he led a team developing comprehensive views of world economic, political, social, technological and energy developments, and applying these to Shell's strategic interests. Among his current projects are strategic planning for the London Stock Exchange and development for them of a business information and commentary service delivered by cable television. With associates, he is starting a futures research institute in Palo Alto.

Previously he directed a group at SRI International studying the business environment. He joined SRI in 1973 to do futures studies, and he worked with the late Arnold Mitchell on his values and American lifestyle (VALS) studies.

Schwartz graduated from Rensselaer in 1968 in aeronautical engineering and astronautics. He served in the Peace Corps in Ghana. He is a co-author with Paul Hawken and James Ogilvy of *Seven Tomorrows: Seven Scenarios for the 1980s and 1990s*, Bantam, 1982, and author of many SRI business intelligence reports and articles. This profile draws on Schwartz' published work and on two interviews.

The audience for his work in the past few years has been the multinational corporation and senior policymakers outside the U.S., except for a collaboration on writing the movie, "War Games." That effort appealed to him as an opportunity to reach a mass audience. He has had less opportunity to reach his own generation, those who came of age in the 1960s, who interest him because they are moving into decision and policymaking positions.

WORLDVIEW

At the end of the 20th century, Schwartz believes, we are experiencing a phenomenon of integration which is shaping the rules for life in the 21st century, just as at the end of the 19th century the technology of the maturing industrial revolution was shaping rules for this century.

The phenomenon is the global spread of information technology. Schwartz believes that technology will produce wealth, and enable the developing global village to be one of great diversity.

There will be conflict, but great varieties of people using many different methods of communication to create substantial links will have a transforming effect. Emerging satellite and television links between the U.S./USSR are an example.

Schwartz is a pragmatic optimist, observing the forces in motion and celebrating the potential for structural change. The changes interesting him most are those affecting multinational corporations. He believes that as large and complex institutions they must anticipate structural shifts to survive and prosper.

Technology and economic and market forces are drivers of change, with values and social and political structures tending to maintain the status quo. Schwartz no longer believes in a national or global change of heart that would lead to a voluntary simplicity of lifestyle. It is unrealistic to expect that people, outside the U.S. and other highly developed countries, who have been living in involuntary simplicity would want anything other than to be comfortable. He does expect that individuals will want to maintain their diversity of values and lifestyles. Diversity is a value, because it enables individuals, institutions and nations to be more flexible and adaptable to change. It is to the advantage of the U.S. that it has a built-in diversity of people, customs and lifestyles.[1]

SPECIFIC ISSUES

The International Economy

The world's financial flow is a system so large it overwhelms any single nation's attempts to regulate it. The new financial interrelationships tend to render domestic economies unmanageable. In 1985 the world financial flow was $65 trillion, 20 times the U.S. GNP and only a minute part was actually needed for trade.[2]

Attempts to influence the international financial flow tend to have opposite effects to those intended.[3] Schwartz believes learning how to manage the flow will result in the creation of new international institutions to make and enforce rules, and new international economic structures which will be able to manage, although not regulate, those flows. The solution will not be simple, such as one international currency with one supervisory body, but a complex structure of institutions and multiple currencies forming a tighter-knit confederation than our current loosely woven structure.[4]

The worldwide flow of money is an unstable system, but is, and must become, less sensitive and more tough. The system has what Schwartz calls a resilient fragility, that continuously pulls through crises and adapts. He believes the system is self-sustaining as long as people continue to have confidence in it. The Japanese appear to have confidence and a good grasp of the system—they now have some of the largest banks.

The financial industry is likely to be one of the largest users of new and emerging global computer and telecommunications links and will, in effect, be establishing rules for the linkages. As another user, the recorded entertainment industry will grow to enormous size worldwide, determining the direction of technological development with its needs.

Information Technologies—Entertainment

The market for entertainment is huge. One half the world's population is under 20 years old and the numbers are growing—this age group loves to watch and listen. Potential sources of material and production are worldwide—the world's biggest movie industry is in India, with Hong Kong as the second largest—with much of the production in English.

Information Technologies—Political Directions

A political question which all nations will wrestle with is—how can information flows be controlled? Schwartz notes that most people live in countries where the state decides to some extent what the people will see. Countries will attempt to slow and channel the flow, but be unable to stop it.

Information Technologies—U.S. Education

The effect of information technologies on education is unlikely to be direct. Schwartz argues that those who believe computers, and computer aided instruction (CAI) in the home, will put schools out of business are working from the wrong premise. For most people computers are home entertainment. Recorded education will always be outproduced and outsold by recorded entertainment. Schwartz believes that the primary structural function of school is to keep children out of the home for a few hours each day, and therefore until parents no longer need this service, the development of CAI will be limited. He is gloomy about U.S. education which he sees as a crippled system. In any event, whatever schools do, their educational input is likely to be overwhelmed by the sophisticated communications products bombarding children at home.

World Regions

Among the uncertainties of the 1990s are the long term economic prospects of countries with an eroding manufacturing base, the North-South gap, the existence of mutually exclusive national political objectives such as wealth creation versus maintaining social traditions, and the movement of economic power away from Europe and towards the Pacific Rim.

Schwartz suggests a scenario in which Europe continues to suffer from a hardening of its economic arteries and a reluctance to risk new ventures, rationalizing their decline as a trade-off for preserving their centuries-old culture and way of life.[5] An alternative scenario has Europe being willing to trade sovereignty for cooperation in developing innovation and technological potential, fostering a resurgence of competition with the Pacific Rim countries and other newly industrializing countries.

The contribution of existing international organizations to world order is doubtful. Schwartz believes that the group of organizations established after World War II, the World Bank, the United Nations, NATO, and others, maintained stability until the 1970s when they began to weaken. Their struggle to restructure themselves, to regain effectiveness, seems likely to be a feature of international politics over the next few years. A positive outcome would be the establishment of a new stable framework for international trading and politics. At the moment, according to Schwartz, there is too much friction in the system. We are using patchwork methods to solve problems such as the indebtedness of Third World nations, rather than working out an enduring solution.

Defense and Disarmament

The world continues to be shaped by the discontinuities of World War II and the Depression. Everyone of the generations that experienced them agreed such events must not happen again. However, forty years of relative peace and prosperity is in itself discontinuous. Such conflicts as we have, in the Mid East, for example, are familiar, continuous, and therefore less frightening.

The most likely conflicts which might involve the U.S. are:[6]

- A revolution in Mexico—for various reasons, Schwartz suggests one generated by the right-wing would be more likely to draw in the U.S. than one organized by the left. Left-wing struggles in South America are likely to drag on, especially as long as the U.S. remains a drug market, financing the revolutionary effort.
- A war along the Asian ring—the Soviet Union, China, Viet Nam, Afghanistan, Turkey—could be presaged by the Soviet Union's involvement in Afghanistan, an Iranian breakthrough in Iraq, and so on. This conflict would tend to draw in the U.S. and the Soviet Union.

According to Schwartz, the most likely next big war is a Sino-Soviet one, growing out of demographic pressures—500 people per square mile on one side of the border compared with 1 per square mile on the other side. Another trigger might be the downhill economic slide of the Soviet Union and its needs for radical change and a boost to its economic activity.

Another potential discontinuity could be a devastating plague, most likely in Africa, which is already on the verge of collapse and chaos through economic failure, war and famine. Schwartz believes economic and political conditions in Africa are decayed and ineffective. The bright economic promise of some African countries in the 1960s, Ghana, for example, has disappeared and most of central Africa is on the edge of breakdown. This may have less affect on the rest of the world than might be expected because the world has already demonstrated little interest in or concern for the stability and economic health of Africa, and is likely to offer little help in the event of disaster.

Technology

Schwartz believes nanotechnology, the ability to manipulate matter on a molecular scale, will be the most important technology to human life.[7] Using the design principles by which biological systems—or machines—can replicate themselves we may be able to replicate in simpler structures small-scale molecular machines, which enable us to manufacture from the molecular level.

Some practical applications may be expected in five years. One of the first applications may be in super-strong, super-light alloys, created from the redesign of cellular structures. If predictions of nanotechnology's potential are correct, many things will happen in 50 years which we would not otherwise have expected for 1000—organically manufactured spaceships, for example.

The Future of the Multinational

The multinational corporations face a highly uncertain environment which Schwartz characterizes as periods of growth, turbulent transition, then further growth. We are now in a 20-year transition, following 20 years of growth after World War II. During the transition, oil price shocks resulted in a shift of capital to oil exporters, less developed countries fell behind on their long term debts partly as a result of faster financial flows and higher interest on short term loans. Other less developed countries became newly industrializing countries. A few countries with flexible, adaptive, developing economies, such as Japan, did well.[8]

The fundamental challenge for the multinational is complexity, both internal and external. We need new tools for managing complexity, according to Schwartz, and to develop the capacity of individuals to adapt to, function in and manage complex systems. Schwartz believes Shell is probably one of the most complex systems ever built and it works uncommonly well because it is internationally decentralized and employs highly qualified people. Many other corporations have managements that tend to oversimplify problems.

Most fantasies of world government by multinationals are only fantasies. What multinationals can do is to get things done: the international transfer of information and skills, for example, the global search for energy sources, promoting training and education in a country by publishing hiring requirements and developing programs of education, ensuring that trade flows continue to work, opening borders, increasing the level and rate of social change.

As an example of the latter, Schwartz notes that imposing sanctions on a country where you want to increase social change is less effective than sending in trade goods—Coca Cola and computers, for instance. Markets can work as a powerful force for peace.

Schwartz believes market forces have enabled multinationals to develop faster than other international institutions. This benefits them in that the political institutions of the countries in which they operate will not be able to get together to regulate them in any effective way.

However Schwartz believes multinationals need to welcome emerging international organizations which support wealth creation even if part of their agenda is to regulate multinationals. Without adequate controls on international corporations, the aggressive pursuit of wealth is likely to lead to instability that is not in the long term interest of corporations.[9]

The next period of expansion and growth is likely to present different business conditions from the last. Schwartz argues that manufacturing technology has advanced to the point where manufacturers will be expected to produce a range of different products for markets that are increasing in number and variety. Schwartz implies the next period of growth will take off when protectionism wanes and free trade expands. Capital, labor and products will move freely around the world, competition will sharpen, entrepreneurialism flourish, and governments restrict regulation to alleviating laborforce distress by encouraging mobility and retraining.[10]

If the world economic system maintains or increases its variability of performance, however, multinationals are likely to be rewarded less for their economic performance and more for their contributions to solving the social problems of nations.

Energy

Schwartz is optimistic about energy in general and oil in particular, believing potential problems can and will be managed effectively. Although world per capita demand for energy will grow with rising expectations and world population, developed nations will continue to use more than the developing nations by a large margin. Even if oil demand of the industrialized nations drops from 80% of world share today to 60% by 2000, improvements in energy efficiency by the advanced industrial nations will continue to exert great leverage on world demand.

There has been a somewhat condescending assumption LDCs will use the castoff energy technology of the industrialized nations or, put more academically, that developing countries must follow the development path of the advanced industrialized nations. Instead it is already clear that they are leapfrogging advanced nations to use the most efficient energy technologies available. A Korean steel mill today is four times more efficient than one built ten years ago which was then equal to the average efficiency of steel mills in fully industrialized countries. Some of the less efficient energy related technologies are likely to be seen in LDCs, but alongside highly efficient alternative forms. In transportation the old, large automobile may still be in use, but alongside greater numbers of fuel-efficient versions and other more economical forms of transport such as motor scooters. Schwartz excepts Africa from this trend toward greater energy efficiency.

He anticipates oil demand in the U.S. could fall more than 50% by 2000, if prices do not fall too low. Innovative energy policy action may be needed to maintain higher prices artificially—at or above $20 a barrel—in order to continue pressure to reduce demand. Plausible outcomes for the U.S. of maintaining the price of oil will be highly efficient cars and no net imports of oil.

Schwartz suggests an energy threshold exists of about eleven hundred dollars per capita, beyond which people may begin to consume a great deal more energy but at the same time work to improve efficiency and conservation, limiting the overall demand for energy.

Transportation

Jet air transport changed the scope of organization, making it possible to run national companies, and have personnel in New York serving accounts or equipment in Chicago. A hypersonic airline providing passage to Sydney in a few hours would have a similar effect, enlarging national corporations to global organizations.

U.S. Political Directions

Schwartz expects business as usual from the U.S. government, with regret that there seems little likelihood of an anticipatory mechanism for the U.S. being created at a federal level, or of the developing of a political process either new or renewed that will provide a greater sense of national leadership for the 21st century. Some U.S. organizations other than government, corporations and associations, for example, are developing foresight capabilities, but the international corporations are ahead in this field. Certain other international organizations, such as the World Bank, have effective global foresight efforts.

On the other hand, Schwartz believes the 1990s may be a time of economic and political stability, in contrast with the turbulent 1960s, 1970s and early 1980s coinciding with an integration of computer and communications technologies and a maturing of the policy process, especially in defense.

Values

Schwartz expects entrepreneurial values to spread in the U.S. and among populations worldwide. He believes individuals are more willing to put themselves at risk and to seek local and individual solutions for problems rather than waiting for government to act. An increase of individual interest in physical health and fitness is one indicator of a trend towards more personal responsibility autonomy. To some extent this may be an outcome of the greater access individuals have to information and more powerful information gathering tools, such as television, VCRs, personal computers and their connections to databases, and conference networks.

On the other hand, U.S. society is creating a permanently excluded subculture of several million, many of them black, young, violent, under- or unemployed, who support themselves by preying on others. They usually have neither the skills nor the inclination to join the societal mainstream. As a troublesome group that is too large to be re-educated or imprisoned, the subculture is one of many factors influencing a potential surge of conservatism on values and on family and social issues. There are other pressures towards a moral shift, for example, a failing educational system, drug abuse issues, disease, business scandals and white collar crime, and concerns about toxic waste dumping.

An AIDS epidemic could raise new public concern for moral values and behavior. On the other hand the disease may create a hedonistic subculture of those who either have, or believe they will have the disease. This group will no longer plan for the future, save money, build homes, or postpone gratification.

UNDERLYING CAUSES

Being a highly diverse and inventive species, humans have a tendency to use their technology to create systems which grow and become more complex than any one individual or group can control. The system then develops a life of its own which may be adapted to, or managed, but not controlled. The most important task for any individual or group is to understand the nature of complex systems in order to anticipate their direction, go with the flow, or be able to get out of the way.

EXHIBIT 20-1

FORCES INFLUENCING THE FUTURIST THINKING OF

PETER SCHWARTZ

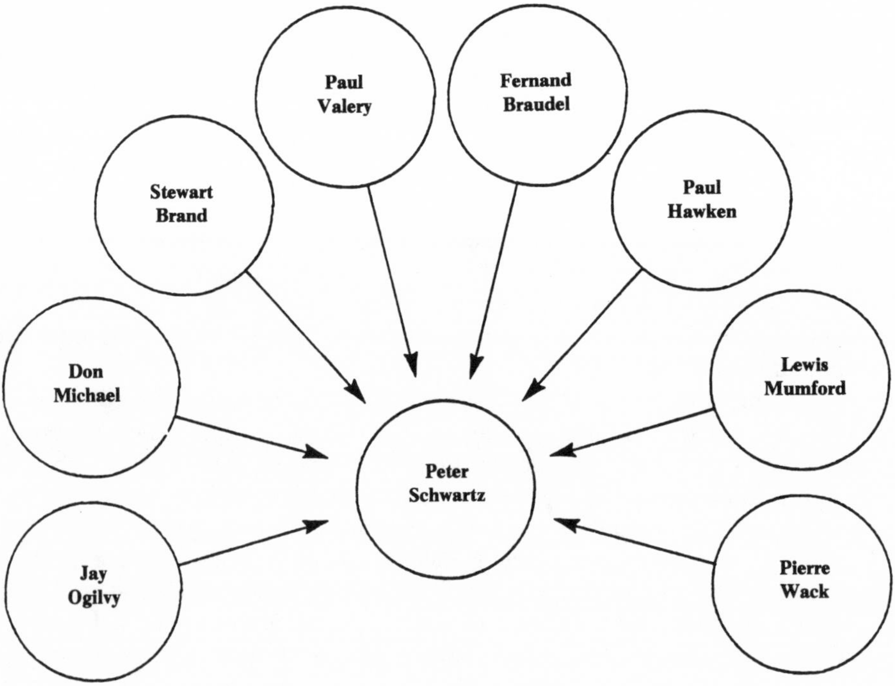

REFERENCES

1. Interview with Peter Schwartz, October 9, 1986.
2. "The World Information Economy," *Whole Earth Review,* Stewart Brand interviews Peter Schwartz and Jay Ogilvy, Winter 1986.
3. Schwartz has worked with the Group of Thirty, which is a periodic gathering of wise men in the international financial system, including former heads of the World Bank. The members of the group have reflected that they do not know how the system is controlled.
4. *Whole Earth Review.*
5. P. Schwartz and J.J. Saville, "Multinational Business in the 1990s—A Scenario," *Long Range Planning*, 19:6, December 1986, pp. 31-37.
6. Interview with Schwartz, October 9, 1986.
7. Eric Drexler, in his book, *Engines of Creation*, explores the potential of nanotechnology.
8. *Long Range Planning,* 19:6, December 1986.
9. *Long Range Planning.*
10. *Long Range Planning*, p. 35.

CHAPTER 21

ROBERT THEOBALD

Early in Robert Theobald's career as an economist he began to argue against the accepted wisdom that the undeveloped world should follow the economic strategies of the developed nations. He has continued to buck the intellectual tide since then. He is a transformationalist who believes we will have to build the transformation ourselves, at the grass roots. He is most likely to be found, anywhere in the U.S., patiently listening and talking to a small group of people about current conditions and their role in bringing about change. Theobald is virtually unique among futurists in combining broad scale analysis with cogent arguments for the ability of individuals to instigate change.

KEY VIEWS ABOUT THE FUTURE

1. The industrial era is over. We are beginning the communications era. What worked then will not work now, in economic policy, in education, in culture or in leadership.
2. We are burdened with myths, such as maximum economic growth as a goal. We need to recognize what our realistic alternatives are and rethink our values accordingly.
3. Cultures change not because one great person demands that they do but rather because many individuals decide to act, often in only slightly different ways.[1]
4. Infoglut is a problem of these early days of the communications era.
5. Terrorism is an unacknowledged form of war and the most likely one in the future, as the have-not nations come into conflict with the haves. Because their economies continue to depend on weapons production, and their consequent sale, industrialized nations are arming their opponents.
6. The family is experiencing turbulence as the industrial age gives way to the information society. At the height of the industrial era, the average male spent about 40% of his life at work. Today he spends barely 14%. We can, and will, have more satisfying work and family lives.

BIOGRAPHICAL NOTE

Robert Theobald was born in India, studied economics at Cambridge, worked in Paris for the Organisation for European Economic Cooperation and Development, spent a year at Harvard in 1957, and wrote his first book, *The Rich and the Poor*, published in 1960, about his belief that economic systems depend on social systems and values. In 1969, he founded Action Linkage, a networking organization which is intended to encourage, support and inspire networking for the challenges of and opportunities for social change. The group has about 800 members. Theobald is now chairman of Knowledge Systems, Inc., which incorporated in 1986 to publish the works of social entrepreneurship and to develop the knowledge base for social action.

His books include *The Challenge of Abundance*, 1961, (in response to John Kenneth Galbraith's thesis in *The Affluent Society*), *Free Men and Free Markets*, which raised the issue of guaranteed annual income, and *The Triple Revolution*, 1964, on the shift from industry to a new, non-industrial era and the potential impacts of automation. In the 1960s, Theobald began to write extensively about social change—the need for a guaranteed income in the new society was one of his arguments. After a few years, however, he became more interested in the process of change and the importance of the communication of ideas and the role of individual and local action in influencing societal change. *An Alternative Future for America*, in 1970, was an early work reflecting these new concerns. He first tackled the problem of drawing together diverse ideas for a debate on realistic objectives for social change in *Social Policies for America in the Seventies*. In the 1970s, he wrote *The Economics of Abundance, Habit and Habitat*, and *Futures Conditional. Beyond Despair*, in 1974, described the types of social shifts Theobald thinks necessary for a move into an information/communications society.

In the 1980s, he wrote *At the Crossroads* and *Avoiding 1984*. In 1986, he published *The Rapids of Change*, which distills what he has learned over 30 years about the reasons for change, the directions in which we are moving, the forms of leadership required, the new ways of thinking about the world, and the ways in which coming crises can be used to force change. The book is intended, among other purposes, to serve as a discussion guide for small groups debating change and planning social entrepreneuring. Robert Theobald propagates his ideas by meeting and talking with small to large local groups across the country. This chapter is based on observing him at these events, his writings, his correspondence with the authors and their conversations with him.

WORLDVIEW

Theobald has undergone substantial change in his approach to the future. Earlier in his career, Theobald, like many social analyists, followed his problem assessment with a coherent set of action steps and solutions. As he himself says, he talked with people likely to agree with him, and sought to build support for his ideas of what should be done without expecting that he or his supporters would accomplish great change. Over time he became more interested in the process of change and the social dynamics necessary for convincing people their actions can make a difference. He now finds at least as interesting the building of a network of people of diverse views, who support and contribute to positive change.

He is convinced a radical transition is occurring, that the future will be profoundly different from the past, and that the systems and institutions preserving social order for past generations will no longer function effectively. From taking informal polls, he concludes that most people believe there is an urgent need for extensive change in our culture and in our institutions. There are still many, however, who do not see opportunities for change, and believe the culture does not give them permission to talk or think about how they would like to make changes.

Whether or not everyone agrees on the need, several factors are driving change, nationally and globally:

- the technologies of microelectronics and communications,
- worldwide needs for energy and raw materials,
- population problems and their related environmental issues, and
- the development of a global labor force.[2]

In *Rapids of Change*, Theobald identifies more drivers of change:

- the revolution in weaponry that removes war as a means of resolving conflict,
- revolutionary technology, in computers and robots for example, removing the need for muscle power in work,
- the limiting effect on growth of a finite and relatively fragile environment,
- an international movement on human rights that is raising the expectations of millions,
- migration, especially in the Third World, of rural inhabitants to cities, and, where possible, to other countries where a marginally better life is available,

- our developing ability, although not necessarily our competence, to remodel life, to use biology to power our own evolution, and
- the shift to a world interconnected by information and communications systems, described by Theobald as knowledge systems.[3]

For Theobald, these are not solely issues for government, for the National Science Foundation, The Department of the Interior, the European Economic Community, or the Kremlin. These are issues for each individual to consider. Each person must be his or her own hero or heroine and act before the crises overwhelm us.

> *. . . we have a personal responsibility for the society in which we live. The second is to accept that there are no pat answers but that each of us must struggle to apply the values of faith, honesty, responsibility, humility and love to real-life situations without judgement.*[4]

A transformationalist who does not fit the usual mold because he does not expect a spontaneous shift in values—he believes we will all have to work for it—Theobald nevertheless advocates societal values common to transformationalists; a more humanistic society, one more based on cooperation and interdependence than competition and conflict between autonomous groups and nations.

He describes himself as a hopeful realist about the future, striking a balance somewhere between the pollyanna optimism which seems to him characteristic of some transformationalists—and some politicians—and despairing pessimism.

> *Visualizations of hopeful futures will help bring them into existence, both in personal lives and in societies.*[5]

SPECIFIC ISSUES

The U.S. and International Economies

Long term cycles, as argued by Kondratieff, exist as a balancing mechanism for the economy, but the slump at one end of the 50-year cycle and the hectic boom at the other are increasingly risky for world stability. Theobald doubts the competence of nations to manage these cycles partly because of their tendency to react to rather than anticipate the upswings and downswings of their economies. Nation states, as business managers and as defenders of their realms, are obsolete. Both of these functions can now only be managed or understood at the global level.

Theobald likens the U.S. economy—and those of most major nations—to a recalcitrant drunk, going on and off the wagon, deaf to messages of disaster and staggering ever closer to the gutter.

He suggests that the production methods developed in the industrial age and used in all sectors, including agriculture and energy production, have been so successful that the chief problem of advanced nations in the 20th century has been producing more than people can buy. This leads to over-extension of credit to individuals and nations, the consequent build-up of debt, and, in Theobald's view, to economic collapse, possibly as soon as the late 1980s.

He believes we need to buy time for managing the big issues of the economy by breaking them up into smaller ones. Our aim should be policies which achieve optimum growth, not in the economy, but in quality of life. He suggests several directions of approach:[6]

- reducing debt loads, as equitably as possible,
- decreasing population growth,
- cutting back on waste, and dumping policies that encourage waste,
- forcing polluters to bear the cost of clean-up,
- creating economic opportunities for the poor and putting a ceiling on wealth.

The emerging communications era will demand a better understanding of global economic interdependence. The international economy is in a debt crisis, for example, with more money loaned than can be paid back. If countries are not to collapse, some debts will have to be written off.

If world management is to emerge, it will do so at several levels, for example:

- the global level will be one of networking and exchange, rather than world government or international debate,
- the bioregional level, will, by abandoning old national boundaries and redrawing them around natural regions, create new ecologically based units of self-government,
- the community level will determine most local issues, with the limits on their power to make choices being a question with variable answers.

Cities

Megacities, especially those anticipated for the Third World, are no more viable than nation states. Some forecasts of potential growth in metropolitan systems are greater than can conceivably be expected to happen.

Housing

U.S. housing stock is unsuitable for emerging households, and inadequate to house the poor. Furthermore, we will become aware of the need for a new form of domestic architecture that works with nature rather than against it.

U.S. Regions

Rather than cities, the regions in deep trouble are in the heartland, in rural areas. We need to pay attention to the quality of rural life if rural areas are not to be depopulated.

Theobald suggests we accept 100 miles either side of the U.S. Mexico border as an Am-Mex territorial region with all its cultural implications—because we do not have the choice of an alternative.

The Future of the U.S. Corporation

Theobald observes the corporation actively changing, flattening its management hierarchy, introducing more flexibility, downsizing, moving to smaller profit centers, and so on. He assumes these trends will continue as the organization sheds bulk in an attempt to remain light on its feet in a period of economic turbulence. However he is not sanguine about the corporation's ability to lead, or join in, a social transformation. He questions corporate willingness to abandon certain values: maximum growth; the power of money in achieving goals; migration to lower cost, such as moving to the South or seeking cheaper labor overseas; and its reluctance to operate from a good citizen, rather than a self-interested, point of view.

On the other hand, a corporation that embraced social change would tap into an extraordinary fount of energy in the culture. A public relations campaign focused on needs for change would resonate with many people.

Unions

Unlike corporations, unions are not changing much, and seem unable, or unwilling, to recast their agendas. Two unfavorable factors are: one, corporations and labor are moving away from an adversary approach to labor and towards win-win strategies that do not necessarily include a role for unions; and two, the public is aware that unions are lagging change and, consequently, sees them as part of the old order of the industrial era, not of the new.

U.S. Political Directions

The 1988 presidential election may be more volatile than many think, especially since the possibility of a recession in the late 1980s cannot be ruled out.[7] However, effective change is not likely in Washington because much of the governmental structure is based merely on adjusting self-interest. Many of the non-profit, political action, social change groups who concentrate on the Hill are ineffective because they work from a one-issue, volunteer advocacy model. In Theobald's view, change will occur where people of diverse views establish a climate supporting local and individual action. His model is of a small town or city away from Washington, where the community leaders are willing to work with a broad vision of improving their town's quality of life. From the point of view of effecting positive change, federal and state governments are obsolete structures on an unstoppable downward spiral. Building an alternate structure with a more positive dynamic seems the only possibility, but such restructuring has never been done without great disruption. He suggests building new service clubs for change, on the model of the Kiwanis, or the Girl Scouts. Such national groups also have local and small units and, in some cases, were founded to accomplish social reform.

Defense and Disarmament

It is a paradox that even though we cannot use war to resolve conflicts any more, we are still behaving as if we could and continue to build up armaments.

On the other hand, the question of how we can move beyond war may already be answered because modern weapons have prevented conflict between advanced nations many times since World War II.

Terrorism is an unacknowledged form of war and probably the most likely one in the future, as the have-not nations come into conflict with the haves. Industrialized nations are inadvertently arming their opponents for this war, as their economies continue to depend on weapons production, producing more than they can use or stockpile themselves.

Technology

Technology has been and is a major driver of society, especially in the U.S. Technological developments are likely to continue to provide us with an enormous number of surprises—the new superconductors are just one—but we continue to underestimate the impacts of technology on society and lag in our efforts to counterbalance and shape technology by social choice. We are willing to follow where technology leads, but now that we have the means to upset global systems we have few social mechanisms to temper that power. These mechanisms can only be produced out of a re-examination of spiritual and moral values.[8] The recent surrogate motherhood court case, although not based on new technology, illustrates the effect of approaching a serious human issue from a casual, technical viewpoint of, if it can be done, do it.

Telecommunications and Computers

We dramatically underestimate the effects still to come of developments in telecommunications—on the workforce, on how we do work, and on lifestyles. Within x years this chapter would be written by a computer in voice consultation with the authors. No one knows, of course, the value of x.

Education

Theobald's views on education run counter to current belief that children need more time in school to learn the skills demanded by an emerging information society. This assumes, Theobald believes, that education is completed in school. If we assume, as we should, that learning is lifelong, we can cut schooling and teach people what they need to know, when they need to know it, rather than laying up a store of knowledge to be used—or forgotten—later. Our concepts of work are changing, people are likely to hold a variety of jobs, to need to learn new skills, and to know how to use unemployed times productively. For this reason community colleges are a more useful model for lifelong learning than four-year universities. In *Beyond Despair,* in 1976, Theobald made several proposals for opening up the educational system:[9]

- permit parents to encourage schools they believe most effective by sending their children to them,
- allow more people to teach without extensive credentialing and thus liberate more practical information and knowledge for the student, and

- assume that other sources of learning are available, lower the age limit for compulsory schooling so that parents are not forced to send their children to high schools that have become destructive environments for young people.

One of the problems may be in communicating to teachers that children ought to be prepared for a different future. Theobald finds educators generally believe parents are satisfied with the present structure of education, if not with its results.

Health

Hospitals, insurance companies, corporations and others are challenging people to keep themselves healthy, but even with this positive approach directed at keeping health care costs down, there will not be enough medical care to go around. Theobald notes many societies are already rationing care and anticipates further rationing, based on two primary models:

- the wealthy will get more, or,
- those with the best chance of survival will get more.

Neither of these models, in his view, frames the debate adequately. For an information age society, there are issues of individual responsibility for health and risky behavior in light of much greater available information on health risks; moral and ethical issues of who should be kept alive; and who pays, and how much.

Crime and Justice

In an increasingly diverse society laws based on a model for a more conforming age are less respected and ineffective in maintaining order. Theobald suggests a three-part strategy for developing an individual's sense of personal responsibility, reducing the need for enforcing laws.

- Recreating personal discipline in minor matters, obeying traffic laws, for example.
- Expecting more groups to discipline their own members, as professional societies are expected to do.
- Undercutting the criminal culture by finding ways to prevent young people from entering it. Taking the glamor out of self-destructive behavior, such as drug use and drinking, would be a step.[10]

Energy

The energy debate is in recess. This is unfortunate because we ought to expect at least one energy crunch in the near future. Theobald believes we will have to take another look at nuclear fission and begin to explore nuclear fusion because the coal alternative is too environmentally damaging in its contribution to the greenhouse effect. Resource issues are all energy related and are likely to be resolved, or not, depending on how we answer the questions about future energy supply.

Transportation

Transportation's future will be determined by the availability of energy, its effect on the environment, and whether communication will be substituted for travel.

The Environment

Learning to live within environmental, ecological and resource limitations may be a significant damping factor on world economic growth, but one which may not be avoided. The potential for a human-induced greenhouse effect is a warning the environmental response to unlimited human activity may be severe.

Information Age Societies

Too much information glutting the channels is likely to be a continuing problem for individuals in an information society. The most enterprising people will discover how not to receive junk information, but others will retreat and flee from the flood. The infoglut is confusing public debate and is likely to be a barrier to an individual or a group trying to attract attention to their ideas for change, because so many others are trying to do the same or similar things.

Theobald believes strategies for involving people in social change will not work for long if they add to the logjam of information. People will not respond to being urged to come to one more meeting, read one more book, contribute to one more good cause.

They may be enticed by an appealing approach requiring little effort. This minimum effort on their part returns a growing understanding of how to sort and manage information to achieve a dynamic balance between its complexity and diversity and how to set realistic goals for individual efforts for change.

Values

Industrial era values are held by many people in the U.S., especially those in academe, politics and the media. As the movers of information, their views continue to influence our culture, obscuring a shift towards new values by many people, especially those in small communities, in the central states and outside the business-political-educational structure prevailing on either coast. This discontinuity may make difficult a full shift to what an individual might consider good values for society. People may have shifted their ideas about education to the extent that they will work for its improvement, but do not necessarily see the same need for change in another system, such as health care. It is not usually apparent to people that their individual choices about what to buy, or in their lifestyles, can influence the national economy. A certain proportion want to be protected from hearing, seeing or thinking about any societal change, which is a reason, according to Theobald, for President Reagan's popularity. He suggests that if another presidential candidate offers to build a wall of ideology that will provide the same type of protection, the public will elect him, or her.

Theobald cites the United Way as an organization seeking to anticipate change and to act nationally and locally with sensitivity to diverse values among its members.

Families

Theobald believes it is a mistake to assume that changes in family life are irreversible, or that society or worklife cannot be rearranged to provide a more satisfying and acceptable family life that puts greater emphasis on childrearing. Some changes in the family are outcomes of turbulence as the industrial age gives way to the information society. At the height of the industrial era, he estimates, the average male spent about 40% of his life at work. Today he spends barely 14%. For Theobald, this shift implies there will be further restructuring of work and family life to make a happier adjustment with the new society.

UNDERLYING CAUSES

Theobald's thesis is that nearly all changes in society are incremental, built on individual choices and decisions at the grass roots. By a commitment of will, individuals can by their efforts alter the future course of society in a more positive direction. Individuals are likely to join organizations or to create new ones to tackle larger issues, but

Theobald believes these organizations must stay small to be effective. Beyond a certain unspecified size—a size Theobald calls 'X'—organizations cease to nurture and promote diversity of opinion and solution and are consumed by struggles for advantage and self-interest. For this reason, most governmental institutions, national and state governments and large organizations are no longer functional solvers of new problems, although they may continue to seek solutions to old ones.

EXHIBIT 21-1

FORCES INFLUENCING THE FUTURIST THINKING OF

ROBERT THEOBALD

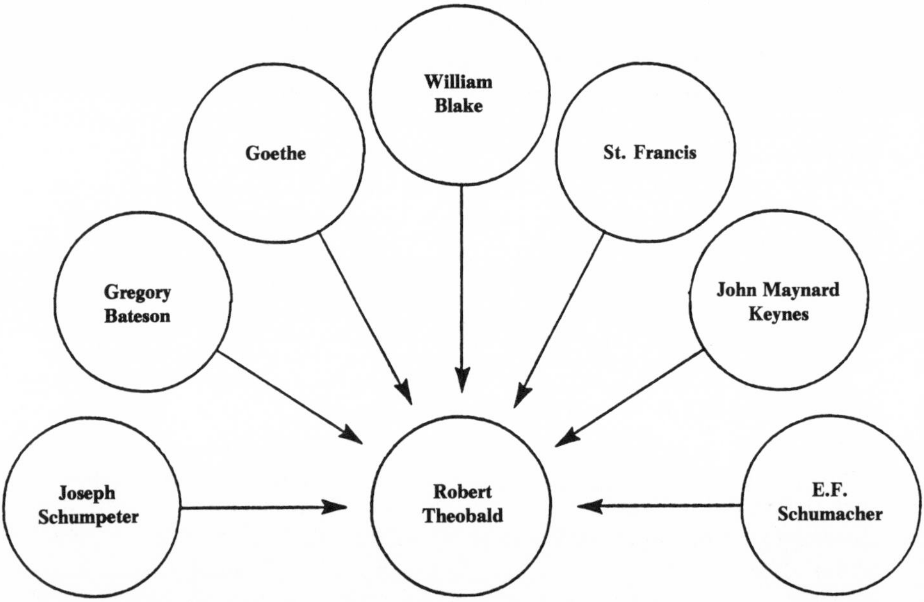

REFERENCES

1. *The Rapids of Change; Entrepreneurship in Turbulent Times*, Knowledge Systems, Inc., Chicago, 1987, p. 232.
2. "Managing Uncertainty: Economic Decision-Making in the Eighties," *Risk Management Reports*, July/August 1982.
3. *The Rapids of Change*, 1987, p. 32.
4. From a looseleaf version of the *The Rapids of Change*, 2:2.40.
5. *The Rapids of Change*, p. 44.

6. *The Rapids of Change*, p. 176.
7. Comments to a meeting of the Action Linkage and others in Washington, DC, April 2, 1987.
8. In conversation with Robert Theobald, August 3, 1987, he describes the social activist, Jeremy Rifkin, as raising the right kind of questions about biotechnology, but not in a manner or from an expressed moral position that encourages many others to join the debate.
9. *Beyond Despair*, The New Republic Book Company, Inc., Washington, DC, 1976, from the chapter on education.
10. *The Rapids of Change*, pp. 74-77.

PART THREE

CHAPTER 22

AS WE SEE THE FUTURE

The authors, Coates and Jarratt, present their views of the future in this chapter. We make no attempt to relate our views to the others discussed in earlier chapters. In this independent chapter we limit ourselves to a moderate time horizon of 15-30 years and emphasize topics of interest to the American corporation.

OVERALL TRENDS SHAPING AMERICAN SOCIETY

Fifteen areas in which trends are shaping the future of the United States are discussed in the following pages. These include demographic change; political direction; education; technology and science; telematics, (that is, information technology); the national and the multinational corporation; the domestic economy; religion; civil and criminal justice; regional differences; cities and housing; food and agriculture; the environment; health; defense and disarmament; and energy. These topics are indicative rather than exhaustive of the primary and secondary drivers shaping the domestic situation.

A discussion of values and the likelihood of any major changes in the values shared in American society is followed by a discussion close to the heart of any futurist or forecaster, and that is the question of discontinuities. What, if any, is the potential for sudden or sharp breaks from behaviors or patterns that could have a major effect on society? They are examined in exemplary rather than exhaustive fashion. Finally, international and global long-range trends are discussed, illustrating what was a questionable political slogan half a century ago and is now an undeniable reality of the future—one world.

The chapter ends with some conclusions specific to the role of, and the actions open to, the corporation. The corporation is the largest single factor in our society capable of shaping our political and social agenda positively, although still unorchestrated and inchoate in its goals and directions.

TRENDS AND DEVELOPMENTS IN THE UNITED STATES

Demographic Trends

Many of the most significant demographic trends are familiar and widely discussed, such as declining fertility, changing family size, the aging of the population, and the movement of the baby boom age group like a pig through a python across the future of the U.S. The impacts of many of these trends on labor markets, products, and culture will generally be ignored in this section, not because they are unimportant but because they are so familiar.

An uncertainty worth noting with regard to the baby boomers is whether their enthusiasm for innovation and change will persist through their middle years as they become more numerous and influential in corporate life. Their age clustering as they move through the corporation, when tied to the dearth of entry labor behind them and the cap on upward mobility created by downsizing, strongly suggests that new reward systems and new organizations of work within the corporation will evolve.

The mass entry of women into the workforce is the most significant demographic factor affecting the future of the corporation and the nation. Women are rapidly approaching men in parity of numbers. They are staying in the workforce full-time for full careers. They are briefly dropping out to have children and returning, on an average, after only three months. The lower wages paid to women (currently 71% of that of men) is due to occupational selection, some patterns of part-time working, but most significantly to prejudice. That issue will be dealt with the way all labor grievances have been dealt with, through legislation, regulation, suits, unionization, strikes, and so on.

All that is merely important. The radical effect of women in the workforce lies in the creation of millions of dual-income households, including many millions of full-time working couples and dual-career couples. Now millions of families have the opportunity to set aside enough income so that they can, for the first time on a mass scale, exercise independence at the workplace. The corporation has no choice but to cope. If workers do not like the organizational situation, after some modest warning, they will feel free to pick up and leave. This independence will first show up among the most critical, best educated, and brightest of the workers. It is common sense that the best and the brightest marry the best and the brightest, and they will have the greatest desire and latitude for independence. The corporation cannot exercise a two-tier labor strategy on a mass scale; i.e., different sets of rules for different groups.

Mass entry of women into the workforce is raising the question in millions of families: Do we need 80 hours per week of income equivalent? Increasingly, the answer is no, leading to a new work flexibility, not the flextime of the day or the week or the month, but flexibility over whole working careers. This is leading rapidly to a new economic unit in U.S. society, the working family, which will orchestrate and arrange its time and commitments to jobs and income to its collective needs and tastes.

Moving up the organization with some speed and generally concentrated in staff roles, women usually find themselves unable to break through the "glass ceiling" to the top of the pyramid. That situation will change as women move into operational or line roles and as they become more effective, visible forces in government, in client and customer corporations, and throughout the world of business.

Underlying that move of women into increasing power in the corporation is a core, biologically-driven question, the answers to which are unknown: Are women sufficiently different biologically from men that they will radically alter the work environment? From another perspective: Have men created a workplace riven by conflict, adversarial, and competitive behavior because of their surplus testosterone, a driver largely absent from the biology of women?

Demographic factors when coupled with continuing prosperity and education and the expansion of the middle class, drive the workforce toward a diversity of needs, expectations, and demands, which must evoke reciprocal flexibility from the corporation.

U.S. Political Directions

Democracy in the U.S. is facing multiple crises. First is the rise of the middle class to numerical and political dominance. Never in history have so many people known so little about those matters most important to their occupational, social, personal, and political future. This epidemic of ignorance is a powder keg of potential overreaction during our stressful integration with the global economy. Should the search for simple, easy solutions fail, the disappointed and stressed middle class may seek to line up behind the charismatic tyrant.

The second threatening trend building over the last 40 years is reliance on procedure rather than substantive understanding, specific knowledge, and political resolution. A quagmire of governmentally imposed or stimulated individual and corporate procedures reduces our flexibility, fritters away our opportunities, and on balance caters to fear and ignorance rather than encouraging opportunity. Proceduralism has put in the hands of every major and minor interest group the capability to invoke selective paralysis.

A third trend is the steady deterioration in the quality of political leadership in the federal government. The Congress lives in dread of special interest politics. The rise to national office increasingly depends on the telegenic smile, the glad hand, the nerveless spine, and the vacant skull.

Education

The potential future for education has never been better. Information technology holds the promise of making real the three long-term goals of education in our democratic society: mass education, lifelong education, and individually-tailored education. Whether we have the will to restore to education the goals of knowledge, learning, and civic virture, however, is doubtful.

Education in the U.S. while the most celebrated, effective, and democratic in the world, has been in 40 years of decline relative to its earlier excellence. Decades of expanding prosperity lured the best away from teaching and left elementary and secondary education in the hands of vapid incompetents. Legitimate but misplaced programs to raise standards by encouraging advanced degrees have stimulated a disastrous system of credentialism in which form has virtually displaced substance. The forces to reverse this trend are weak and disorganized.

At the university level, decades of prosperity have led to inattention to the quality of the output and created a perverse indifference or hostility to business and invention, the very factors which have made that education possible. While hope is rising that the situation will change, the single most important actor in reshaping the goals of education and making the needs for standards of excellence central, has stood back in near silence. Acting in a way characteristic of good deportment of earlier decades, the corporation remains nearly silent on the critical issue of education and the quality of the workforce. Some business organizations at the national level issue reports and deplore lack of progress, but where the corporation is most powerful, at the state and local level, it has remained the most quiescent. Internal training programs cannot compensate for twelve or sixteen years of faulty education. There are positive signs, however. For example, a group of corporations has founded a school run on business lines in Chicago.

Technology

Technology is the godsend to our faltering economy and quavering democracy. Whether that gift can be realized is an open question.

Independent streams of development in science separately and together promise radical enhancements in our capability to manage our affairs. For example, the material sciences are witnessing a flood of scientific capabilities which sooner rather than later will allow us to design almost any desired characteristics into new materials. Initial costs will be high, but they will steadily decline as the new materials go through their product and process lifecycles. Materials science will give us flexibility through new choices in more durable or tailor-made materials and, to a large extent, eliminate many traditional distinctions between substance and function in the design of our physical world.

The present early phases of applied genetics follow the traditional pattern of all new developments, to provide substitutes for present materials, processes, or products. While "inevitable" is a word to be used with discretion and care, biotechnology will inevitably give us products of an unprecedented degree of specificity, purity, and functionality. Its early application to esoteric products will be complemented by applications to produce commodity chemicals, an arsenal of magic bullets to devastate diseases and pests, and capability to reduce or correct environmental threats from chemical and biological materials. The tailoring of genes will give us nearly absolute control for producing plants and animals optimally suited to each environment. The elimination of genetic diseases and defects in plants and other animals will be quickly followed or even preceded by the capability to virtually eliminate inherited diseases and undesirable genetic proclivities in humans. Schizophrenia could disappear in the U.S. within the reader's lifetime. And again within that lifetime, mastodons will walk the earth, and passenger pigeons will fly again, once the secret is discovered of how to unlock the genetic message built into every body cell.

While genetics promises a boundless cornucopia of benefits, as we convert the science of genetic memory into applied technologies, our other two biological memories are semi-independently undergoing revolutionary transformation into practical applications. Immunology, the memory of our protein exposures, is becoming a practical, quantitative experimental and clinical science, which is likely to drastically alter our management of the built environment and other situations in which we are exposed to annoying, hostile, or threatening proteins and other chemicals.

Neuroscience, in dealing with our psychological memory, is nearly every month laying low another of the beliefs that human behavior is primarily determined by the social environment. New technologies directed at influencing our behavioral and mental processes will be based on neurochemical phenomena which are site and chemical specific in the brain and themselves primarily determined by the genetic code. While the direction of the science and the emerging technology is clear, how far that direction will carry us must remain an open question.

Telematics

The technologies of telecommunications and computers are rapidly melding into a new national and global infrastructure as the practicalities of science and commerce wash away the debris remaining from origins in disparate regulated and unregulated sectors. Telematics is giving a nervous system to the muscle and skeleton of national and international business, to government, and to every private interest group. It is in this nearly infinite, boundless, and intrinsically uncontrollable network that the hope of democracy lies.

Every large agency and corporation, i.e., bureaucracy, is characterized by the regulated flow of information externally and internally. That regulation is now severely stressed by the uncontrollable flow of information in every direction as telematics in the form of electronic mail and local area networks permeates business and government. Internal to the corporation, telematics is reducing the need for bureaucratic apparatus and eroding the importance of hierarchical status as we move to an organization driven by what you know, rather than where you are organizationally. The same technology caters to the worst side of the managerial autocrat by permitting new degrees of centralized control. On the other hand, it makes real the possibility of new and more effective modes of management based on decentralization.

Less in the factory but more in all other jobs, telematics reduces that 200-year-old trend and need: to go to work. The technology now makes it possible to carry the work to that half of the workforce that deals in information. The contemporary worker can work in a suburban center, at home, on the road, or even in the traditional office with equal facility and effectiveness. This, of course, is leading to a reversal of 60 years of land-use planning where the goal was to separate work from home and leisure. Off-site work also stresses organizational supervision and raises unfamiliar issues of liability.

The new information technology, by being intrinsically complex and requiring a great deal of time to be understood, invites abuse, crime, and unconventional uses. Put briefly, no one who plans, designs, builds, or operates a large system fully understands all it can do. The corporation, government, and society at large must learn to live with that information age reality.

As these and a dozen other characteristics of telematics work to change the organization of American society, a new revolution based on artificial intelligence, and on expert systems in particular, promises further radical change by the turn of the century in who works where, when, why, for whom, and at what compensation. Not far in our future are machines that will talk and listen, sense and move, see and feel, and to increasing degrees, exercise that most special of human qualities, judgment.

To sum up the trends in telematics, by early in the next century the per capita investment in information technology may rival that of the investment in the automobile. Every office and most advanced factories will be totally wired with fiber optics and automated. Homes will have as their core the home-work-study center. As the kitchen was the center of the household in the nineteenth century, and the rec room in the twentieth century, the home-electronic-work-study center will be the centerpiece of domesticity in the twenty-first century. As a capital asset, it will rival the bathroom or even the kitchen as the most expensive element in the home. With 10% to 20% of the workforce in telecommuting, that is, working two or three days a week at the traditional workplace and two or three days a week at home, on the road, in the suburban center, and in the supplier's or vendor's office, new distributed work patterns will alter our lifestyles. There will be one-plus screens per worker and numerous ones per household. Work, education, recreation, and leisure time activities will meld. One of the outcomes will be new forms of work, places for work, and modes of compensation, and the organization of many workers into small and large teams rather than in their present hierarchical structures.

The National and Multinational Corporation

At the end of World War II the U.S. was the global model for marketing, manufacturing, management, and the conversion of scientific research into practical products, processes, and services. Forty years of emulation often stimulated by U.S. government policy have spawned competitors by the score who may not only emulate us but innovate and exceed us in the four primary functions mentioned above. These new actors in international commerce seek above all to crack the U.S. market, the world's largest single market. The net effect has been a declining share of global commerce for the U.S. and an increasing challenge domestically, first in low cost and then in high cost, high quality, consumer goods, and most recently in scientific research and advanced technology.

Finding itself in crisis, the corporation is caught up in an orgy of competitive initiatives, cost-cutting, and reorganization, and the assumption of a visage of lean-and-mean. The outcome is unclear, but several factors are driving the corporation toward a chancy future. For none of our 1000 largest companies is there any criterion of health more basic than growth, yet the simplest arithmetic shows that no significant number of those 1000 can persist for the next 20 or 30 years in any conventional corporate growth objective of 5, 7, or 10% per year. There is a tragic flaw in society's central enterprise when most actors must end up defeated if not eliminated.

Symptomatic of the corporation's inability to address its long term health is the dominance of the paper entrepreneurs, a flood of junk bonds, an endless list of mergers, divestitures, and acquisitions. Most of these have no intrinsic purpose, only the extrinsic purpose of making the paper entrepreneurs wealthy. An erratically volatile stock market continually foreshortens the corporation's horizon, retards capital investment, demeans the value of long term research, and reduces top management's tie to its own organization through short-term expedients such as the golden parachute.

The multinational corporation, at an earlier stage in its history than is the domestic corporation, will surely run relatively unconstrained, if not wild, in the third and fourth world, as the domestic corporation did from 1870 to 1920. And just as surely it will ultimately be constrained by new levels of international control. The forms of control are unclear now. However, one can already see early signs of an emerging pressure for constraint, particularly in the areas of environmental pollution, transborder shipment of toxic wastes, and the evermore visible disturbances of the global commons, our air and oceans.

As the domestic corporation takes the globe as its planning unit for marketing, manufacturing, and manpower, the U.S. domestic polity is increasingly incompetent to cope. In the absence of a corporate long range point of view and corporate collective action the domestic polity is likely to aggressively rein in the corporation as it goes for more job exports, plant closings, and trade imbalances. Exhibit 22-1 notes trends within the corporation. Together they create a complex image of vitality, inventiveness, and change as well as myopia, isolation, and drift into more turbulent times.

The U.S. Domestic Economy

The great irony is that our capability of generating new products and processes to bring greater benefits to all has never been greater, while our political leadership, which has its hands on all the big economic levers, has never been more inept, more ignorant, more lacking in nerve and vision. For example, research must be at the root of our future

Exhibit 22-1

Trends in the American Corporation

1. Continuing commitment to growth.
2. Growing overseas manufacturing and procurements.
3. Domestic/foreign distinctions fuzzy.
4. Shaping up to foreign competition.
5. "Lean and mean" in vogue.
6. Management innovations abound.
7. Competition for consumers and industries.
8. Pressure for higher quality goods and services.
9. New forms of expansion.
10. Predators and prey abound in mergers, acquisitions, and divestitures.
11. Move to new areas of business for growth and stability.
12. Short term vs. long term concerns tipped to former.
13. Paper entrepreneurs increasing in influence.
14. New trends in planning.
15. Lessening commitment to geographic place.
16. Public, private distinctions fading.
17. Weakening creativity and invention.
18. Low public regard continues.
19. A new people orientation sweeping the corporation.
20. Chauvinism continues.
21. Organizational change at a brisk pace.
22. Research-oriented.
23. Increasingly information based.
24. New social missions falling to the corporation.
25. Expanding accountability.
26. Comparative freedom from regulation continues.
27. Suspicion of government continues.
28. Rising political activity and astuteness.
29. Business degrees in growing disrepute.
30. Anti-union behavior increasing.
31. Secretiveness continues.

Source: J.F. Coates, Inc., for the Environmental Scanning Association, 1985.

progress, yet we have no policy, coherent or otherwise, for nurturing and promoting civilian scientific developments. We provide neither information nor incentives to the American businessman for engaging in international commerce; we have no significant or new monetary or fiscal policies for promoting new investment; we have no policy for prevention or control of foreign acquisitions of U.S. businesses and the bargain basement acquisition of American patents and inventions.

The economy remains distorted by a two-pronged defense program. One prong is directed at Star Wars. The challenge in that case is to find anyone not tied to the Department of Defense payroll who has any confidence that it could conceivably achieve its objectives. The second prong is directed at land and sea conflicts and engagements inappropriate for the manpower, the logistics, and the training in vogue for the past 25 years.

The big American corporation's involvement in defense has paralyzed it with regard to the prodigality of the potlatch called national security. While their long-term interests are destructively undercut by the defense budget, short-term fears of a vengeful White House and Department of Defense, and the threat of economic setback from the loss of military contracts, renders the corporate moguls mute. The corporation's and the nation's future is blighted by what Eisenhower warned us against, a military-industrial complex. Patriotism vs. incompetence and waste is not the only choice.

Values

The most important value shifts in the U.S. are the long-term, irreversible consequences of mass education, continuing prosperity, and the shift to a middle class society. The American public will no longer tolerate risks imposed upon it, for the simple reason that it knows such impositions are unnecessary. On the other hand, virtually any risk will be embraced by the middle class if it is confident that it has the competence to make that embrace and there is some important benefit. After all, people do hang-glide. The implications for the corporation should be clear as it reaches the limits of attempting to create risk-free products, processes, and services. A healthy switch is to better, fuller information and a wider choice for its customers and other affected parties.

The second value shift is the erosion of confidence in authority, authority figures, and institutions. The same three drivers of change noted above now put most people in a position where they can become their own authority or at least learn enough to probe and question putative authorities. Just consider how the ***Reader's Digest*** raises repeated challenges to the practice of medicine. Their articles are well-known for motivating questioning patients.

The third value shift is the movement from the showy, the flashy, the quick turnover, and the superficial, as the hallmarks of success in an upwardly mobile society, to amenities, durability, preservation, and quality, the hallmarks of prosperity, education, and middle-class success.

Finally, the rise of pressure for self-fulfillment is reflected in many ways throughout society. At the workplace, the workers demand to be de-robotized and to have more complete use made of all their skills, talents, and capabilities. Any hope that modest or severe economic setback will alter the attitudes of these new workers is unrealistic to the point of foolishness.

Religion

A half-century of research documents that by any measure religion is in long-term decline in the U.S. Adherence to traditional beliefs, e.g., a unitarian god, a personal devil, or hell, declines with education, intelligence, upward mobility, and economic status. Catholics are Protestantizing; Protestants are Unitarianizing (there is at most one God). These trends are leaving behind a nationwide, wealthy husk—the institutional church.

The rise of television preachers and religious fundamentalism is not an exception to this trend, but rather reflects different factors. For the first time after 50 years of public policy neglect, the poor-but-honest folk who traditionally adhered to these basic beliefs have found a public voice. At any time either political party could absorb them by recognizing their elementary socioeconomic needs and responding to their long-time quest for political status. The Republican Party's embrace of the religious agenda of fundamentalists misses the longer term political opportunity to attend to this group's economic well being.

Civil and Criminal Justice

Trends in civil and criminal justice in the U.S. reveal several crippling and pernicious threats to our democratic society. The doubling in a decade of the number of lawyers in the U.S. (estimated incremental personal income $15 billion per year) has created a self-generating monster of proceduralism and hyper-caution. A generation ago the corporation lawyer's function was to tell you how to get on with the business. Today the corporate lawyers concentrate on how to avoid trouble. Their power, reflecting their orientation to the past and their penchant for procedure, is a lead weight on society. There is little hope the situation will improve. They make the laws, define the rules, enforce them, debate and judge the pros and cons of the consequences, and at each stage skim off their income. Law and lawyers have managed to out-do the Mafia in skill and gall in predatory practices.

Criminal justice similarly reflects the pathology of middle class life and excessive lawyering. No justice is speedy, defeating the fundamental scientific knowledge about effectiveness of rewards and punishment. No justice is inevitable or sure to be fair, subverting public regard for the system. The legal system progressively rejects or perverts rather than embraces new scientific knowledge. In the area of administrative law we have allowed willful monomaniacs to intimidate legislators and to employ procedural techniques to thwart, stymie, and ultimately discourage many avenues of research and applications appropriate for a positive social agenda and crucial to effective international competition. As in so many areas the corporation has stood by in silence, only occasionally emitting mild protests.

Regions of the U.S.

Regional differences will persist in ethnicity, language, custom, business, and industrial base, but the dominant trend is toward economic equalization and cultural and social homogenization across regions. This facilitates planning and promotes uniformity in marketing and in plant siting. Homogenization also carries with it a threat to democracy—the mass reaction of an undifferentiated populace to some national crisis. On the other hand, economic homogenization is making it difficult for the corporation to follow its traditional strategies of indifference to the local community and cut-and-run when it does not like the local situation.

Yet, regions are still acquiring new elements of diversity. The southern tier from Texas' Padre Island to Los Angeles is rapidly becoming a bicultural, bilingual Hispanic dominion. The shift of immigration from Europe to Latin America, and South and East Asia is creating in California and the western states massive concentrations of Oriental and Latin populations. They will relive the experiences of all other urbanized immigrant groups since the civil war and bring new culture, recreation, entertainment, foods, and politics to the American melting pot.

Cities and Housing

Regardless of bucolic romanticism and memories of a rural society which probably never existed, the city is and will continue to be the center of civilization, and must continue to grow. The U.S. is today 75% metropolitan. By early in the next century, the majority of the world's population will be metropolitan. The next two decades of American urban life, however, are likely to be bleaker and less pleasant than the early part of the century. Political power is disproportionately low for city dwellers. Local government officials are less professionally trained, less able, more subject to parochial influences and suborning. This is the history of major American cities. The most powerful unorchestrated force in improving the quality of city life is the corporation. Again, it tends to sit back in indifference without a murmur of discontent, much less a cogent plan, program, or threat. The infrastructure rots, the school system decays, housing is a disaster, the central business district is traumatized, and the corporation says nothing.

Internationally, throughout the Third World, the cities and housing situation is moving from desperate to catastrophic. The appeal of the city still dominates throughout the Third World, and the city still offers more opportunity than the countryside. The outcome is unbelievable squalor, as rural customs such as large families and low regard for public health practices are carried over into city life. The large cities of the Third World, with ten to twenty million people each, will prove to be death traps as epidemics eventually decimate them, drive the survivors away, and discourage new immigrants. For a more positive future for Third World cities, the central problem is not food, clothing, or public health, but housing. The commandingly exciting opportunity for modern technology is to provide the means of permanent housing for a family of four for a total capital investment of $1200 and buckets of sweat equity.

Food and Agriculture

The present crisis in the farm belt is a consequence of the failure to attend to two visible trends. First is the decline in political power of the farm bloc. That failure is, to a large extent, a consequence of farmers being blind to the rise of the consumer movement and failing to join forces with that primarily urban power bloc. Second is the failure to attend to the trend, operating over a decade, of increasing agricultural competence, technological investment, and agricultural productivity in the Third World. The expectation of the U.S. being the granary of the world ceased to have reality a decade ago.

In the absence of public policy the domestic trend is toward more industrialized farms and a further expansion in size of the so-called family farm as prudent farmers buy out their bankrupt neighbors. The declining power of the agricultural sector in the voting booth will eventually lead to and allow reform of wasteful subsidy programs and more rational agricultural management partially administered by the federal government.

On the other hand the rise of the self-care health movement, the environmental movement, and the fear of toxic materials, will stimulate new small specialty farms and specialty products. Responding also to the pressure for better cost control and quality control, more food will be grown in controlled environments. Biotechnology, when it gets rolling in agriculture, will create totally new crops, resistant crops, crops with better storage and handling characteristics and perhaps—but just perhaps—restored gustatory quality.

Internationally, the wave of optimism that the global food crisis has passed is hardly sustainable. The present marginal food surpluses and the several transitions from importer to exporter status in the overpopulated Third World, are likely to be only a short term (5-10 year) imbalance favoring food surplus. In the absence of any effective population control throughout the Third World, except possibly China, Malthus must eventually prevail.

Environment

The national problems which started the environmental movement of the sixties and seventies are well on the way to resolution, only to be superseded by problems likely to be both more ubiquitous and less tractable. Assuming no catastrophe such as a nuclear power plant spill, a mid-continent earthquake, or an eruption in the Canadian Cascades, the visibly emerging environmental problems carry multibillion dollar price tags. Groundwater contamination from toxic materials must get worse, and we have no significant technology for modeling, monitoring, containment, or reclamation. Indoor air pollution is likely to radically alter the design, structure, and materials entering into home, office, and workplace. New fears ranking with carcinogenesis and mutagenesis will become prominent as effects of trace materials on the neurological system, the immunological system, aging, and the reproductive apparatus are more fully understood.

Domestic environmental concerns have spread across the globe in two dimensions. First, the now familiar U.S. problems are undeniably visible in the other advanced nations and in the Third World. By general agreement, for example, the most polluted atmosphere in the world is in a city in Brazil. This awareness will influence multinational business in terms of sites, marketing, manufacturing, minerals extraction, employment and public acceptance.

The second shift is to concern for global problems which are not constrained by political boundaries: the greenhouse effect, sea level rise, ocean contamination, deforestation, diminishing biological diversity, perturbations in the ozone layer, etc. Aside from the merits of the arguments for each threat and the reliability of the anticipation of their outcomes, the unifying theme in all of them is to stop something we are now doing. There is almost no interest on the part of the aggressive advocates in solutions, accommodations, or countermeasures, all of which would presumably involve the application of new scientific and technological knowledge. Again, each corporation peeking out of its small niche, draws back from identifying opportunities for positive action in global civil works and planetary engineering.

Health

The long-term trend in the advanced nations is toward squaring off the death rate curve. There is no compelling scientific basis for anticipating general life extension past the ninth decade. While that may come to some future generations, the realistic current goal is to have more of us live happy, healthy, full lives into our eighties.

Overlaying that broad pattern in the U.S. is the emergence of several areas of health technology based on fresh, fundamental scientific insights. Many genetic and most congenital diseases could effectively fall to near zero. Genetic and hence biologically based degenerative diseases, e.g., arthritis, are likely to come under biological prevention and control. The major psychoses, schizophrenia and psychotic depression, will probably become things of the past in the advanced nations by the turn of the century.

The largest and clearest opportunity for improved health lies in nutrition, exercise, altered lifestyles, and—using the automobile analogy—preventive maintenance. Unfortunately, rural, impoverished, small town people and new ethnics tend to be inattentive to these health-promoting factors. They are malnourished and overfed. Ironically and pathetically, the children of America have for well over a decade been on a steady downhill slope in strength, vigor, stamina, and athletic prowess.

Aside from a score of minor new diseases that will become prominent, the emerging centerpiece of private, public, and corporate health concerns will be AIDS. As it currently stands, $250,000 for care from first diagnosis till death will be unacceptable as the Grim Reaper harvests not thousands, but millions. As a practical matter the need is to isolate AIDS from the current health care system so that in the absence of a vaccine for prevention or a definitive therapy society can provide effective humane care at 10-20% of current costs. Perhaps a fair goal might be the equivalent of a year's salary from diagnosis to death.

This need jibes with a continuing corporate agenda of benefits and particularly health care cost containment. While the measures of benefits are difficult, there is little or no evidence that the current high expenditures (11% of GNP) has paid off commensurate with the increased costs.

Defense and Disarmament

Nuclear war is the greatest manageable risk facing humankind. A consensus on that point exists among the people of the advanced industrial nations. Yet we continue only to dabble around the edge of the problem and in many ways actively promote a worsening of the situation. This reflects our chronic inability to deal with anything beyond the moderately important or the sub-critical. We and the other major nuclear powers stand by while unstable, volatile Third World countries build nuclear capabilities.

We continue to promote national defense programs to a large extent framed around a war that almost no one believes ever could or would be fought—on the north German plains. We shunt the nation's outstanding technical brainpower into a strategic defense program—Star Wars—which no competent military analyst not directly or indirectly on the DOD payroll sees as workable, now or ever. We build ground and naval forces incapable of fighting in any of the dozen places most likely to call for our intervention. What fool, for example, would ever wish to be the captain of the $15 billion nuclear aircraft flotilla put at risk by two-bit weapons in defense of an unnameable, unidentifiable, uninhabited backwater of the world? The military-industrial complex continues to call forth new materials flowing into the logistics stockpile not by the dozens or the scores but by the hundreds every year. Few new items are around long enough to be tested, proven, or used. Virtually no senior military officer has the guts or the brains to call a halt to that which cannot work, e.g., the Abrams main battle tank or the Bradley personnel carrier.

The outrageously unprofessional and incompetent state of the military is punctuated by the fact that after 42 years of nuclear weapons and three substantial wars not a single first-class book on military strategy has been written by a U.S. army, marine, or naval officer. There is no powerful force for change short of budgetary pressures, and that is only likely to shrink the pool of assets to be frittered away, rather than to lead to intelligent reform.

Even the traditional argument that a flow of civilian technologies is derived from military and military-space expenditures no longer holds water. The transfers have become trivial compared to the assets expended.

Energy

The energy prospects for the U.S. reveal the long-term pernicious consequences of industry focused solely on the short term, a polity without vision or leadership, living in fear of powerful regional and business interests, and the inability of government's senior officials because of ignorance, ineptitude, and brief tenure to mount any federal program with staying power. The petroleum stockpile could not be filled when oil was too expensive, and now that it is cheaper it is clear, to some, that there is no point to filling it. We deplore the risks of depleting energy stockpiles and yet work diligently to promote the exhaustion of that finite resource, ignoring the vagaries of the world oil supply and the price roller coaster. We allowed thousands of wells to be closed down irreversibly rather than arrange for their temporary capping and future revival. We obliterated our exploration capability, which all interested parties knew we will sooner rather than later need again. We know that we need alternative fuel sources but refuse to either make or promote long-term stable investments for the exploitation of coal and the promotion of solar power. The federal R&D energy program is a shambles. Public policy toward conservation has ceased to exist. We have still not accommodated and promoted new structural designs for home and office which are environmentally satisfactory, cost effective, and energy conserving.

At the international level, the energy situation seems to be worsening as more people place more burdens on local energy supplies for the minimum domestic needs of cooking and shelter. Little has been done nationally or internationally to field a coherent well-funded program of socially, anthropologically, and technologically sound energy technology. The growing world population, even in satisfying their minimum demands for energy, will stress present and future supplies and make half the world captive of the erratic behavior of second and third tier world powers. The U.S. corporation has been neither coherent nor forthright in establishing a sound position on the relationship of energy needs and energy supplies to their or the nation's future. The corporation has been, for unclear reasons, a devoted enemy of stabilizing the long term energy situation.

WHAT ARE THE DISCONTINUITIES?

Discontinuities are the sudden and sharp breaks in behavior or patterns or the unexpected perception of such changes or breaks. They may come in the economic, social, technological, geophysical, or any other domain. They come in all sizes and shapes, and affect businesses in an indeterminately wide range of ways. Some are beneficial, some neutral in their long-term effects, but in the short run, most of them are negative. Some discontinuities that might affect the corporation are displayed in Exhibit 22-2. That list, while long, is highly abbreviated. It does point up the fact that little comfort can be found in any long-term planning grounded in assumptions of continuity.

Exhibit 22-2

A Few Discontinuities That Could Affect the American Corporation

NATURAL EVENTS

1. A major earthquake in the Midwest, California, or Japan.
2. Confirmation of the (carbon dioxide induced) greenhouse effect and associated sea level rise.
3. Multiple volcanic eruptions in the Cascades range.
4. Sustained drought in the U.S.
5. A big meteorite strike.
6. Crop failure—a blight attacks world wheat or corn crops.

TECHNOLOGICAL FAILURES/BREAKTHROUGHS

7. A nuclear accident, involving mass contamination.
8. Star Wars becomes operational.
9. Military or civilian space junk falls on urban area.
10. Terrorist acts aimed at specific companies or classes of individuals, such as key executives.
11. Unanticipated side-effects of new drugs, or drugs in common use.
12. Smart cards in widespread use.
13. Expert systems widespread and commonplace.
14. Intelligent life in space confirmed.
15. A cure for cancer(s).
16. Development of effective genetic screening.
17. Use of interactive cable in retailing, participatory politics and education.
18. Cheap, efficient photovoltaics available.
19. Energy produced from fusion.

ENVIRONMENTAL

20. A worldwide pandemic of a fatal disease, such as AIDS.
21. A non-fatal epidemic with latent or unanticipated side-effects, such as sterility or infertility.

ECONOMIC

22. A group of third world countries collectively abrogate debt.

23. Unemployment rises and stays high, causing a default on the nation's consumer debt.
24. Runaway inflation.
25. A balanced U.S. budget.
26. Volatility of the housing market, falling property values.
27. Crisis of expanding liability and insurance, leads to new definitions of acceptable risk.
28. Merger/Acquisition legislation.
29. Organized crime found to have penetrated several major corporations.
30. Expanded concept of privacy on the job.
31. More computer fraud.
32. Europeanization of U.S. workforce, i.e., extensive legal control on firings and plant closings.

INTERNATIONAL

33. Revolution in South Africa, or Mexico, or the Philippines.
34. Israel falls.
35. Protectionism increases in the U.S.

GOVERNMENT AND POLITICAL

36. A president is impeached after details of an undercover plot to destabilize the government of a European country is uncovered.
37. A durable, sharply unbalanced Supreme Court precipitates a Constitutional crisis.
38. Growth of third party politics.
39. Constitutional convention, which rewrites the Bill of Rights.
40. Concept of the "ideal racial mix" developed to support new U.S. immigration policy limiting influx of Asians and Hispanics.
41. International treaties to regulate multi-nationals.
42. Marijuana and other drugs legalized as recreational.
43. Assassination of a President and the complete succession.
44. Comparable worth legislated nationally.

SOCIETAL

45. Service and information workers' unions gain strength.
46. Educational reform.
47. Terrorists detonate nuclear device in the U.S.
48. Universal service instituted.
49. A messianic millenarian movement.

Source: J.F. Coates, Inc., for the Environmental Scanning Association 1986.

IS A TRANSFORMATION IN VALUES LIKELY?

Some futurists foresee, and some others advocate, a fundamental transformation of American and global society, involving the adoption of radically new structures for employment, organizations, governments, and social institutions, accompanied by widely adopted lifestyles radically different from those at present. In our opinion, such a transformation is not likely in the next several decades. However, that does not mean that the next few decades will not see strikingly different lifestyles prominent across the U.S. The most likely changes are discussed in the following paragraphs.

Expanding diversity in every aspect of American life is driven by education and prosperity. We increasingly are aware that the world does not have to be the way it is. Education and prosperity also provide the tools and mechanisms for promoting change. A sub-theme which will have great visibility in food, clothing, style, and the makeup of the population is the steady contribution of immigration to our net population growth, currently about 25%. Perhaps the most significant organizing principle of the expanding diversity is the thesis of Abraham Maslow or that independently developed by Clare Graves, which implies that as we move from a stressful, struggling, competing, upwardly mobile society to one which is middle class, stable, prosperous, and educated, our individual demands are increasingly for self-fulfillment and the development of the total person. These changes will influence managers and also create a drive to accommodate diversity.

An expanding range of new values and tastes will come out of the Maslovian-Gravesian ideas. The middle class, which is the core of the society (60% to 80%, depending on how one counts—and growing) is increasingly committed to trial, experimentation, and the development of new tastes.

Conservatism will come into play in the economy in many social activities, in sexual deportment, and in a general and pervasive conserving view toward the environment. At the economic level, a somewhat stressed economy will make us more conservative about jobs, about crime, about security, about risk-taking, about guarding income, all of which will be in counter-position to the pressures for diversity, change and flexibility in jobs and workplace. Sexual caution will be driven by fear of venereal disease, particularly AIDS. Conserving materials and energies will be driven by the institutionalization of conserving practices, by putting them on an economic footing.

There will be expanding liberalization throughout the society in politics, in occupations, in careers and recreation, in education, and in lifestyles. For many, there will be an inversion of the traditional relationships of working young, relaxing old to a situation in which more interleaving of work and leisure, travel and employment will dominate. The expanding liberalization lies in the expansion of education and some continuing level of prosperity. Prosperity, to have this effect, does not imply vigorous growth, it only implies tangible opportunity for betterment.

A more experimental attitude will permeate the society. That experimental attitude will be reflected in two distinctly different ways. First will be more testing of social programs, and a more conscious move to social invention to find new ways of dealing with old problems. As an example, how might we approach monetizing the goal of controlling teenage pregnancy?

The second experimental avenue will be in personal development. Perhaps 3% to 5% of adults at any one time will be living a substantially different lifestyle from the mainstream, in a style one might characterize as voluntary simplicity. Such behavior is well known in other cultures. Adult male Buddhists spend an extended period in their priesthood. Contemporary Mormons spend substantial time in various church programs proselytizing. The life of voluntary simplicity does not necessarily involve a religious or proselytizing strategy. The illustrations only point out models of contemporary people allocating large blocks of their life to behavior strikingly different from the usual.

Finally, one can anticipate more elements of society in conflict with each other in their interests, goals, and desires. The test of democracy will be whether those conflicts can be dealt with effectively without hostility and aggression through peaceful trade-offs.

INTERNATIONAL AND GLOBAL LONG-RANGE TRENDS

A global economy has developed, marked by intense and increasing interactions among almost all nations, regions, and markets. Trade patterns are fluid, and there is increasing competition for both raw materials and markets, whether high technology or basic commodities. Political patterns also are fluid. Conventional organizing concepts such as East/West, North/South, advanced nations and LDCs, have become useless or dangerously misleading.

Worldwide, there is increasing urbanization, industrialization, capitalization of agriculture, and disproportionate growth in the service sector. The most advanced nations have become "post-industrial." Urbanization and industrialization in developing nations, the rapid growth of population in the poorer nations, the relative depletion of high-grade accessible deposits of minerals, and the more critical threat of exhaustion of renewable resource systems indicate future demand for food and most materials that can be met only with rapid advances in science and technology.

In the meantime, international businesses increasingly will be operating in an uncertain and hazardous political environment. Aggressive nationalism and cultural assertiveness, shifting alliances, and the politicization of trade and commerce will be more serious problems. International trade will be faced with a marked growth in legal and regulatory constraints imposed through a welter of treaties and agreements by both governmental and non-governmental bodies. Environmental and public health problems are particularly likely to become political issues and result in regulations and restrictions within nations and among nations.

Disruptions of the normal flow of materials, information, and people are likely and will be more troublesome because of the intermeshing of economic activities around the world. Threats to the security of the corporation's representatives, workers, facilities, and property may increase as terrorism becomes associated with a wider range of political and non-political demands and conflicts.

Long-range trends are converging to erode American political, economic, scientific, and technological dominance. On the other hand, a new surge of scientific advance and technological change offers America every opportunity to excel. The telematics revolution, which is changing the world on the same scale as the industrial revolution did, is apt to be followed shortly by a biological revolution that has the potential for equally dramatic impact on all sectors from agriculture to manufacturing to human health and longevity.

The sweeping changes underway in the world system generate unfamiliar international issues that will trouble the next few decades unless they are resolved in some workable fashion. One such issue is stabilizing the world banking system; another is regularizing the development of resources from the global commons. The way in which these issues are resolved, or the failure to resolve them, will strongly affect all multinational corporations.

Exhibit 22-3 shows some 89 trends shaping the global and international situation. This relatively brief list implies that planning based solely on continuity is likely to be far removed from future reality. The complexity of these interacting trends also implicitly points up the need for more positive, collective, and cooperative policy planning and action by the corporation. Exhibit 22-3 was prepared in 1983 for a large petroleum company. Its text is left unedited to make the point that most significant trends are visible for a very long time, that sharp breaks should not dominate thinking about the future, but rather give awareness to the revolutionary potential in steady unrolling long-term changes as the basic strategic background for long-range planning. In examining that exhibit, the reader, we hope, will share with us the observation that some of the trends might be better stated, some might be updated, but of the 89, perhaps only one or two would be drastically altered.

CONCLUSION

The corporation is the dominant economic institution in the United States and in the world. Its role, its responsibilities, and scope of action is increasing. This chapter has reviewed many of the stronger and clearer external and internal forces operating on the corporation, forces which challenge its traditional organization structure, function, goals, and objectives. In order for the corporation as an institution and individual corporations as economic entities to remain healthy, substantial change is called for. Whether these changes are looked at as opportunities, challenges, or necessities is, to some extent, a matter of taste. The reality is that "business as usual" may be fatal.

As a dominant economic institution, the American corporation is acquiring increasing social responsibilities at the same time that its workforce is rapidly changing in its makeup and expectations. It is being challenged nationally and internationally in the market place. The corporation must collectively protect itself from predatory practices and the pernicious myopia induced by an excessively volatile stock market and an increasingly foreshortened time horizon. The corporation must also overcome its indisposition to government, to joint ventures, and to corporate cooperation. In lush times the corporation may enjoy the luxury of basking in the prejudices of unsustainable ideology. Under the severe pressures of economic competition it must recognize that government can be its largest asset and one of its greatest resources in international competition. Government as either facilitator or coordinator in joint ventures and collective action is not the end of marketplace competition, but rather can give it new vitality. Witness the intense competitiveness of the Japanese with automotives and electronics among each other. The American corporation is ideologically and strategically adrift, with no long-term purpose or goal, save the unsustainable and destructive one of growth for growth's sake. This chapter outlines the clearest of the many forces acting to reshape the corporation and the pressing urgency of a new collective strategy for doing business.

Exhibit 22-3

Global and International Trends Affecting the Business Environment

A. ECONOMIC DEVELOPMENT: POPULATION GROWTH, URBANIZATION, AND INDUSTRIALIZATION

1. The world's population will continue to grow: 5 billion now, 6.3 billion by 2000, perhaps 10 billion in 50 years.
2. Ninety percent of the world's population growth will be in very poor nations.
3. Urbanization is increasing in all countries, but especially in Less Developed Countries (LDCs).
4. All LDCs are attempting to industrialize; in the more advanced, industrialization is increasing rapidly.
5. In all nations, agriculture is becoming more heavily capitalized and employment is shifting toward manufacturing.
6. The preponderance of employment is shifting from manufacturing to services in all industrialized nations. As LDCs industrialize, service sectors also expand.
7. International trade and competition in services is increasing.
8. The gap between rich and poor nations is increasing although LDCs as a group have made great strides in the past decade.
9. The gaps among LDCs in economic development are growing.

B. WORLD ECONOMY

10. National currencies, economies, and markets are increasingly intermeshed. Economic activity will lead to more competition for raw materials and markets.
11. All major trade groups are increasing trade with other major trading groups, a sign of increasing interdependence.
12. Industrialized nations are more dependent on imports of industrial critical and strategic materials.
13. Foreign direct investment is increasing for most industrialized nations.
14. The LDCs are increasingly trading with one another, often by barter.
15. Competition among advanced nations promotes redistribution of markets and an international division of labor.
16. The U.S. is falling behind other industrialized nations and its own past in productivity growth.
17. Exports are increasingly important to the U.S. economy.

18. U.S. non-manufactured exports are likely to grow significantly in the future.
19. As the world debt burden grows, it is tending to shift from the public to the private sector.
20. The international banking system is increasingly unstable.
21. American dominance of international business is sharply eroding.
22. Cartels may become more prevalent in European industry.
23. Investment in mining is shifting to LDCs.
24. In chemicals, the U.S. has had a growing share of the market, but the U.S. share may decline in the future.
25. Non-tariff barriers to world trade have shown a tendency to increase, especially during economic recession.
26. Some Pacific nations are rapidly becoming industrialized competitors to the more advanced nations.
27. World tourism and business travel are increasing rapidly.

C. ENERGY AND MATERIALS

28. Energy demand will grow at a slower rate.
29. Automobile use will grow.
30. After 2000, other sources of energy and chemicals will replace a significant portion of petroleum consumption.
31. The possibility of another successful oil embargo is decreasing, but other disruptions of imported oil are likely.
32. Coal exports from the U.S. will increase.
33. Nuclear energy use has not increased as much as anticipated worldwide, and may continue to be constrained by rising costs, waste disposal problems, and political resistance.
34. The costs of basic minerals will steadily increase. This includes both economic and environmental costs.
35. Demand for minerals will grow at a slower rate.
36. Mining of the ocean bed will increase; the U.S. will be at a disadvantage.

D. FOOD, RENEWABLE RESOURCE SYSTEMS, AND ENVIRONMENTAL PROBLEMS

37. Production of food is projected to increase by 90% between 1970 and 2000 without significant scientific interventions, as compared to a population increase of 55%.
38. Scientific and technological development could radically transform food production in the future.

39. The major threat to global well-being is from the threatened depletion of so-called renewable resources.
40. World forests decreased 9% from 1967-1977 and may be reduced another 40% by 2000.
41. The primary uses of wood may change in the future.
42. The United States and Canada may supply a large part of the world's need for wood in the future.
43. Soil erosion and desertification will be major problems in all food producing countries in the future.
44. The world catch of fish is likely to decline.
45. Many regions face severe water shortages.
46. Environmental issues will increasingly become matters of international political controversies. Regulation will grow everywhere.
47. Protection for threatened and endangered species will become an international objective in the future.
48. Actions directed at understanding, monitoring, reporting, and controlling weather will grow.
49. Changes in climate as a result of CO_2 accumulation may be important within 35 to 50 years.

E. LABOR FORCE, EMPLOYMENT, AND AUTOMATION

50. Telematics (the convergence of telecommunications, computers, and other information technologies) is a worldwide revolution comparable to the industrial revolution.
51. Automation will change all manufacturing activities.
52. More female labor force participation in all industrialized nations reinforces declining birth rates.
53. Employment and economic activity in the public sector increases with economic development.
54. Education is increasing in all countries, with emphasis on science, mathematics, and computer literacy.
55. In the least developed societies, internal barter is rapidly disappearing.

F. SCIENCE AND TECHNOLOGY

56. Science is internationalizing.
57. U.S. dominance in virtually every area of pure and applied science is in general and steady decline.
58. Industrial technology is in a pattern of multiphase migration from the industrial nations to somewhat less advanced nations, and then to those in early industrialization.

59. Local industry and some multinational corporations are exploiting land, labor, and environment in third and fourth world countries in ways unacceptable at home.
60. The scientific workforce is internationally mobile.
61. Indigenous technological and scientific capabilities are developing in many third and fourth world countries.
62. International cooperation in science and technology is increasing but simultaneously science and technology are becoming increasingly politicized.
63. Biological sciences will be the leading edge of scientific discovery and technological development in the next decades.
64. The general trends toward miniaturization of technology and widespread use of remote sensing will continue.
65. The continuing spread of computers and telecommunications poses many international issues and problems.

G. INTERNATIONAL AND REGIONAL POLITICAL CONDITIONS

66. International politics is increasingly multipolar or non-polar.
67. Telecommunications will strongly impact foreign affairs.
68. Economic sanctions are decreasingly effective.
69. Nationalism is no longer tied to geographical boundaries.
70. Terrorism is increasing.
71. There is a recent trend toward democratizing in LDCs.
72. There is a small but growing movement toward "culturally appropriate development."
73. Mexico is on the road to being the New World's Bangladesh.
74. There is a great increase in military and economic ties between Latin America and countries other than the U.S.
75. Latin America is likely to undergo economic contraction in the next few years.
76. Brazil, Venezuela, and Peru are increasingly vying for political leadership of the continent.
77. The Islamic Revival will continue. There is a definite possibility of "religious-nationalistic" warfare in the Middle East.
78. Cleavage between Northern Africa and Sub-Saharan Africa will continue to dominate that continent.
79. There will be increasing instances of political upheaval in the African states.
80. Indonesia's development may be constrained by economic and political troubles.
81. The economy of the USSR grew rapidly and industrialized from 1950-1980, but growth slowed significantly during the last decade.

82. The USSR is a society with serious internal problems that do not, however, threaten the stability of its government. Instead the problems may open the government to try to satisfy pent-up consumer demand by internal free markets and more imports.
83. The USSR along with China are the two largest potential new markets for the U.S.
84. The USSR's military policy continues to combine strength and caution.
85. The Soviet Bloc of European nations faces severe and increasing economic problems.
86. Hungary is increasingly bound to the West by economic ties.
87. China is continuing its initiatives toward modernization through opening up to the West.
88. West Germany's economic growth may be losing momentum.
89. Europe is steadily developing cooperative mechanisms to enhance its regional international competitiveness.

KEEPING UP AND DIGGING DEEPER: A GUIDE TO THE FUTURES LITERATURE

The best single source of timely and up-to-date information on books, articles, and reports about the future is *Futures Survey*. This is a monthly publication of abstracts, published by the World Future Society (4916 St. Elmo Avenue, Bethesda, MD 20814). They are collected yearly into *Future Survey Annual,* seven volumes of which have been published as of mid-1987. Eleven to twelve hundred abstracts are published each year.

GENERAL FUTURES PERIODICALS

Futures-related articles appear in hundreds of general and specialist publications. Eight accessible publications dealing with the general area of futures research are noted below. Through them one can keep up with general trends and interests as well as methods and techniques.

Futures: The Journal of Planning and Forecasting. Butterworths, U.K.
Futures Research Quarterly. World Future Society, Bethesda, MD.
The Futurist. World Future Society, Bethesda, MD.
Impact Assessment Bulletin. International Association for Impact Assessment, Georgia Institute of Technology, Atlanta, GA.
Journal of Forecasting. Wiley.
Project Appraisal. Beech Tree Publishing, U.K.
Technological Forecasting and Social Change, Elsevier, New York, NY.

There is of course also the planning literature, well-known in the business community. Conspicuous among these Journals are *Long-Range Planning,* Oxford University/Pergamon; and *Planning Review,* North American Society for Corporate Planning, Oxford, OH.

BOOKS AND MONOGRAPHS:

Keeping up with significant books and monographs in the area of futures is particularly difficult, because of the six months to two years delay in reviews. Consequently *Futures Survey* is quite helpful in that regard, as is the semi-annual catalog published by the World Future Society's bookstore. The bookstore is eclectic and uncritical. The fact that a book is offered by the bookstore does not indicate a judgment of high quality, intellectual substance, or even worthwhileness.

We recommend that readers turn to the detailed bibliographies of the seventeen futurists discussed in this report. No notation of their books and articles is repeated here. There is however a substantial number of other authors and topics which are timely and appropriate to rounding out futurist thinking. A few of them are noted here because they expand, complement or contradict positions noted in this report.

Adams, John H., et al. *An Environmental Agenda for the Future.* Washington, DC: Island Press, 1985.

Battelle Memorial Institute, Columbus Division. *Agriculture 2000.* Columbus, Ohio: Battelle Press, August 1983.

Beckwith, Burnham P. *Beyond Tomorrow: A Rational Utopia.* Palo Alto: B.P. Beckwith, 1986.

Beckwith, Burnham P. *Ideas About the Future: A History of Futurism, 1794-1982.* Palo Alto: B.P. Beckwith, 1986.

Davidson, Frank P. and John Stuart Cox. *Macro: A Clear Vision of How Science and Technology Will Shape Our Future.* William Morrow & Co., 1984.

Forester Tom, ed. *The Information Technology Revolution.* Cambridge, MA: MIT Press, 1985.

Gallup, George Jr. with William Proctor. *Forecast 2000: George Gallup, Jr., Predicts the Future of America.* New York: William Morrow & Co., 1984.

Heath, David, ed. *America in Perspective: Major Trends in the United States Through the 1990s.* Boston: Houghton Mifflin Co., 1986.

Marien, Michael and Lane Jennings, ed. *What I Have Learned: Thinking About the Future Then and Now.* New York: Greenwood Press, 1987.

Martino, Joseph P. *Technological Forecasting for Decision Making.* Second Edition. New York: North Holland, Elsevier Science Publishing Co., 1983.

Meadows, Donella, John Richardson, and Gerhart Bruckmann. *Groping in the Dark: The First Decade of Global Modeling.* Chichester: John Wiley & Sons, 1982.

Mitchell, Arnold. *The Nine American Lifestyles: Who We Are and Where We're Going.* New York: Macmillan, 1983.

Porter, Michael E., ed. *Competition in Global Industries.* Boston: Harvard Business School Press, 1986.

Simon, Julian L. and Herman Kahn, ed. *The Resourceful Earth: A Response to Global 2000.* Basil Blackwell, 1984.

Stableford, Brian and David Langford. *The Third Millennium: A History of the World AD 2000-3000.* New York: Alfred A. Knopf, Inc., 1985.

Winston, Patrick H. and Karen A. Prendergast, ed. *The AI Business: The Commercial Uses of Artificial Intelligence.* Cambridge, MA: MIT Press, 1984.

SECOND THOUGHTS

Each of the seventeen futurists profiled in this book was invited to prepare a 500-word commentary, since some time had passed since the profiles were written. While each of the profiled futurists was given the same opportunity to provide these brief appended statements, several declined for the rather obvious reasons, usually connected with congested schedules; we greatly appreciate all of their cooperation throughout the writing of this book. For those who have contributed these afterthoughts, special appreciation for their willingness to push one additional notch further forward. They are: Roy Amara, Robert U. Ayres, Kenneth E. Boulding, Victor C. Ferkiss, Barry B. Hughes, Richard D. Lamm, Michael Marien, Peter Schwartz, and Robert Theobald.

ROY AMARA

Future Methods

There is perhaps no subject on which futurists disagree more than whether the field or activity has any common base of methodological tools from which it draws and what the applicability and value of such tools and approaches may be. Indeed, the commentary on strengths, weaknesses and gaps (Chapter IV) specifically notes that futurists have little common ground, are very thin in the use of quantitative techniques, and are not normally explicit about their assumptions. In the last decade, the most important trend in the use of planning tools has been the move away from methodological formalism and doctrinaire approaches.

The use of expert judgment has remained, and very likely will remain, a mainstay of our work, because the tools of the econometric modeler or the statistical forecaster are not applicable—historical data are unavailable or time horizons are too long. However, Delphi, as practical in the 1960s and 1970s, has proved too slow, too expensive, and too blunt as an instrument for most applications. We have become far more eclectic in using tools for eliciting judgments, opinions and attitudes, focus groups and customized surveys.

Spreadsheet-like tools such as cross-impact analysis have always been high on the futures planner's list, for representing and for checking the consistency of logical connections between all possible factor-pairs. It has not proved an effective tool in very complex environments where basic structural changes are occurring—for example, in the communications industry after divestiture.

In such situations, our preferred modeling tools often are "softer", qualitative descriptions of interactions or clusters of interacting variables, represented by simple logical block diagrams or simple structural models.

We now use scenarios more frequently both as end products and as "front ends" for issue generation or for evaluating options. A scenario is a description of an internally consistent, plausible future.

Our best guess for methodological advances in futures planning (FP) are:

- Setting agendas
- Detecting and describing structural change
- Interleaving planning and acting

Problem solving is about selecting agendas, generating options or choices. Decisionmaking is about evaluating given agendas and variables. Artificial intelligence may provide the basis for new understanding in agenda setting or problem solving, even though people and computer generally use quite different processes.

Structural change is basic change in the pattern or makeup of a system. Sometimes, it happens unexpectedly. Often, it happens with forewarning, but the exact form it will take is not clear. However it occurs, it represents a sharp break with history. We do not have good theories about structural change, how it occurs, how it can be detected early; even small advances here could pay rich dividends.

We may gradually be approaching the point at which the analytic arm of FP becomes more and more invisible. The result will be the ability to integrate planning and acting so intimately that the two become almost inseparable. The key here is computer simulation long used for war gaming, flight training, and the design of complex physical systems such as telephone and weapons systems. The complexity of most environmental scanning, forecasting, and planning systems probably does not yet permit full simulation of such systems, but the software tools are being fashioned piece by piece to allow simulation of portions of, and perhaps ultimately more complete, systems. These are not just computational and numerical processes that result in long printouts of hard-to-digest data, but full-scale models that provide graphics and animated video images of the dynamics of complex structures and systems.

ROBERT U. AYRES

Commentary

It is tempting to comment on a number of points, both to "clarify" some of the characterizations of my views in the foregoing text, and to explain how they have changed with the passage of time. As to the latter, let me admit that my views on a number of issues have evolved significantly over the years. For instance, I now put less emphasis on "motivation" and "attitudes to work" than I once did. I also see a much greater potential for energy conservation than I did in the 1970s, which means that I do not foresee any serious energy crisis in the medium-term future provided appropriate policies are adopted. It is by no means certain that policies encouraging conservation will be adopted in the U.S. anytime soon, given the consumer-orientation in this country. Nevertheless, I will say here that fossil fuels (and also other minerals) are grossly underpriced due to the free use of common property resources—"environmental assimilative capacity" is the technical term—and as a consequence it is still much cheaper to waste energy than it is to invest in the technologies needed to use it efficiently. Co-generation and heat pumps are two of many examples. This is not the place for a detailed discussion, however.

There are two other topics that deserve explicit attention here. One is the impact of Gorbachev and "perestroika" on the Soviet Union and, indirectly, on world order. I freely concede that I never would have anticipated the possibility of a voluntary loosening of the repressive Leninist-Stalinist system, yet it is occurring. There may be setbacks, to be sure, and the "thaw" might even be reversed. Much depends on the political genius of one man. But, as I have pointed out in the past, the right man at the right time can sometimes "tilt" a country in a new direction. It seems to be happening now, and it is the best news since the end of World War II.

Unfortunately, there is also bad news. I wish I could say that I was wrong about the Japanese drive to world dominance. No such luck. In fact, the situation is worse than I expected in 1979. This is partly due to the fact that the Reagan administration has persistently ignored the problem. The situation might have been ameliorated if determined action had been undertaken as late as 1980. Today it is probably too late. The U.S. has become technologically and industrially dependent on Japan, even for its military needs. This is now a fact, though few people yet recognize it.

Where do we go from here? It is not really in the Japanese interest to continue killing the goose that has laid so many golden eggs for them. Yet the Japanese mandarinate shows no more sign of understanding the current situation than does the industrial establishment in the U.S., which continues to abhor "industrial policy" and cherish the freedom to close U.S. manufacturing facilities and become ever-more dependent on its strongest adversary. There is no sign at all that the Japanese will agree to restrain their export juggernaut except under extreme duress. I have feared for some time that the rise of Japan to "number one" status would be accompanied by severe instability in the world, as many countries begin re-evaluating their political alignments. I now have an additional fear: that the U.S. industrial decline is moving so rapidly that a major protectionist backlash will develop in the U.S. The end result could be a legislative nightmare that triggers a massive worldwide depression.

KENNETH E. BOULDING

Commentary

Perhaps the greatest danger which faces futurists is their failure to recognize the profound uncertainties of the future and hence to think about structures which will handle these uncertainties. This danger is understandable in light of the fact that futurists are interested in developing clear and consistent images of the future. The very variety of the images which are presented in this volume, however, suggests that the uncertainty of all of them is very important. It is especially important to recognize that in any system involving information and knowledge as an essential element there is a nonexistence theorem about prediction, if only because information has to be surprising or it is not information. We cannot predict what we are going to know in the future or we would know it now. Sometimes we can estimate the probabilities of different futures, and then we can have insurance. This is what my old teacher, Frank H. Knight, whom I should have mentioned, called "risk." He defined "uncertainty," however, as that which cannot be insured, partly because of an inadequate universe of similar events, more fundamentally because of the inherent unpredictability of the future.

A critical question here is: What institutions protect us against disastrous decisions based on mistaken images of the future? One answer to this in personal life, of course, is liquidity, diversification, not putting all one's eggs in one basket and, most important, being constantly ready to learn from mistakes. Indeed, I would argue that failure is by far the most important human learning process. All we learn from success is what we thought we knew already. If the success is a result of random forces, as it frequently is, it can be very dangerous. Knight saw the profit system as an adaptation to uncertainty. It may well be that market-type societies have a better chance of learning from failures than do centrally planned economies, though one cannot be sure of this. I would urge futurists, however, especially when giving advice, to stress these uncertainties, to develop constantly alternative images of the future, and to develop the concept of an optimum degree of commitment to them, which should not be too rigid. If we are totally uncommitted we get nowhere; if we are too committed the future will take us over a cliff. The great problem of the future is not how do we maximize anything, but how do we avoid the cliffs and turn away from them when we find ourselves going towards them?

VICTOR C. FERKISS

Commentary

Nothing in the past several years has caused me to fundamentally alter my views about the race between a revolution in consciousness and catastrophe, but, while remaining—indeed if anything becoming more—pessimistic about mankind's future at an intellectual level I am somewhat less concerned from an emotional and normative point of view. In general, I tend to see things in a less dichotomous fashion and be even more open to the possibility of radical disjunctures in causality that we cannot predict, and willing to accept whatever future emerges as the inevitable will of God.

Specifically, in the short run, I am increasingly convinced we may—especially perhaps in the United States—witness an economic catastrophe even before ecological catastrophe fully strikes, though obviously the two are related. The United States economy is becoming more two-tiered as the result largely of the "information revolution," with a growing upperclass and a growing lower class and a shrinking middle class, while average standards of living measured in constant dollars as well as largely unquantifiable quality of life factors diminish. This is, I would argue, part of a world-wide development as the division between rich and poor is no longer primarily on national lines but within nations as well. The American position is special, however, since our inability to live within our means—a special case of the global stress on fixed resources—has led to a debt which puts us at the mercy of other nations, above all in time the Japanese, who will turn out to be less merciful than classical free traders would have us believe.

This change in global patterns of economic strength, with the United States weakening largely due to self-inflicted wounds of various kinds, will be played out within a pattern of increasing ecological problems. The planet's seas become filthier by the moment, while the greenhouse effect promises to create climatic changes virtually unknown to recorded human history and so vast that they will make traditional conservation meaningless. Human nature being what it is, there will be little done to halt these changes before it is too late, and mankind will have to learn to adapt to them. But adapt it will. If there is anything more characteristic of humanity than its unwillingness to react until the problem is so obvious that it is unsolvable, it is its ability to live under adverse conditions. Not only will the race survive physically, but some sort of civilization will continue and, on its own terms, flourish. Alas, it will not be a life that most of us today would find fulfilling.

Note that I discount the possibility of major nuclear war. I am perhaps naively optimistic in doing so, but I am more than ever convinced that our decline will not be due to miscalculation but to lack of imagination and to procrastination; it will be much slower but just as inexorable.

BARRY B. HUGHES

Commentary

Much futurism (especially outside this volume) falls into basic categories of generalized enthusiasm or pessimism across issues as diverse as technology, the environment, international economics and global politics. Such portrayals of the future as either technological utopia for a prosperous and contented humanity or as environmental hell for an unequal and contentious human population are simplistic.

Technological advance in food provision, health care, energy systems, manufacturing, transportation, and communication will continue. Life expectancies will rise further and the average level of basic human need provision will climb. But technological advance in conventional and nuclear weaponry will also proceed, as will fossil fuel exhaustion and the accumulation of toxic chemicals in soil and carbon dioxide in the atmosphere.

Decline in population growth rates in almost all regions will gradually lessen the burden of support for young dependent populations. But the equally wide-spread growth of older, dependent populations will substitute other human care and public policy problems.

The newly industrialized countries and additional members of that club will further amaze us economically and increasingly share in the processes of discovery and invention, to the benefit of all countries. But the greater dynamism of those economies will also threaten the more technologically mature and slower growing United States. At the same time the economic stagnation of some less developed countries will persist and will appall us.

U.S.-Soviet relations will continue gradually and irregularly to improve as the two countries adapt to restricted world roles for what is, after all, a total of only 10% of humanity. But nuclear proliferation and rapid growth of conventional forces in the Third World will proceed. And neither superpower will graciously accept their relative (not absolute) decline as the rest of the world overtakes them technologically, demographically, economically, and eventually militarily.

We need to look for understanding of the future to important fundamental forces, especially the ongoing march of technology, the growing human impact on the global environment, the long-term and powerful dynamics of the demographic transition, and the continued spread and evolution of the industrial revolution (no, it is not complete, and it will not be for many generations). These forces promise long-term, generally positive global progress, but also danger, disruptions, distortions—even disasters. Our policies need to anticipate the opportunities and when possible to avoid—or at least to compensate for—the set-backs. There will be large numbers of both opportunities and set-backs; the futurists of this volume have done a remarkable job of identifying many in advance.

RICHARD D. LAMM

Commentary

I stand pat. I believe even more fervently that the United States is headed for trauma. A nation that has only balanced one federal budget in 27 years; that then adds staggering trade deficits year after year; becomes the world's largest debtor nation; whose students test below almost all their competitors' students; whose workers have among the lowest rate of productivity growth; whose goods contain many more defects than their competitors' goods; that country is headed for trauma.

The United States has allowed too many of its basic systems to become dysfunctional. No one spends more money on health care than the U.S. yet we do not keep our people as healthy as our competitors do for a fraction of our spending; we spend more for police and law enforcement yet live in the most violent and crime-infested country in the world; we are the home of a vast majority of the world's lawyers, adding additional transactional costs to our goods and services; all this bodes ill for our long-term competitiveness.

American management is driven by short time lines and quick profits while our competitors have an ethic of savings, long-term investments and patience. American corporate raiders help make long-term planning impossible and American workers have little sense of loyalty to their employers and *vice versa.* We are consuming more than we produce and spending more than we are willing to tax. We have debased our currency, adopted hedonistic values and lost our culture of hard work. Our political system responds only to crises and sometimes not then, and a massive **"For Sale"** sign hangs on American politics.

Indeed, I am gloomy: with some little reason.

MICHAEL MARIEN

Some Comments from An Atypical Generalist

Overall, *What Futurists Believe* is a valuable study. It is original and thought-full, offering much for a variety of users to chew on. But there are some major flaws, as one might expect in any ambitious project. The symptom is that two of the most worrisome problem clusters for the immediate, mid-term, and perhaps even long-term future—pollution and over-militarization—are scarcely mentioned.

The "commons" in which we all live and work is increasingly affected by pollution, and by misinvestment of our wealth into unnecessary and dangerous militarization. If one has tried to canvass all futures-relevant books and periodicals of recent years, as I have with *Future Survey,* one must conclude that these two threatening megatrends should be at or near the top of anyone's list of concerns. Yet, in the Coates and Jarratt list of what 17 futurists agree on, disagree on, or are uncertain of, pollution is not mentioned at all, and militarization is seriously understated. Why?

The gross neglect of these two broad issue clusters has to do with flaws suggested by the very titling of the project, *"What Futurists Believe."* The problem lies in defining "Futurists" and the past and recent-present orientation of "Believe."

There are no qualifications for being a futurist. A futurist is someone who says that he or she is a futurist, and/or someone who is seen as such. Lacking credentials, discriminations are sometimes made about the "professional," "serious," or "prominent" futurist. Coates and Jarratt summarize the Right Stuff traits of the "exceptional futurist" as being strong in both history and forward vision, in both coherent description and developing action strategies, in both credible portrayal and enlivening spirits, and in both depth and breadth of understanding. They graciously state that "All of the futurist panel meet these essential criteria to varying degrees." That's the glass-half-full argument.

The glass is also half-empty, and perhaps much more. It is strongly implied that all of the prominent futurists are generalists, but most in fact specialize in a broad and long look at certain problem areas, or clusters of areas. And thus the problem of Great Big Glaring Blindspots (GBGBs), notably pollution and militarization. It is not that the futurists have fully considered the evidence for these problems, and then assigned them less-than-priority status, but simply that these problems have not been looked at, or considered only superficially.

The GBGB problem is illustrated by Exhibit 3-3 which arranges the 17 futurists along two axes of present and long-term perspectives, and optimism and pessimism. In doing so, the chart also inadvertently shows four non-communicating clusters of what might be termed corporatists (short-term, optimistic), technophiles (long-term optimistic), social scientists (short-term pessimistic), and environmentalist/globalists (long-term pessimistic). The so-called "optimists" simply do not look at social problems (including militarism) and environmental problems. The "pessimists" who do so are pessimistic because of the inescapable conclusions of what they look at and not, I think, as a result of disposition. I know of no one with a strong corporate orientation (Exhibit 3-2) or a strong technological emphasis (Exhibit 3-2) who has even a minimal appreciation of the pollution and militarization problem clusters. Thus, *if* an unadulterated Big Picture is desired, those who consult with pro-corporate and pro-technological futurists, no matter how prominent, are being seriously misled.

The second major flaw has to do with the strong implication of durable beliefs. This is suggested by the Coates and Jarratt statement that "most futurists are structuralists whose interest is in long-term shifts and not in quickly changing fashions and enthusiasms." As an atypical generalist, who surveys present changes in future outlooks every month, I am prone to see this as another glass-half-full argument. There are of course many fashions and enthusiasms. But, in a world that surely is complex and turbulent, new threats, opportunities, technologies, and insights are constantly being introduced. Coates and Jarratt provide an excellent list of such potential discontinuities in Exhibit 22-2.

Such is the stuff that makes thinking about the future both fun and frustrating. Because of constant change in our world, a futurist's beliefs about the world should also be in flux—"lifelong learning" should mean more for a futurist than any other profession. And yet I find many futurists who not only narrow their view in space (thus creating GBGBs), but are frozen in time. The "frozen futurist" may have formed a reasonable worldview, say in 1970, but has not thoroughly updated it, if at all.

In sum, what we believe today is not what we will—or ought to—believe tomorrow.

PETER SCHWARTZ

Commentary

The essence of good intelligence is good questions. If we knew the outcome of several issues we would know a great deal about the world at the turn of the 21st Century:

- **A SOCIALIST SURPRISE?** Will the radical structural changes now underway in the socialist world progress successfully? Will the Soviet Union and China become modern economic giants or will the inertia of history and bureaucracy overwhelm the progressive movement now underway? Will those internal economic and political transformations lead to continuing reductions in international tensions?
- **EUROPE POST 1992?** Will Europe succeed in the integration efforts being set in motion in 1992? Will the imperative of economic progress overcome historic barriers to integration? How rapidly will it

proceed? Will the European game be open to foreigners or will a fortress Europe develop? How deep will the integration go? For example, will Europe develop an integrated set of financial and currency markets? How will the new Europe develop its relationships with the U.S., Japan and the Eastern Bloc?

- **THE USA-JAPAN LINK?** Will the United States and Japan find a new mutually beneficial political and economic relationship appropriate to their new circumstances? Will the U.S. restore its competitive strength through investment, education and intelligence or will the strength that it retains flow mainly from its huge scale? Will Japan adapt to its new political role appropriate to its new role in the world and with respect to the U.S.? Or, will economic friction between them lead to political problems contributing to a more volatile and uncertain world?
- **NEW NICS?** Will a new group of rapidly industrializing nations emerge to take the place of Korea and the other Asian Tigers? Will we find a way to lift the burden of debt which has put a lid on the growth of many key countries such as Brazil and Mexico? Will the ideology of market-oriented solutions now sweeping the developing world lead to greater prosperity and social progress?
- **NEW RULES OF THE ROAD?** Will an adequate framework of international financial and trade organizations emerge to minimize the friction in the global economy? Given the scale of global integration, will we extend the scope of international institutions to handle modern global securities and currency markets? Will we develop a structure of trade rules and practices appropriate to a global information economy?
- **AN INFORMATION ECONOMY?** Will the potential of information technology be effectively employed? Recognizing the exponential growth in the power of information technology, how rapidly will organizations and work patterns adapt to productively use its full potential? Will we succeed in the difficult and complex issues of breaking down the barriers to integration of all information systems? How rapidly will people develop the skills needed for the new technology?
- **RESILIENT FRAGILITY?** Despite signs of fragility (e.g., massive debt) will the global economy remain sufficiently resilient to withstand continuing volatility? Having survived the rigors of the shocks of the seventies and eighties, will possible large swings in prices or interest rates or economic downturns—and whatever other shocks we can imagine—finally trigger a downward break in economic growth? If the U.S. deficit continues near current levels—

which may be very likely—how will the international system cope with the massive imbalances that creates?

- **A "GREEN" NINETIES?** Will major environmental problems prove to be the key organizing issue of the nineties? Will the world be forced to address greenhouse warming and ozone depletion? Will we have to save the rainforests and clean up the acid rain? Will we find an acceptable way to deal with solid and toxic wastes? Will the momentum toward more efficient use of resources be sustained? On the other hand, might nuclear power come back for environmental reasons?

ROBERT THEOBALD

Commentary

When Joe Coates approached me to participate in this volume, he told me that I was the only futurist he knew with a profound concern for global issues and a deep bias toward local action. Let me take my 500 words to explain why I take this stance and what I am doing now.

I believe we are caught in the rapids of change and that we must learn to run them if we are to survive. I find that most people have realized that the above statement is true but are failing dismally to challenge their professions and institutions to change fast enough to prevent a catastrophic upset.

It is my belief that the ideas and models we so urgently need will arise as crises infringe on specific systems. Helping these systems to recognize that there are new possible directions, rather than necessarily remaining mired in the past, seems to be a critical task.

But I am increasingly aware that we need a more compelling myth to encourage enough activity. I have recently begun developing a scenario by which the Dynamic Balance Party wins the 1992 election. The science-fact scenario draws its energy from the boredom of citizens and the stupidity shown by participants in the 1988 campaign. (A science-fact approach is a scenario set in the future which tries to give life to desirable trends while recognizing that actual events will differ from those prefigured in the text. My previous effort along these lines was *Teg's 1994,* co-authored with my wife.)

I am assuming that a broad range of people can buy into the following four statements and would like to see what they would mean for the political process of the twenty-first century. (I am using the word politics in the anthropological sense of the way cultures settle disagreements and decide priorities—not the "party political" sense which is now commonplace.)

Here are the four assumptions:

- Warfare is no longer an acceptable way of settling disputes because of modern weaponry. This requires a rethinking not only of international dispute resolution systems but also forces us to move toward all-win thinking in our personal and group lives.
- Ecological stress is so great that we are required to reduce the rate of increase in population and, even more importantly, decrease the amount of waste and pollution resulting from production.
- These shifts are enormously stressful for human beings because they challenge many of their most deeply held beliefs. The stress will be increased by the challenges of the aging of the population, new medical and biotechnological discoveries, the skills of computers, etc. Directions and policies must therefore be developed in ways which limit stress to the greatest possible extent, rather than entering it as we did in the sixties.
- Directions and judgments must be made on an explicit value base which recognizes the centrality of spiritual/religious values.

There will be a wide range of opportunities to be involved in this science-fact development. If you would like more information, please contact me at Box 2240, Wickenburg, AZ 85358.

NAME INDEX

KEY WORD INDEX